SECRETS CAN BE MURDER

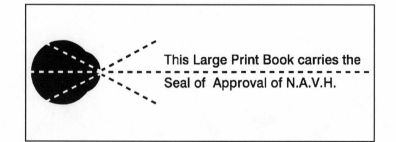

This Large Print Book carries the
Seal of Approval of N.A.V.H.

SECRETS CAN BE MURDER

WHAT AMERICA'S MOST SENSATIONAL CRIMES TELL US ABOUT OURSELVES

JANE VELEZ-MITCHELL
WITH FOREWORD BY
NANCY GRACE

THORNDIKE PRESS

An imprint of Thomson Gale, a part of The Thomson Corporation

THOMSON

™

GALE

Detroit • New York • San Francisco • New Haven, Conn. • Waterville, Maine • London

LIBRARY OF CONGRESS CATALOGING-IN-PUBLICATION DATA

Velez-Mitchell, Jane.
    Secrets can be murder : what America's most sensational crimes tell us about ourselves / by Jane Velez-Mitchell.
        p. cm. — (Thorndike Press large print crime scene)
    Originally published: New York : Touchstone/Simon & Schuster, c2007.
    Includes bibliographical references.
    ISBN-13: 978-0-7862-9857-0 (lg. print : hardcover : alk. paper)
    ISBN-10: 0-7862-9857-X (lg. print : hardcover : alk. paper)
    1. Crime — United States. 2. Victims of crimes — United States. 3. Trials — United States. 4. Large type books. I. Title.
HV6789.V45 2007
364.10973—dc22   2007023176

Published in 2007 by arrangement with Simon & Schuster, Inc.

Printed in the United States of America on permanent paper
10 9 8 7 6 5 4 3 2 1

To my mom, Anita Velez-Mitchell

CONTENTS

FOREWORD: AN ABANDONED AND MALIGNANT HEART

I spent the bulk of my trial career in the various courtrooms of an old and stately courthouse in inner-city Atlanta. The levels of violent crime at that time were raging . . . at their highest. Incoming shipments of crack, powder cocaine, heroin, and pot would first enter the country in Miami. "Mules" would hotfoot it up the interstate north to New York and all points in between. First major pit stop? Atlanta.

The increasing drug trade only served to fuel violent crime in a city already bursting at the seams with newcomers, both legal and illegal. Billed as the city "too busy to hate," Atlanta's legitimate business was thriving. The drug and crime business thrived right along with it. As I battled violent felons day in, day out, I noticed that, along with the culture of crime came the victimization of those who need society's protection the most: women and children.

How often during those ten years in Atlanta courtrooms did I find myself staring across a paneled courtroom . . . at the defense table. Seated there would inevitably be the defendant, predictably well dressed and well groomed, surrounded by a phalanx of his defense attorneys. The lawyers didn't interest me so much. I had them — and their tricks — pretty well figured out. No, it wasn't the highly educated and well-paid lawyers that fascinated . . . it was the defendant.

Fixing a steady gaze on the accused, I typically had memorized a file folder full of facts about him that the jury would never hear due to the restrictive nature of the rules of evidence, created to protect the defendant under the Constitution. Past convictions, bad acts, psychological reports, and a host of other inadmissible evidence would run through my mind as I openly looked. Sometimes I would watch the defendant become obviously nervous as I stared over. At times they would actually try to physically hide behind their attorneys. While they may have suspected that I was completely repelled by them and their bad acts, more often than not, I stared in pure fascination.

How could one person cause so much pain? That was my usual thought. How could one seemingly ordinary person sitting quietly in a suit and tie — looking like the corner banker or an accountant or science teacher — wreak so much havoc? So often their crimes would include a complete and reckless disregard for the lives and feelings of others. Sometimes in the law this is called an "abandoned and malignant heart." Sometimes the law refers to it as a "black heart."

It often seemed as if the suffering they inflicted on others meant nothing to them. I became completely obsessed not only with "who," but also with "why?" I would work tirelessly to understand the criminal mind and the so-called "black heart." It took me years, literally years, to accept that I could never understand "why?" I had to accept that my job as a prosecutor was to seek a verdict that would speak the truth, a true verdict as the law says. My job was to determine whether a crime had taken place and take the state's position before a jury. I poured my heart, body, and soul into the representation of Atlanta's victims of violent crime.

But on many a night, as I left the court-room and trudged to my car with arms full of files and evidence, I wondered. As I drove home through the maze of traffic, I wondered. And to this day, I still wonder. With every case I cover, every missing person or lost little child whose body is found discarded, I wonder. I wonder "why?"

My job was to make the streets of Atlanta safer for the innocent. That in itself was a daunting task. In the pages that lie before you, my colleague JVM, as I call her, gives us answers to the question that still plagues me with each case: Why?

— NANCY GRACE

INTRODUCTION

As a TV news reporter for three decades, I've visited crime scenes coast to coast, watching cops hunt for killers and listening to district attorneys theorize about motives. What I've gradually come to realize is that the key to understanding a crime often lies in discovering the *secrets* that led up to it.

With insights from well-known criminologists, forensic psychologists, fellow reporters, and the families of victims, this book analyzes the most sensational crimes of our times, flushing out the secrets behind the sinister acts.

The truth is, law-abiding citizens share many of the same secrets as criminals. And people who have never suffered a crime share many of the same secrets as victims. That's why, when a secret is exposed at trial, we often experience a flash of recognition! Sometimes the only difference between us and the criminal is that his secret was threatened by exposure, and he did something unthinkable to protect it. Sometimes the only difference between us and the victim is that we were lucky.

What exactly is a secret? I posed this question to many experts. One intriguing answer came from Los Angeles psychotherapist Lew Richfield, who defined a secret this way: "It's a lump of unfinished business that you carry with you wherever you go." And, just as you would with a concealed weapon, you pretend that you are *not* carrying it. So secrets automatically make you duplicitous and turn you into a liar. You may think you know somebody but you don't, unless you know their secrets.

Secrets are based on shame. A secret needs to be revealed or it will slowly poison the person who is holding it. Says Dr. Richfield, "Secrets prevent people from moving forward comfortably in their lives."

Living a lie takes a huge amount of energy, which can be debilitating. The deceit, which often starts as a minor cover-up, increases exponentially. Secrets build on secrets and lies must be protected by other lies. Resentment and rage over the clandestine life creates a climate of hostility. Anger and shame about the false exterior can lead to alcohol and drug addiction, fueling the toxicity of an already volatile situation. Sometimes a crime is committed in a desperate attempt to preserve the secret. Violence can also erupt when the truth is finally discovered.

The best way to purge a secret is to own it. That means we have to accept this shameful truth and embrace it. We need to get comfortable with it. We have to learn where it came from and why it formed. Once you accomplish that, the secret loses its power over you. Shakespeare said it best: "To thine own self be true, and it must follow as the night the day, thou canst not then be false to any man."

The process of dismantling a secret can be humbling, demanding self-honesty. But consider the alternative. What if your secret was exposed in the worst possible way? What if the one thing you've never told anyone was suddenly broadcast to the entire world? What if everyone suddenly found out what you're really like, behind the mask?

Trials fascinate us because the criminal court system is one of the very few venues in our society where we get to see somebody else's most closely guarded secrets spill out into the open. Most of the secrets discussed in this book were uncovered during the course of criminal investigations and trials.

Unlike a psychiatrist's office, a lawyer's

office, or a person's bedroom, we are *all* allowed into the courtroom to discover what's really going on beneath the polite appearances and what really went down behind closed doors.

This book dives deep into the deceits behind each criminal act and looks at the greater social implications of lying . . . to ourselves and others. These sensational trials mirror the darkest corners of our own interior lives. In a world ruled by superficiality, these are the corners we pretend don't exist.

Look at Imette St. Guillen, the young student murdered after a night out drinking in Lower Manhattan. How many women have, at least once in their lives, stayed out late at night, alone at a bar?

Consider the Natalee Holloway disappearance. How many moms have fretted as their teens went off on a graduation trip where there was bound to be a lot of partying? Those parents may realize how lucky they are that their teenagers returned home safe.

How many Scott Petersons are out there? How many lying, cheating husbands who don't want kids but who feel saddled with a pregnant wife? While Scott's double life led to the death of his wife, Laci, many disgruntled husbands just live out their days in quiet desperation. They flick on the TV to catch the latest development in some big murder.

It's no fluke that these crimes give us a vicarious thrill. They get us high. For a few moments, we're the criminal, but without any of the consequences. These terrible people got rid of someone they didn't want around. We all have a few people we'd prefer to live without. But, thankfully, we're not likely to do anything violent to get rid of them. When we see a criminal finally brought to justice, we congratulate ourselves for not acting on our worst impulses.

Sometimes we relate to the victim, breathing a sigh of relief that it wasn't us — because it could have been. Sometimes, we see similarities between ourselves and those on the periphery of crimes: neighbors, friends, lovers, and relatives who get caught up in a high-profile case and find their secrets exposed. What if your good friend or lover disappeared and police suddenly started investigating *you?* What would they find?

Sex is usually the most secretive part of our lives. Many crime stories that get a lot of TV coverage involve sexual secrets. Take the cases of British citizen Neil Entwistle, accused of killing his American wife and their baby, or Florida teacher Debra Lafave, who had sex with an underage boy. Both cases were steeped in secrets. Sex is the one area of our lives where our real thoughts, feelings, and urges are most deeply hidden behind a charade of so-called normalcy.

But the secrets can also be about money, as in the case of wildly eccentric real-estate heir Robert Durst. In the case of music legend Phil Spector, accused of murder, the secrets unearthed involve suicide and guns.

Deceptions can be about sex, class, pedigree, race, sexual orientation, sexual abuse, fetishes, family, religion, childhood trauma, money, or addiction. The list is long. But they all have one thing in common: secrets are toxic. They make you sick inside. Secrets create the need for deceit, hypocrisy, and phony façades, which rarely can be maintained forever. Usually, somebody slips up or just can't take it anymore.

These sensational cases, and many others, reveal how our culture encourages double lives by demanding rigid conformity. America's addiction to "family values" is creating a cynical society bursting with deception, as everyone tries to live up to an impossible ideal.

Aiming for perfection in your children, your spouse, your relatives, or anyone will create an environment prone to drama and distress. Creating a self-serving agenda and demanding that somebody else adhere to it will create a fertile ground for deceit, tragedy, and violence. These truths are evident in the trials that fascinate America.

Throughout this book you will be reading my theories about why the key characters behaved the way they did. Feel free to disagree with my opinions and conclusions! I don't pretend to be able to read anyone's secret thoughts or feelings. We all know that's impossible. The aim is to get you, and by extension our whole society, to reexamine the values our culture injects into us and to remind us that we always have a choice between secrecy and honesty.

1
WOMEN AS PREY

The murders of Imette St. Guillen and Teresa Halbach are so obscene, so disgusting, it's terrifying even to think about them. These cases produced allegations of grotesque sexual torture. The details are pornographic in the extreme. The sadistic nature of the crimes makes it almost impossible to delve into them without feeling like you're victimizing these women again just by telling the story of how they died. Each sad saga has left a huge controversy in its wake, one about the rights of the falsely accused, the other about the rights of women. Each case reveals the secrets of the men accused, secrets that are remarkably similar to those of millions of law-abiding American men.

Imette St. Guillen was a slim, smiling beauty who was on the dean's list at Manhattan's John Jay College of Criminal Justice. About to turn twenty-five, she was popular and set to graduate with a master's degree in criminal justice. Imette was on a fast track to career achievement and she had plenty to celebrate when, one Friday night in February 2006, she decided to go out on the town with a friend. As the evening became early morning, she and her friend split up. The friend went home. Imette decided to stay out.

Imette was last seen at a trendy bar in lower Manhattan, where she was drinking alone at about 4 a.m. It was closing time and the bouncer, a muscular forty-one-year-old ex-con, escorted her out. He has been charged with her murder.

The accused, Darryl Littlejohn, said publicly that police simply got the wrong man. Prosecutors say they have a wide array of forensic evidence against him, including a DNA match with blood found at the crime scene.

Seventeen hours after Imette St. Guillen left that bar, her naked body was found in Brooklyn, where it had been dumped in a ditch on the side of an isolated service road. A white athletic sock was stuffed down her throat. Some of her long dark hair had been chopped off, her hands had been bound with heavy-duty plastic ties behind her back. Her feet were bound. Her body was battered and bruised and had cuts and scrapes.

She was wrapped in a colorful king-sized comforter. Authorities said she had been sexually assaulted.

PART OBJECT

To me, the most unnerving detail was this: Imette's head was *completely wrapped in opaque packing tape,* in effect mummifying her.

The killer "tried to dehumanize her completely," says Dr. Stephanie Stolinsky, a Los Angeles forensic psychologist who specializes in sexual issues. "Whenever you hide someone's face, it means that you don't want to see them as a human being. You want to pretend that they're just an object." In fact, says the doctor, the psychoanalytic term for viewing a person this way is as *part object.* "You only see a part of them. And it's a grand extension of what some people have as a fetish."

SECRET SICKNESS

We've all heard of foot fetishes and the like — but shoving a sock into her mouth, wrapping her head in packing tape, and torturing her until she suffocates? That goes way beyond fetish to freakish. The medical examiner ruled the cause of death to be asphyxiation. Why would any human being get a sexual thrill out of dehumanizing another human being? To better understand, we have to delve deeply into the mind of the killer and uncover the secrets, the dark fantasies and sadistic desires, that lurk there. But how do we do that? How can we ever possibly know what goes on in someone else's head? The unpleasant truth is that the answer lies in our own heads, in our own dark secrets, in our own disturbing fantasies, the ones we think about but never reveal, not even to the person who shares our bed.

The unspoken reality is this: The person who killed Imette St. Guillen did not have unique fantasies. Human beings tend to obsess about a handful of sexual themes that often revolve around power and surrender, dominance and submission, sadism and humiliation. We are terrified of addressing these sexual issues as a society. We pretend that only criminals have "dirty" thoughts. But, secretly, many of us have indulged in fantasies involving cruelty, either dispensed or received. That's why we want to hear all the sick and sadistic details. They titillate us even as we cringe.

The first step to solving any problem is to acknowledge the truth and understand it — to own it. The only way we can really understand and shape the forces at work in violent sex crimes is to recognize their seeds. We must face ugly truths about sex, rage, and violence, and how men and women are trained to relate to each other as hunter and prey. Only then can we revolutionize the cultural dynamics that mold both murderers and the lesser sadists who merely abuse women and children.

To suggest this is to invite the self-righteous among us to beat their chests and denounce us as apologists for criminals and purveyors of moral degeneracy. To them I say: Look around you. Look at sexual molestation scandals involving priests. Look at *Dateline NBC*'s "To Catch a Predator," which shows that sexual predators come in all shapes, sizes, and professions, from teachers to religious leaders. Spend a day at a rape crisis center, or at an urban police station. Our society is dripping in sexually charged violence, and it's crippling us.

Something has to change! A good beginning would be for each of us to start being honest with ourselves about our own dark secrets. Ask yourself what secret thoughts you have about sex that you've never told anyone. What occurs to you about how you developed these fantasies? What are their roots?

In the aftermath of Imette St. Guillen's nightmarish end, an emotional debate arose over whether the victim should have been out at a bar by herself drinking at that time of night. Earlier on, Imette had gone with her close friend to another hot spot, a bar called Pioneer. At about 3:30 a.m., the friend decided she wanted to go home, but Imette chose to stay out. She is believed to have walked a few blocks through the darkened streets of lower Manhattan to another bar, the Falls. At about 3:50 a.m., the friend says she called Imette on her cell phone, and Imette told her she was going home soon. Imette was reportedly still at the bar at closing time, and was escorted out by Darryl Littlejohn, whom police allege later murdered her.

The New York Times reports that a co-owner of the Falls told investigators that after Littlejohn took Imette out a side door, he heard arguing and then a muffled scream. Two homeless people in a nearby park reportedly told cops they saw a man fitting Littlejohn's description putting an unsteady woman matching Imette's description in a van and speeding away.

"The first thing that pops into your mind when you hear a situation like that: What in the world was she thinking, to be out at that hour of the morning, after having been drinking all night in an area where she was very vulnerable and in situations where she had no protection whatsoever?" This observation comes from Dr. Janice Shaw Crouse of Concerned Women for America, a conservative evangelical organization that bills itself as the largest women's public policy organization.

As the revolting details of Imette's murder emerged, talk radio was blaring similar sentiments. "As tragic as it is, your first reaction is she should not have been out alone at 3 or 4 a.m. in the morning, because look at what can happen," scolded one indignant male talk radio host.

Oh, really? Easy for a man to say. He isn't bound by the same restrictions. If a man was out having a drink at four in the morning, would we be blaming him for putting himself in harm's way? Would we be asking ourselves, What was he thinking being at a bar alone? Of course not!

THERE BUT FOR THE GRACE OF GOD . . .

Imette's family, in Boston, was understandably disturbed by the criticism directed at her for being out alone that late. Her mother, Maureen St. Guillen, told a *Dateline*

NBC correspondent, "To those people who spoke, were they ever twenty-five? . . . What did they do at twenty-five? I mean, you can't live your life in a bubble."

She raises a very valid point. How many of us have done something in our twenties that might pose a similar level of risk? Be honest. Are women in our society not entitled to be adventurous? Is questionable judgment an option reserved only for frat boys?

Even the dismay of Imette's family pales next to the anger expressed to me by one woman, who says she was sober and with friends when she was assaulted by a bouncer at a nightclub after complaining about bad service.

"I think bouncers are notorious for having a raging-bull temperament. That's part of what makes them able to carry out their job," says the woman, who didn't want to give her name because she was pursuing legal action against the club. She feels that the hour and the location are irrelevant to the crime committed against Imette St. Guillen. What is relevant is the hostility and rage this male bouncer apparently felt toward a woman who was a total stranger. *Newsday,* citing police sources, said witnesses in the bar claimed Imette directed a "racially tinged comment" at Littlejohn, who is African American. Imette's family found that hard to believe. In any case, it's hardly a justification for the murderous violence of which Littlejohn was accused.

FLIP THE GENDERS

The fact that some people suggest that Imette herself was to blame is a grotesque illustration of how *male*-centric this society is. It's as if to say: well, men are men and they can't control themselves, so it's our own fault if they grab us. It's a hunter/hunted relationship, pure and simple. That's crazy. Turn the tables and consider what would happen if, for even *one* week, women began killing with the same frequency that men are now killing. Just imagine the six o'clock news chock-full of female killers.

Really, try to visualize it! What if *men* were told they had to stay home after a certain hour because they were in danger of being raped and murdered by marauding women? What if *men* had to hope a gallant woman would walk them to their car, thereby protecting them from other, more violent women? What if *men* were lured into vans by women who reassured them, *Don't worry, I'll take you home,* only to rape and murder them? How long do you think *guys* would put up with that before marching on Washington?

NOT LONG!

Many women, however, seem to accept inequality as just the way it is. Some women even encourage the double standard, because it emphasizes traditional gender roles that are comforting to them.

WOMEN ON WOMEN

Much of the criticism of Imette's judgment comes from women themselves, such as Dr. Crouse of Concerned Women for America: "Women do not have the upper-body strength, women are not able to protect themselves in the same way as men do. . . . Some of the feminist rhetoric gets so distorted that they want to, somehow, live in this idealistic world that shows no comparison to what is real."

Rita Smith, who runs the National Coalition Against Domestic Violence, feels that women who express the traditionalist view that women must adjust their lifestyles to protect themselves from male aggression have been "trained" to think that way: "Women shouldn't be too vocal about these issues because then men will see us as, somehow, shrews, or worse yet, lesbians."

So women who challenge gender stereo-types risk being perceived as man haters. But is there even a word for a man hater? Can you think of it? *Misandrist,* says the dictionary. Doesn't come up much, does it? On the other hand, *misogynists,* or women haters, are all over the place, hence our familiarity with the term.

At the risk of being perceived of as the rare man hater, I must ask the following questions. Do women really have to accept, as an unwritten rule, that we are prey to men? Is safety for *all,* regardless of gender, just some utopian fantasy? Is our societal secret that we really don't believe the male gender is capable of evolving beyond vio-lence?

Instead of women having to curtail their behavior to accommodate the aggressive tendencies of men, why can't we as a society somehow *modify the behavior of men?*

EX–CON MAN

Let's take a look at the suspect in the Im-ette St. Guillen murder case, Darryl Little-john. Only five feet seven inches tall, he may have compensated for his lack of height by being "built," as they say of men who are particularly muscular.

Raised in humble surroundings in Queens,

New York, Littlejohn has a long rap sheet that includes about half a dozen felony convictions, including one for armed bank robbery in the mid-nineties that kept him behind bars until 2004.

Numerous reports indicate Littlejohn often dressed in military-style garb and posed as a member of law enforcement, wearing caps and T-shirts emblazoned with U.S. Marshal logos. Sometimes he would wear a bulletproof vest; other times handcuffs or a handgun would reportedly dangle from his hip. Darryl Littlejohn appeared to be trying to live up to some comic-strip macho ideal of what it means to be male. He clearly seemed to have an exaggerated, even cartoonish sense of what it means to be a man.

A bartender at the Falls wrote an article in *New York* magazine about the claims Littlejohn and another bouncer made of being "federal marshals who hunted fugitives by day and moonlighted together at night. . . . They even had shiny gold badges." The bartender wrote of being regaled by tales of house raids, busts, and prisoner transports — all, apparently, complete fiction.

Why make up a story about being U.S. marshals? Is it because the oldest federal law-enforcement agency in America is the stuff of legend? U.S. marshals fought for law and order in the Old West by hunting desperadoes like Billy the Kid and the Dalton Gang.

GENDERCIDE?

"The Wild West mentality is still with us," Mary Anne Warren explained to me. She coined the term *gendercide,* and wrote a book by that name. *Gendercide* means "practices that cause more deaths to one sex than the other . . . usually motivated by people's ideas about the relative value of males and females and their appropriate uses and roles."

Warren says some psychoanalytical theories trace aggressive male behavior back to childhood: "The young boy has to de-identify with his mother in order to become male. He has to separate himself from his mother and from everything that's like her in order to be seen as male . . . in order to feel male. This is arguably one source of hostility toward women. You try so hard to suppress the feminine in yourself, you become hostile toward feminine individuals."

There's definitely something to that. Boys, trying to fit into muscle-bound male stereotypes, suppress the feminine within themelves and feel shame about the feminine traits that they've stuffed inside. The *shameful feminine thing* they hate to acknowledge inside themselves is what they end up attacking outside themselves.

CARTOON HERO/MURDER SUSPECT

The man they arrested for St. Guillen's murder was secretly a teen trapped in a man's body. He was apparently fascinated by comic books. Littlejohn used several aliases that he stole from cartoon characters. One of them was Jonathan Blaze, which just happens to come from the comic book *Ghost Rider;* Jonathan Blaze is the character's alter ego. Littlejohn also went by Darryl Banks, the name of a comic-book artist famous for his contribution to the *Green Lantern* series. Finally, the man accused of killing Imette also used the name John Handsome, which observers have connected to the detective in the *Green Lantern,* named Handsome John Riley.

"He's locked into being thirteen to eighteen years old emotionally," says psychologist Stephanie Stolinsky. "Something probably happened in his school days that locked him there. Those were the last days that he felt happy. Those were the last days that he felt powerful. After that, he felt very inadequate and lacked self-esteem. And the only way that he could get that esteem was to be somebody else and to be many other people." His criminal record is a clue to this secret inferiority complex. When Littlejohn was just a teenager, he was sent to prison for robbery, locking him up — and locking him in.

What's astounding is that when Darryl was working at the bar, this forty-one-year-old man's emotionally stunted behavior didn't set off any alarm bells with his colleagues. That says less about his colleagues than about the vast number of emotionally stunted men leading false lives. Many men are secretly still boys on an emotional and psychological level.

So many people, male and female, are trapped in surfacey, immature lives that being a walking cartoon fails even to raise an eyebrow. After all, American men today have been infantilized in many respects. Popular culture encourages wives to treat their husbands like overgrown children. The airwaves are awash with commercials in which women scold their clumsy men and assign them errands. The women are portrayed not as sexual partners so much as mothers. Their husbands are their kids.

Such stereotyping is robbing American males of a healthy and appropriate sense of power in their intimate relationships. No wonder they retreat to the privacy of their computers, where they can act out all sorts of sexual fantasies, dominating abstract women through Internet porn in a way they can't do in real life. Family Safe Media claims 60 million Americans purposely visited Internet porn sites in one year alone. This organization says 70 percent of those surveyed indicated they keep their online porn use a secret. The group says there are more than 4 million porn sites on the Internet. And the number is growing fast.

I know of several men who admit that their wives are completely unaware of their secret lives on the Internet, where they go to explore areas of sexuality that are off-limits in their marriages. If your husband insists on not being disturbed when he surfs the Web, watch out. He may be checking out more than sports scores.

If we had healthier, more honest relationships with our natural sexual urges and could share them with our mates in an open, playful way, then this secretive, shame-based sexuality wouldn't be rising from the bowels of our psyches, sometimes spilling over into reality when a disturbed individual loses track of what's real and what's fantasy.

Put simply, if we could be real about sex and put all our fantasies out in the open with our lovers and spouses, then we wouldn't have such a need for a sordid fantasy world. As it stands now, the typical American is sexually bipolar, phony when it counts and real only in those secret times when nobody else is watching. That's when we unveil the nasty secrets we share with dangerous criminals. And if you doubt this, just go online and do a search for the words *bondage, submission, S&M,* or any other taboo topic. What comes up is America's secret life. The sexually graphic photos that pop up show women who look very much like Imette must have appeared as she was being violated and murdered.

Sex is often about power, and power exchange is a charged experience. But it doesn't have to be demeaning or sick. It only becomes dirty when we consider it to be. We could learn to accept sexuality for what it is and explore power exchanges through role playing and other means. Then all the need for secrecy around sex would evaporate. But that requires being honest with ourselves.

There is also an interesting psychological analysis of those who would point to Imette's behavior as her downfall. All humans have a very basic need to feel safe in what's clearly a dangerous world. A vicious crime like Imette's murder so shatters everyone's sense of security and safety that we become desperate to take the randomness out of it, because the randomness is precisely what makes it so scary. You can't defend yourself against something that's totally random. If people can point to the victim's behavior as the cause, then they feel as if — by avoiding that same behavior — they can remain safe. It keeps them, psychologically, in the safety bubble. But in real life there is no safety bubble! Just take one glance at the FBI crime statistics if you want to feel insecure about your personal safety. Pick a city — *any* city. How about Albuquerque, New Mexico? In the first six months of 2005, that quaint southwestern city along the Rio Grande saw 14 murders, 152 forcible rapes, 530 robberies, and 1,542 aggravated assaults, for a total of 2,238 violent crimes. That does not include the 2,901 burglaries and 10,586 larceny/thefts and 1,706 motor vehicle thefts the people of Albuquerque endured. That's for only *half* a year! Expand that image all across America and you have an idea of what's going on from sea to shining sea.

Hardly anyone in America can guarantee his or her own personal safety. Most American homes can be broken into relatively easily. Even in affluent gated communities with private patrols, there are so many support staff coming and going, it's virtually impossible to make absolutely sure a home owner is always protected. And even if you are living in a fortress with a safe room, you could be sharing that home with a violent man, as many women are. The Department of Justice reports that in one typical year, 2002, almost a quarter of all murders were family murders. That is what's really frightening. A woman can curtail all her personal freedoms and still become a target of domestic abuse, home invasion, or any number of other common crimes. And we're not even considering psychological and emotional abuse, like intimidation and belittling. Clearly, the answer is not to keep women off the streets and in their homes.

"Women have to wake up," says an anonymous female assault victim. "We have been sleepwalking. It's no wonder we are easy targets. We have to demand in no uncertain terms that men stop acting like terrorists."

Critics of this line of reasoning may be outraged, wondering, How the hell can you indict all men based on the crimes of a few? Well, how the hell can you curtail the freedoms of all women based on the crimes of some men? If you take the "she shouldn't have been out" argument to its logical extreme, you'd have to keep women at home and out of the workforce. The gruesome slaying of Teresa Halbach is a case in point.

IN THE LINE OF DUTY

Blond, five foot six, and 135 pounds, Teresa Halbach had everything going for her. Pretty and ambitious, the twenty-five-year-old loved taking wedding and baby photos. She was snapping pictures of cars for sale as a temporary way to supplement her income and had been over to the Avery family's auto salvage yard a number of times, according to my conversation with her brother. Still, Teresa was virtually a stranger to Steven Avery when he called a car sales publication, reportedly using a false name, and asked that Teresa be sent over to take photos of a minivan for sale. It was October 31, 2005 — Halloween — when she arrived.

Tim Halbach, a subdued and thoughtful

business attorney, still cannot fathom why this crime happened to his kid sister: "The hardest thing is that a stranger did this to a stranger, essentially, and so I don't know what can keep a stranger who's got some mental issues from doing crimes of these violent natures."

Avery admitted he saw Teresa that day in the driveway of his trailer home, which is on the salvage yard's grounds. He said he paid her forty dollars and she gave him an *Auto Trader* magazine. But Avery insisted he knew nothing of Teresa Halbach's death.

However, authorities say Avery's pasty-faced sixteen-year-old nephew, Brendan Dassey, provided a chilling narrative of what allegedly happened that day, in a videotaped confession that lasted several hours. It sparked intense outrage. Here's how the prosecutor recounted the boy's story in the criminal complaint filed in the case against him.

After getting off the school bus, Dassey biked to pick up the mail. He noticed there was a letter for his uncle Steve and went over to deliver it to him. Dassey allegedly told authorities that as he approached, he heard a female voice screaming, "Help me!" coming from Avery's trailer. A sweating Avery invited his nephew in and then asked him "if he wanted to get some 'pussy.' " According to Dassey's confession, Avery admitted, in extremely vulgar terms, that he had raped Halbach, and encouraged Dassey to do the same.

Then Avery allegedly escorted the boy into his bedroom, where a naked Teresa Halbach was face up and "restrained to the bed with handcuffs and leg irons." Halbach begged the boy not to rape her, but Avery encouraged him. The criminal complaint says, "Dassey stated that he then had sexual intercourse with Teresa Halbach while Steven Avery watched." Halbach was crying.

The hellish scene would become even more surreal and grotesque. Dassey said he and Avery went back into the living room and watched TV for ten to fifteen minutes as Halbach remained shackled to the bed in the next room. According to the same court document, "Avery told him he did a good job and that he was proud of him" and then announced his plan to kill Teresa Halbach and burn her body.

According to the complaint, the nephew said he and Avery returned to the bedroom; Avery held a six- to eight-inch knife from the kitchen in his hand. Avery told Teresa Halbach he was going to kill her and threatened her for a while before actually plunging the knife into her stomach. Avery then gave Dassey the knife "and told Dassey to 'cut her throat.' Dassey stated that he then went over to Teresa Halbach and cut her throat with the knife." Halbach was still alive when Avery further instructed his nephew to cut off some of Teresa's hair. Avery then "put his hands around Halbach's neck and strangled her for approximately two to three minutes." They then unshackled Teresa, believing she was dead, but Avery proceeded to shoot her about ten times anyway. Finally, they moved her body to a nearby burn pit and set her corpse on fire.

Avery is a father of four and had a girlfriend at the time. Months after his alleged confession, Dassey took it back in a short letter to the judge, claiming that on that fateful Halloween he was watching TV and playing video games at home until his uncle Steve invited him to a "bombfire."

Dassey's shifting stories sent the prosecution's case against his uncle Steve into a tailspin. Because the rape and kidnapping charges against Avery were based on his nephew's detailed confession, and because Dassey kept changing his version of events, the sexual assault and kidnapping charges against Avery were dismissed, just as his trial was about to start in the winter of 2007. Considering that Halbach's body was burned so far beyond recognition that mere fragments were left, proving sexual assault — independent of the nephew's account — seemed virtually impossible. Avery's defense attorney has been quoted as saying there was not one detectable trace of Halbach's DNA, hair, or blood anywhere in his trailer. Still, prosecutors contended they had a strong case and moved forward with the remaining charges against Avery, including first-degree intentional homicide, mutilating a corpse, and possession of a firearm by a convicted felon.

In the days following her disappearance, Teresa's Toyota Rav 4 was discovered hidden on the salvage yard's grounds. Authorities found her car keys in Avery's trailer, along with handcuffs, leg irons, weapons, and ammunition. Bone fragments and teeth were found in the fire pit. Authorities say DNA from the charred remains was found to be consistent with Teresa's DNA. Authorities also report that the blood found in Teresa's vehicle matches Avery's DNA profile.

In the wake of this nauseating litany of sadism, a public outcry arose over why

Steven Avery was walking free when Teresa Halbach innocently walked into his orbit.

BACK TO THE FUTURE

Two years before Teresa was murdered, Steven Avery had been freed from prison with considerable media fanfare. He had become a living symbol of judicial injustice. Avery had served almost eighteen years for a rape he didn't commit. Given the technological advances in DNA testing in the years since Avery's original 1985 conviction, lawyers at the Wisconsin Innocence Project examined Avery's claims of innocence and filed motions that resulted in new DNA tests on hairs that had been preserved as evidence from the crime scene. The DNA evidence showed the male pubic hair did not belong to Avery; rather, it implicated another man, Gregory Allen, who by that time was behind bars on a sixty-year sentence for a subsequent sexual assault.

As Avery walked out of prison, his nineteen-year-old daughter was there. A gaggle of TV news cameras recorded the historic event. "I'm out!" Avery cried. "Feels wonderful." He was even given high marks for expressing no anger toward the rape victim who singled him out as the perpetrator. "It ain't her fault," said Avery. "They put it mostly in her head." In the wake of his release, a legislative task force was formed to change the laws so that this kind of miscarriage of justice couldn't happen again.

But in the wake of Teresa Halbach's murder, there are those who believe the Wisconsin Innocence Project is guilty of myopia.

"I sit here and think that had the Wisconsin Innocence Project never taken up this case, he'd still be in jail and my sister would still be alive," says brother Tim Halbach as he sits in his law office, his quiet voice choking with emotion, as he recalled his younger sister's hopes and dreams and how his family's world was so violently shattered.

Keith Findley, an impassioned law professor who is the co-director of the Wisconsin Innocence Project, told me he felt deeply saddened over Teresa Halbach's murder, although he didn't want to prejudge Avery's guilt or innocence. "I regret very much what happened to Teresa Halbach. That doesn't change, however, the fact that Avery wasn't guilty of that prior crime. And, if your criminal justice system is going to have any integrity . . . it has to be focused on getting to the truth."

But truth can be an elusive concept. And we must also ask — the truth about what?

THE BIG PICTURE

It is true, say authorities, that Steven Avery had a history of violence that predated the 1985 sexual assault case. His rap sheet included two burglary convictions, reckless driving, misdemeanor theft, and cruelty to animals. Prosecutors say he tortured and killed a cat by pouring gas on the animal and throwing it onto a bonfire to die. Cruelty to animals is a very common predictor of subsequent cruelty to humans. Teresa Halbach's remains were found in the burn pit near Avery's garage.

But far more ominous than his rap sheet are the threatening letters that authorities say Avery sent to his wife from prison as his marriage crumbled. It ultimately ended in divorce in the late eighties while he was still incarcerated. "If you don't brang up my kids, I will get you when I'm out," reads one missive scrawled in large, childish lettering. "I hate you, you got your divorce. . . . Now you will pay for it," reads another page. "Daddy will git mom," he purportedly vows in an Easter card.

The local police department also filed a report on a cassette tape Avery's wife said she received in 1988. According to a police department transcript, in between profanities and accusations, Avery says, "You're going down; you're going down deep. . . . I hate you so much that I won't even tell you what I'll do to you; hell no." Avery also allegedly threatened to burn her car when he got out. Experts say a preoccupation with fire, like animal abuse, is a predicator of violent behavior.

Professor Findley of the Wisconsin Innocence Project said he was not aware of the threatening letters Avery allegedly sent to his wife until long after he was freed. He addressed the larger criticism of his efforts: "If you're asking me, do we try to judge these people and decide which of the innocent are deserving of being exonerated, the answer is no. We look to see if the system got it right in this case."

In hindsight, it appears that Avery's rage was building during his long imprisonment. The false incarceration, the unraveling of his marriage, an apparent tug-of-war over visitation with his children — all were making him feel like the victim. And there's nothing more dangerous than an enraged man in the throes of what he feels is righteous indignation.

Interestingly, Brendan Dassey, Avery's

nephew, is listed a number of times on "Inmate Request for Approval of Visitor" forms, indicating the boy may have visited his uncle behind bars as a child. Years later, that boy would be accused of becoming Avery's apprentice in crime.

THE PLAN

Of all the haunting details to emerge about Avery's time behind bars, the biggest bombshells can be found in a March 2006 legal document. In it, the special prosecutor in Avery's murder case offered some jaw-dropping reasons why bail should be denied to the defendant: "Steven Avery has demonstrated an intent, plan, and motive to abduct, rape, torture, kill, and mutilate young women, as evidenced by conversations with inmates, and showing diagrams within the Wisconsin Corrections System, of a 'torture chamber' Avery intended to build upon his release from prison."

That's right. Prosecutors say that before the Wisconsin Innocence Project got Avery released, while he was still behind bars, he was planning the very sort of crime he was later accused of committing. The prosecution's motion continues, "Steven Avery has demonstrated an intent, plan, and motive to dispose of the victims' bodies through burning, as evidenced by conversations with inmates," which "also included a detailed demonstration on how to bind victims to be held against their will."

The Wisconsin Innocence Project says that if authorities thought Avery posed a danger, they should have pursued that as a separate legal matter. They insist it is very unusual for wrongly convicted men to commit violent crimes once they're freed, adding that the work they are doing is crucial, given that advances in DNA technology have turned up many wrongly convicted individuals in prisons across the country. Since its formation in 1992, a national organization based out of Yeshiva University, called simply the Innocence Project, says it has helped free 181 innocent people, including fourteen who had at one time been given the death sentence.

Still, Teresa's brother says he wishes the Wisconsin Innocence Project had looked beyond the DNA and focused instead on the big picture of Steven Avery's criminal history, his behavior in prison, and his mental state when deciding whether to champion his cause.

One more fascinating fact. Freed after serving almost two decades behind bars for a rape he did not commit, Avery sued

49

authorities for $36 million. But after his arrest for Teresa Halbach's barbaric murder, Avery ended up settling his wrongful conviction suit for a tiny fraction of the amount he originally sought, $400,000, much of which may well be absorbed by legal fees. Avery claimed he was being framed for Halbach's murder by authorities because of his multimillion-dollar suit. But prosecutors believe that the rage and hatred Avery accumulated over two decades in prison was so all-consuming that he was willing to walk away from tens of millions of dollars and sacrifice his hard-won freedom just for the chance to act out his lust for violence and his sadistic fantasies on a woman he barely knew. Such a choice would be pure evil. Not to mention stupid!

Authorities reportedly claimed they found pornography in Steven Avery's home. But some reports indicate what Avery had was probably not that much different from the adult materials in thousands, maybe millions, of homes across the nation and the world. It is undoubtedly being viewed in your neighborhood right now, by a neighbor who walks his dog and smiles at you like he's the most trustworthy guy in the world.

WHAT NOW?

Like so many relatives of murder victims, Tim Halbach says he's thought a lot about how to make sure his sister did not die in vain. Some lawmakers used his sister's murder to push Wisconsin to adopt the death penalty. Others want Wisconsin residents to be able to carry concealed guns. Tim seems to lean against both of those ideas. "What kind of society is it that someone has to carry around a gun to be safe?" Good question, Tim. What kind of society tries to solve violence with more violence? The answer is: a society that is addicted to it.

TRAINED TO BE TURNED ON BY VIOLENCE

America is hooked on violence. America is particularly hooked on sexual violence. If you don't believe me, do a little test. Turn on the TV and start channel surfing. See how long it takes you to stumble onto an act of violence or an example of male aggression against females. You won't find nudity or nonviolent erotic sex on the regular channels. That would be a violation of *our standards of decency"!* But you will find a ton of fully clothed men in aggressive pursuit of women in various states of un-

51

dress and helplessness.

In the Victorian era, when it was risqué for women to show their ankles, a man could become aroused just by the sight of a woman's ankle. That's what men were socially conditioned to find erotic. Today it would be a real challenge to find a man who could get turned on by the sight of a woman's ankle, unless he had a fetish for it. "It's called classical conditioning," says psychologist Stephanie Stolinsky. Like Pavlov's dogs, we can be trained to be aroused by whatever stimulus we're fed.

Today we have created a warlike attitude toward sex. The "pursuit" is no longer an abstract concept. Now it's a real hunt. Men are the hunters. Women are the prey. Now that is what turns us on! And of course, our culture is what's training us to find this exciting. To remain competitive and original, creators of TV shows and movies feel they must continuously raise the bar (or lower it) when it comes to depictions of sexually oriented violence. That's what we're being conditioned to find arousing. And the abuse and murder of women is a by-product. The National Coalition Against Domestic Violence maintains that one in five women has experienced an attempted or completed rape and one in four women will experience domestic violence during her lifetime. Still, many so-called opinion makers urge us to accept this grotesque reality as *just the way it is,* and scold women that they must shield themselves by limiting their own freedoms.

ULTRAVIOLENCE

In the hideously violent film *Sin City,* we saw women being dismembered, with their heads put up on the wall as trophies. They were actually kept in a dungeon, where they were tortured. Many very intelligent critics gave this movie good reviews based on the absolutely breathtaking visual effects. And it was groundbreaking in its use of green-screen technology, which brought Frank Miller's graphic novel to life. In that sense it's a masterpiece, but at what price?

There's an interesting parallel here. One criminologist described St. Guillen's murder as "unrestrained, cavalier cruelty and sadism." That description could have just as easily been applied to this movie and many others that are just as violent. One review called *Sin City* "brutal, crude, and relentlessly juvenile, a work designed to appeal to the antisocial thirteen-year-old inside all of us."

A well-educated and sophisticated movie

reviewer might see the stylized violence in *Sin City* as harmless because it's so unreal. But that movie reviewer is not the one we're worried about! We're worried about emotionally stunted, violence-prone men who already live in a cartoonish, fantasy-based world. Anyone come to mind? How about the suspects in these murder cases? A man like Darryl Littlejohn, who names himself after comic strip characters and wears a shiny fake badge, may not grasp the nuances and subtle distinctions between highly stylized cartoonish violence and real blood. And what about all the latchkey kids killing hundreds every day on their Xboxes?

There's a slogan going around: "Fear No Art!" I agree. I feel art needs to be protected. I know art is meant to disturb and provoke, not reassure. But if it disturbs us, we also have a right to discuss the ways in which it disturbs us.

Ella Taylor is sometimes disturbed by the violence she sees onscreen. The movie critic for *L.A. Weekly* told me she's also a former sociologist and a mom. But, says Ella, all movie violence is not equal. "You would not be able to show a holocaust movie without showing violence and be true to the material. The problem comes when it's empty violence." Taylor says she believes only a very small percentage of violent crimes are motivated by specific movies. She worries more about the impact of *a steady diet of violence* that's all around us, in films and television. That includes local and national news, cable shows, prime-time dramas, the works. "It gives people a tremendously skewed vision of society," she believes.

Everybody's showing violence ostensibly in order to denounce it, but further numbing us to it in the process. Enough! We get the point. How about doing a masterpiece of green-screen technology *without* the highly stylized violence?

But would that sell? See, it's a vicious cycle. Filmmakers, while spouting off about the artistic message behind stylized violence, are really trying to make a hit movie. In today's world, that often means a movie dripping with the kind of sexually charged violence that will appeal to teenage boys. They're demanding "sexy" violence because they've been conditioned to it, and they're conditioned to it because it's what we're feeding them.

"There is no question that watching violence brings out violence. . . . Watching violent rapes on television minimizes what rape means," says Dr. Stolinsky, adding, "They are habituated to the horror of it.

55

The more you watch it, the less it matters to you at all." And we are watching a lot of it.

Women have the power to stop the cycle. According to *Business Week,* "Women earn less money than their counterparts — 78 cents for every dollar a man gets. But they make more than 80 percent of buying decisions in all homes." Message to women: Start flexing your consumer power! Stop buying the violence against you. Say it: No, I'm not going to that movie, it's too violent. Let's choose something else. Let the movie executives figure it out. Money is the only message that gets through to them. Meanwhile, it costs Americans billions of dollars a year to cope with the aftereffects of violence against women, from lost work days to health care, from police and ambulance services to the costs of the criminal justice system. Imagine what we could do with all that money if we didn't have to spend it cleaning up the carnage.

Cases like those of Imette St. Guillen and Teresa Halbach make me think of a scene from the classic movie *Network,* in which people opened their windows and bellowed, "I'm as mad as hell and I'm not going to take it anymore!"

2
DESPERATE HOLLYWOOD

Hollywood is like no other place in the world. This town can turn you into a living, breathing cliché. A good percentage of the people who go to Hollywood dream of being famous. Often they've grown up as the best-looking, most popular people in their small towns. Their secret is that they are convinced they are naturally special and destined for greatness. They feel their dream is unique. When they get to Hollywood, they can't help but notice that there are an awful lot of really good-looking, charismatic people just like themselves strolling around and sipping soy lattes. Still, that reality won't faze world-class dreamers. They often have little self-awareness that the part they're playing is as predictable as a sitcom laugh track.

Two Hollywood stereotypes include the wide-eyed blond bombshell who's past her prime and works as a nightclub hostess, still desperate to get ahead in showbiz, and the eccentric musical genius, almost half a century past his biggest hits, who becomes a dangerous recluse. His secret is that he still dreams of some kind of magnificent eleventh-hour comeback that will astound the world. Hollywood has a way of turning people into B-movie characters. This is the sad story of two classic Hollywood characters colliding one February night in 2003 with deadly results.

February 3, 2003, was a typically stressful Monday in the world of Los Angeles television. I was working as a reporter on the nationally syndicated TV show *Celebrity Justice*. The *CJ* newsroom was a blur of activity. Everyone was on edge because a big celebrity story had just broken and it was the start of "the February book." February is a key "sweeps" month, one of the highly competitive ratings periods when TV shows scramble extra-hard for viewers in the hope of getting good ratings. Ratings determine a show's survival. That day, I too had been turned into a walking Hollywood cliché: the hungry reporter chasing a hot story under deadline pressure.

Word had come down early that morning that a young woman had been shot to death inside the castle of legendary music producer Phil Spector. The now-reclusive millionaire had worked with a slew of famous artists, including the Ramones, the Ronettes, Ike and Tina Turner, and the Beatles. Spector had worked on the Beatles' final album, *Let It Be,* released in 1970, although Paul McCartney reportedly hated the rich sound Spector had layered into it. Earlier in his career, Spector had produced hits for the Righteous Brothers and the Crystals, among others. In 1989, he was inducted into the Rock and Roll Hall of Fame, where he reportedly gave a rambling and incoherent speech.

Only in L.A. would a murder suspect live in a castle. I raced out the door.

Being a journalist in Hollywood is like being trapped on the back lot of a soundstage. You're walking through what looks just like New York City, except there's nothing on the other side of the brownstone windows. What looks so impressive on film often turns out to be just another flimsy façade when you finally get close enough to see the details. So it was with Phil Spector's "castle."

KING OF THE HILL

Most of Hollywood's rich and famous live in Beverly Hills, Malibu, Bel Air, Pacific

Palisades, Brentwood, West Hollywood, or Santa Monica. Some live in Venice or the Valley. But imagine my surprise when I was instructed to start heading toward East L.A. and wait for instructions to Phil Spector's castle, which turned out to be east of East L.A., in a very working-class neighborhood called Alhambra.

I parked as close as I could and began hiking up the steep block that led to the gated entrance of Spector's estate. Looking around, I realized that virtually all the other homes in the area were extremely modest cottages. This eccentric genius lived in an ornate 1920s Spanish-style mansion that was surrounded, comparatively, by shacks. This was a ridiculous case of having the biggest house on the block.

Crowning the steep hill was Spector's "Pyrenees Castle," which had about thirty rooms and even boasted turrets. He'd reportedly bought it for just over a million dollars, certainly a bargain price for a castle that might impress some women out there. He had been divorced from his second wife, Ronnie Spector, lead singer of the Ronettes, in 1974. While he had significant relationships after that, fathering twins, Nicole and Phillip, in the early eighties, reportedly with a business assistant, that marriage also

60

ended. At the time of Lana Clarkson's death, Spector lived alone and was not known to have a girlfriend.

A sizable media swarm had already formed behind the yellow police tape by the time I'd arrived. I joined a packed line of reporters and photographers angling for good shots of the crime scene and some hard information. We were all trying to figure out exactly what had happened in the predawn hours. The black Mercedes sedan that Spector had been chauffeured around in the night before was still sitting near the front gate. Detectives pored over it.

The chauffeur had reportedly told police that he had been outside, waiting in the car, at about 5 a.m., when he heard a "popping sound." Soon after, the driver claimed, the sixty-two-year-old Spector, short and slight at about five foot seven and 135 pounds, emerged from his castle, holding a gun, and blurted out, "I think I killed somebody," or words to that effect. When police arrived, they reportedly had to use a taser stun gun to subdue Spector after he failed to obey police orders to take his hands out of his pockets.

The female victim was found slumped in a chair in the foyer. According to the autopsy report, she was wearing black underwear with a Brazilian or tango-type cut made by Frederick's of Hollywood, a black Felina bra, a black Vertigo Paris jacket, a black slip-dress, black nylons, black Nine West shoes with straps, amber glitter–painted toenails, and a choker around her neck. A lipstick container was tucked inside her bra, a common habit among actresses in L.A. In her leopard-print purse, which was next to her, were a black skirt dress and a pair of gloves with long sleeves.

Information was also pouring in on Spector's fetish for firearms. What might have been a secret to the general public was no secret in the music industry. It turns out that Spector's passion for guns was common knowledge among his colleagues, and people quickly began coming out of the woodwork with horror stories, claiming Spector had pulled guns on them in the past. It was quite a day at *Celebrity Justice.*

Big Girl, Little House

My weekday routine involved leaving my house in Venice at 6:50 a.m. to beat the city's infamous morning traffic crunch. Trying to catch up on the latest Hollywood gossip by listening to the morning radio shows, I would bob and weave my Prius hybrid electric vehicle about thirty miles northeast to Glendale in time for our daily 7:30 a.m. meeting.

But on Tuesday, February 4, the day after the woman's body was removed from the castle, I was racing out the door when my phone rang. I was being diverted. The dead woman wasn't an ingénue in her twenties after all, as some news outlets had originally reported. She was forty years old but apparently looked much younger. Our assignment desk had just learned that the female victim, an actress, lived along the Venice Canals. The narrow waterways began just a few blocks from my house. They didn't have the exact address, just a general description. It was a tiny cottage painted bright yellow near a popular bar that was a local landmark.

I was told to locate the woman's house and see if I could talk to someone who knew her, a neighbor, friend, landlord, or — best-case scenario — a relative. I was also told to bring my own digital video camera, because my photographer would be heading out from Glendale and would undoubtedly be stuck in traffic. I agreed (like I had a choice in the matter), but then panicked when I realized I had lent my own camera to a friend as a favor. Now I was on a big story with no way of recording it.

I called my friend and said I needed my

camera immediately. I headed out and began looking for the house, which was easy to find. Right across the canal and a few doors away from the well-known bar was a little house painted canary yellow. I parked nearby and met up with my friend, only to discover that he'd drained my camera batteries and I needed to recharge them. I got a local store to let me hook up my charger and walked around the corner to check out the little house. It was still early, but already I was fretting about other news crews getting there and grabbing interviews before I could get a full battery charge.

The quaint little yellow cottage was the polar opposite of Spector's palace. While you can only see the full expanse of Spector's property from a helicopter, the victim's home was so tiny it had the feel of a dollhouse. Where Spector's home was imposing, hers was cheerful.

As I stared at it, the assignment desk called to make sure I had the latest information about the victim, details that had actually started seeping out the prior evening. Her name was Lana Clarkson. She was said to be a beautiful blond actress who stood almost six feet tall. She had a long string of credits. Her first movie was the 1982 classic comedy *Fast Times at Ridgemont High.* I would later rent it and find that she spoke literally one word in the film. She also had a bit part in the camp classic *Scarface*. But Lana went on to bigger roles in B movies like *Barbarian Queen* and *Barbarian Queen II: The Empress Strikes Back*. One of her nicknames was "The Original Xena."

My camera batteries finally charged, I approached her house and started knocking on doors, always my least favorite thing to do. The task makes me nauseous. But I also know it's an inevitable part of the job of being a reporter. Every time you watch a friend or neighbor of a victim talking on TV or read a quote in the paper, keep in mind somebody had to convince that person to talk. And sometimes what they have to say is important.

Finally, I found a neighbor who would speak to me, and as he did, he began sobbing. "People should know what a wonderful person she was. . . . The person who did this should pay for it. We can't ever bring her back." He was a wreck. Lana's sister stopped by and didn't want to speak. I understood and backed off to give her some space. After she left, Lana's landlord arrived. She was devastated and wanted to let us know what a considerate and responsible tenant Lana had been. The landlord said

Lana would write a long apology letter if she was even a day late with her rent. It was becoming clear that people just loved this woman. One neighbor called her a "goddess." This was more than just being polite.

The famous movie producer Roger Corman knew Lana well because he'd produced the *Barbarian Queen* series, in which she was the star, during the mid to late eighties. He issued a statement calling her beautiful, brave, and adventurous: "She performed all of her own stunts, and showed unusual fortitude and athleticism in her horseback riding and fight sequences. On and off the set, Lana was a warm and loving person."

It was a stark contrast to what was seeping out about Spector.

HOUSE OF BLUES

After seeing my report, an acquaintance of Lana's faxed me a letter she said the actress had recently written to her. It was dated 1-2-03, almost a month to the day before she was killed. It reads, "Happy New Year! This is just a quick note to update you on my situation. I just received a great job offer from the House of Blues. . . . I start training on the sixth and will be the new (and very first female!) Senior Door Hostess for the VIP Foundation Room at the Private West Hollywood club. This is a full-time night position and will enable me to continue to pursue my acting and writing opportunities during the day. All the best wishes for a fantastic New Year! It's certainly going to be better than the last. . . . Sincerely, Lana."

What exactly had gone wrong in 2002? What was the glamorous and vivacious Lana's secret reality? A friend explained that Lana had taken a bad fall at a party about a year earlier and had broken both her wrists. On her official website, it said Lana required several surgeries. This injury prevented her from pursuing the kind of athletic acting roles that she'd been known for, perhaps exacerbating the already harsh career challenges most female actresses experience when they enter the forty zone.

That fateful Sunday night, Lana Clarkson was manning the Foundation Room door. It was quite late when Phil Spector walked in with a female friend, reportedly a waitress at another well-known restaurant. Lana, who towered over Phil, apparently didn't know who he was at first. But she soon found out. The friend left and Phil struck up a conversation with Lana.

OFF THE WAGON?

In a deposition, Spector refused to acknowledge having more than possibly one cocktail that evening, even though he had spent time in at least two other restaurants that night before coming to the House of Blues. The producer also insisted he never took illegal drugs and swore he was not intoxicated at the time of his arrest. But the Associated Press reported that the producer's own driver told a grand jury that leaving the House of Blues, Spector appeared inebriated and was helped into the car by Lana Clarkson because he was stumbling and slurring his speech. The driver reportedly said Clarkson initially refused to go home with Spector but finally agreed, while telling his driver she wanted it to be a fast trip and that she only wanted one drink.

Prosecutors would later claim Spector had a track record of violent behavior that got worse when he drank alcohol. The *Los Angeles Times* reported Spector had a history of drinking problems, but a friend told the paper the troubled producer had given up drinking a few years earlier. "He was supposed to be on the wagon," Pat Lalama, a reporter for *Celebrity Justice* who also covered the case extensively, told me. She explained that "he wasn't supposed to be drinking, which is all part of his treatment and therapy, because there are accounts from various musicians that under the influence of alcohol he became a maniac."

According to published reports, singer-songwriter Leonard Cohen told the BBC that while recording a song in the late seventies, he had to deal with Spector's "megalomania and insanity and the kind of devotion to armaments, to weapons, that was really intolerable." Cohen is quoted as saying that Phil had a bottle of wine in one hand and "shoved a revolver into my neck and said, 'Leonard, I love you.' I said, 'I hope you do, Phil.' " Still other published reports claim John Lennon and Dee Dee Ramone had both seen the muzzle end of a Spector gun while collaborating with the producer. Where legend ends and the real details begin is hard to say.

As someone with twelve years of sobriety, I know that people who sober up often drastically modify their erratic behavior. But I also know that if you say you're sober, or on the wagon, that means not one drop of alcohol. It doesn't mean having even one drink, as Phil Spector reportedly claimed he might have had the night Lana died. People with drinking problems cannot safely have just one drink any more than people with a heroin problem can safely shoot up just one more time. One drink can trigger a binge, which accounts for the saying "One drink is too much and a thousand isn't enough." A police report quotes the chauffeur as describing Spector as "completely drunk" when he emerged from the mansion after the shooting.

For his part, Spector later claimed that Clarkson was drunk and loud when they left the House of Blues and that she brought a bottle of tequila with her. The autopsy reportedly showed alcohol and Vicodin in her system, two substances that doctors will tell you shouldn't be mixed. But all of her friends I spoke with insisted Lana was not a drunk. Therefore, they say, she was entitled to have a drink or two after she went off duty and may have taken the painkiller earlier in the day, given that she was still recovering from her terrible fall more than a year before.

Whatever their respective conditions, we do know that Phil and Lana left the House of Blues in Spector's car and were driven back to his castle, where they disappeared inside at about 3:15 a.m. They were apparently the only two people inside the massive home when the single gunshot rang out about an hour and a half later. The big question is, Who fired the gun? And why?

As the days and weeks went on, I found myself doing story after story on the case, each with a slightly different explanation of events as Spector's interpretation of what happened seemed to shift.

GUNNING FOR TROUBLE?

According to published reports, an Alhambra police officer told the grand jury that after officers arrived at the castle, they shot the unruly Spector with a taser and handcuffed him. The cop testified that Spector then said, "What's wrong with you guys? What are you doing? I didn't mean to shoot her. It was an accident." But that alleged statement was not tape recorded. The prosecutor reportedly told the grand jurors that Spector later changed his story and told two separate officers that Lana Clarkson had blown her own brains out.

Spector's attorney condemned the release of the grand jury transcripts. "Much of it contains lies, half-truths, and slanted testimony and is biased, prejudicial, and unfair," said defense lawyer Bruce Cutler, a large and imposing man who is famous for having represented mafia legend John Gotti.

Cutler claimed that Spector was suffering

71

from withdrawal symptoms from *seven* prescription drugs when he allegedly told cops he had shot Lana. The defense lawyer accused police of refusing or ignoring Spector's requests for his medications. The medications were for treating depression, seizures, stomach acid, migraines, and pain, according to the defense.

Cutler's response to the murder charge against Spector is "Where is the motive for this? Does it make any sense? She was a stranger to him. This was an unfortunate accident, I believe, and he did not shoot this lady."

But wait: Was Spector's camp arguing it was an accident or a suicide? Phil Spector gave an interview to *Esquire* magazine in which he reportedly said that "she kissed the gun." The *Los Angeles Times* says Spector told cops that Lana sang two of the biggest hit songs he'd ever produced, "You've Lost That Loving Feeling" and "Da Doo Ron Ron," before she grabbed his gun and shot herself. Interestingly enough, while the autopsy report says the chauffeur saw Phil emerge with a gun in his hand, police later found the weapon that killed Lana lying on the ground near the chair where her body was found.

The autopsy on Lana concluded her death was a homicide. But the report also theorized "the weapon was in the mouth" when it was fired: "The entry wound is located at the oral cavity." The shocking news that the gun was in Lana's mouth when it went off started a round of wild speculation. What secret could explain that bizarre circumstance?

As the district attorney's spokeswoman put it while discussing the case, "Just because the gun was in her mouth doesn't mean she put it there."

"Guns are absolutely associated with being phallic symbols because of all the things they do," New York clinical psychologist Dr. Judy Kuriansky told me. Guns shoot "in the same way that a penis shoots. And it's shaped like a penis. So there are many analytic associations that can validly be made between a gun and a phallic symbol." Dr. Kuriansky said, while it's all speculative, one possible scenario is that they were playing some kind of sex game, or that he was forcing her to play against her will. Either way, it could have involved him putting the gun in her mouth, or forcing her to put it in her mouth. The psychologist adds, "It's an act of domination for one, and an act of aggression for another. It is certainly an act of control."

Using guns in sex play is not an uncommon practice for those who engage in sadomasochism, according to Dr. Kuriansky. How does it work? "The gun is the penis and the mouth is the vagina," says the doctor, leaving us to our imaginations. If you're upping the ante, this game can be played with a loaded gun that might even be cocked, so to speak. The turn-on is the total control one person is exerting over the other. Essentially, the dominant is holding the life of the submissive in his hands.

With most violence between men and women, there is a sexual undertone, and the common refrain is power — who's got it, who is giving it up. If we could just get comfortable with this unalterable plotline in sexuality, we might be able to relax and enjoy it, instead of repressing it to the point that it only pops up in hideous displays like dangerous gun-play or other violence.

In truth, many men desire to experience being submissive to a woman and many women would like to know what it feels like to sexually dominate a man. Talk to any practicing dominatrix and she'll tell you many of her customers are highly successful, married business executives who are tired of wielding power and desperately desire that delicious sense of freedom that comes with surrendering control. But these men feel they can't be totally honest with their own wives, whom they presume want them to be the eternal breadwinner and protector. So they pay their mistresses to fulfill their fantasies. Too bad. Chances are the wife would secretly love to break out the riding crop.

Sexuality can become a safe game practiced by loving adults — if they get over being so ashamed, embarrassed, and repressed. Until that happens, this aspect of sex will remain in the closet, only bursting out in self-destructive and hostile ways that are often dangerous, even deadly. America, with its stubborn puritanical streak, seems intent on exposing itself to all the dangers of repressed sexuality while robbing itself of all the fun of healthy and open sexuality. This attitude is what is responsible for so many of our secrets, secrets that are cracked open when repression gives way to obsession that leads to crime.

Jim Holcomb, a former cop who is a law enforcement expert, told me during an interview for *Celebrity Justice* that he's seen numerous homicides that have occurred as a result of sexual fetishes, but stressed that this theory is just one of many possible explanations worth looking at.

There are less kinky but equally kooky scenarios that have been entertained by those trying to solve the puzzle of why the muzzle was in Lana's mouth. "They could have been playing a wacky game of Russian roulette," says Pat Lalama. "It's anybody's guess." Except with Russian roulette you generally have only one bullet in the gun, hence the suspense of whether the click is going to kill you or not. In this case, the gun was reportedly fully loaded, with the exception of the one bullet that had been fired into Lana's mouth.

Some experts used their law enforcement experience to move beyond guesswork. While I was working on this case at *CJ*, Holcomb and I analyzed the defense's explanation. At that time, Spector was being represented by attorney Leslie Abramson, of Menendez brothers fame. She claimed that Clarkson could have put the gun in her mouth as a threat of suicide without meaning to pull the trigger, or out of grandiosity, or curiosity, adding "anything can happen when a person is under the influence of that combo," meaning alcohol and Vicodin.

Former cop Holcomb told *Celebrity Justice* that he believed the defense theory had a huge flaw. "In law enforcement circles, it's pretty well understood that women generally don't shoot themselves in the head, especially in the face area, because . . . they're very concerned about their looks throughout their life, and this kind of carries over as part of their instinct. That would certainly raise a red flag . . . as to maybe there's something else going on here."

Holcomb's point would be especially true with an actress like Lana, whose entire life had been centered around her beauty. One friend described her as "stunning, absolutely stunning. Perfect body, beautiful blond hair."

A publicist who claimed to be a friend of Lana's told reporters that the two of them used to go to target practice together. He said that Lana had become an expert markswoman because she needed to handle guns for many of her roles in TV shows like *Vice Girls.* He insisted Lana would never have pointed a gun at herself for any reason, given that the first rule of firearm safety is never to aim a gun at yourself. But if not by accident, what about intentionally?

"Suicide is absolutely out of the question," Lana's close friend Jann Castor told me, in her slightly Polish accent. Jann said he was supposed to be with Lana that very night;

she had invited him to meet her at the House of Blues, but he couldn't make it. "She was actually happy," he told me. A composer, he was working with her on a one-woman show she was planning about Marilyn Monroe. Lana hoped to impersonate the screen legend and sing some of her most famous songs.

Victim Bashing

So what about the speculation that she might have been depressed because she'd gone from starring in movies to being a hostess? "It's a lot of crap," said Jann. Another friend laughed at the suggestion that Lana would go on a suicide mission to Phil's house to blow her brains out, calling the theory "tortured." Why not kill yourself in the comfort of your own home?

The idea that Lana was depressed or suicidal was also ridiculed as nonsense by Elizabeth Prince. A collector of theatrical daggers and swords, Elizabeth said she'd become friendly with Lana because they both had booths at Los Angeles–area fantasy conventions like Monsters Among Us. Elizabeth told me that just weeks before Lana's death, she was upbeat, "posing with her fans, signing autographs for them," and exhibiting a great sense of humor and enthusiasm. While Lana may have been struggling in her career, the fact that she still had fans lining up for her autograph was certainly evidence that she didn't regard her career as over.

As debates over Lana's state of mind raged on, many of her friends became increasingly furious, watching helplessly as Lana's reputation was trampled in the media. "They will do everything. They will call her a prostitute or whatever. They will use everything in the book," Jann fumed.

The fact is, that very accusation was made in published reports just a few months after the deadly shooting. *Vanity Fair,* in an in-depth article on the case, claimed that a source said that in the early nineties Lana was a $1,000-an-hour call girl, using the name Alana and working for then–Beverly Hills madame Jody "Babydol" Gibson, who was said to cater to some of Hollywood's rich power players. The article quoted a co-worker as saying, "Oriental guys loved her. . . . She was the type who'd get booked in a second on a $10,000 Paris deal." In an interview that aired on *Celebrity Justice,* the article's author said he'd picked up no indication that she'd done that since the early 1990s, stressing it doesn't change the fact that Lana was the victim and that a good woman was dead.

Lana's best friend, a live-music promoter named Punkin Pie, told me, "It's very upsetting," echoing the common feeling among Lana's friends that the accusation was planted as part of a campaign to blame the victim. "Never," Punkin insisted, did Lana ever mention anything about being a paid escort, something Punkin is sure Lana would have revealed to her, since they'd been inseparable for the last decade. "We talked twenty times a day."

Others said it was just the typical Hollywood case of people trying to get their own publicity spin on a terrible tragedy.

And in Hollywood, the lines can get very blurry. Punkin Pie told me, "She would go on trips with people, all expenses paid, of course. We all do that." But, Punkin explained, that's vastly different from being a call girl. And it's true, in Hollywood, all-expenses-paid junkets are very common, provided by lots of companies and individuals hoping to get branded the next big thing.

Hollywood is always throwing around "free stuff" that isn't really free because it comes with strings attached. In the L.A. game of telephone, gossip can turn from silly to savage in the time it takes to paint a toenail. With all the talk, Lana's friends were livid over what was happening to her memory.

Frank Strausser, the author of a play that Lana appeared in called *The Powder Room Suite,* told me, "She had a very gentle spirit." He called her a gentle giant, saying he was surprised at how easily intimidated she was by other actresses, even though she physically overshadowed them. He theorized she may have been intimidated by the short but infamously aggressive Phil Spector.

PAYBACK TIME

In the wake of the murder charge filed against him, Spector's reputation came back to haunt him. It would seem that some people were just itching for the opportunity to tell *their* Phil Spector stories. And there were so many stories to tell.

The police have their own story to tell, reportedly having found at least ten guns in Spector's house on the night of the crime.

According to the *Los Angeles Times,* grand jurors heard several women testify about incidents in which Phil Spector allegedly threatened them with firearms. One woman said that in 1999 she was throwing a holiday party at her Beverly Hills–area home when Spector appeared. She didn't know who he was and reportedly described him as a "drunk Dudley Moore." After he flicked an ash from his cigar on her boyfriend's dog, she asked Spector to leave. She claimed he then pointed a handgun at her cheek. He said, "What are you going to say now?" according to published reports quoting the woman's testimony. After a brief but tense standoff, she said, he left.

A woman who once dated Spector reportedly told the grand jury the producer threatened her with a gun in the house where Lana died. This witness said that when she refused his commands that she go upstairs to the bedroom and undress, he hit her while holding a gun. She called the experience terrifying and said she ran out of the castle to her car sobbing, only to turn around and see Spector pointing a gun at her as she drove away. A third woman reportedly testified that she had gone with Spector to a party in New York and was later confronted by him in her hotel room. She said a gun-wielding Spector blocked her door with a chair and wouldn't let her leave. She managed to call the cops while Spector apparently thought she was on the phone with her mother.

Similar stories from still other women circulated in the media. At a later hearing,

Spector's attorney, Bruce Cutler, accused some of the women of being "sycophants and parasites." But the prosecutor said the stories showed Spector had a "common plan or scheme" when it came to women and guns.

"He's lucky he's gotten away with it this long." That was reporter Pat Lalama's conclusion after investigating Spector's history. She added, "He's an emotionally tormented, angry genius who tried to turn that torment on others and finally pushed the envelope to find himself in a murder trial."

Spector has acknowledged that he is, at the very least, eccentric. In a 1977 *Los Angeles Times* interview he confessed, "Being the rich millionaire in the mansion and then dressing up as Batman, I have to admit I did enjoy it to a certain extent. But I began to realize it was very unhealthy." As if a parade of bitter women wasn't enough, one of Spector's adopted sons publicly accused his father of bizarre and abusive behavior, calling him a psycho.

Spector even got into a legal war with his former personal assistant. After he accused her of stealing, she claimed sexual harassment. She accused Spector of sometimes appearing naked in front of her and once asking her to find him a prostitute. She reportedly claimed Spector proposed marriage to her to keep her from testifying against him at this trial, since spouses cannot be forced to testify against each other. She declined the offer.

To Know Him is to . . .

Phil Spector was born in the Bronx in lower-middle-class surroundings in 1940, the son of Russian Jewish parents. When Phil was about nine years old, his father is believed to have committed suicide. Phil's dad, reportedly depressed over money troubles, is said to have poisoned himself with carbon monoxide from his car's exhaust pipe. The tombstone on the father's grave read TO KNOW HIM WAS TO LOVE HIM, reminiscent of the title of Phil's first hit song, "To Know Him Is to Love Him."

Dr. Judy Kuriansky says these simple facts explain Phil's life trajectory: "To have his dad kill himself over money, the anger that a kid develops as a result of that is overwhelming. Which is not to say that every kid whose father commits suicide ends up being aggressive himself, but it is a major trauma for a child."

And yet this very trauma also pushed Phil

to wild success in the music business. This scrawny kid with no connections turned himself into a musical phenomenon who shaped the direction of pop and rock. Why does trauma motivate some people to greatness, while others just fall apart? Phil Spector has been described by many as a genius. The apparent suicide of his father over money appears to have given him enormous motivation. He used his intelligence to succeed financially, to make up for his father's lack of success. Undoubtedly feeling he had something to prove, Spector became a millionaire by the age of twenty-one. At the same time, he was smart enough to seek psychiatric help for his demons. According to *Reckless,* Carlton Smith's book on the producer, way back in 1960 Spector began seeing a psychiatrist with whom he discussed his anger over his father's death. Spector reportedly continued seeing the doctor for years. Despite all his efforts, it would appear Spector failed to heal inside, even as he was becoming more successful and more famous in the world at large. That ultimately became a dangerous combination: a tormented, angry man with the power and influence to intimidate people and get away with it. Why couldn't this brilliant artist find a way to heal his pain? According to author Smith, Spector showed early signs of being bipolar, a disorder marked by wild mood swings from manic euphoria to depression. This suggests that he wasn't an otherwise well-balanced boy who simply experienced one awful family tragedy. It suggests that Phil's demons are in his psyche's hard drive and he can't exorcise them — that he may indeed be a mad genius.

GET SHORTY

Dr. Kuriansky says the fact that Phil is physically small is another factor that would make the producer feel insecure and produce the desire to overcompensate and manifest his stature in other ways.

In the book *Phil Spector: Out of His Head,* author Richard Williams claims there was another incident that scarred Phil's psyche. It came early in Phil's music career, when the "short, skinny boy with mousy hair, a pursed mouth, and recessed chin" was touring with the Teddy Bears. The author quotes a close friend of Phil's who "told it like this: '. . . Phil went to the men's room. He went to the urinal, and four guys who'd come to see the show came in right after him and locked the door. They all urinated on him. I think this was the most shocking thing of his life.' This, indeed, seems to have triggered Spector's obsession with his personal security, leading him to surround himself at all times — even in the studio — with bodyguards and to equip himself with guns." In other accounts, some of Phil's acquaintances have doubted the story, but it would certainly explain a lot.

Phil's eccentricities no longer seemed as strange when put in the context of his physically tiny stature, his humiliation during that alleged assault, and his father's suicide. Suddenly, this small man's desire to display signs of power makes sense. While he cannot change the fact that he's short, he can make everything associated with him larger than life.

He became famous for his "wall of sound" recording technique, which used layer upon layer of instruments to create an orchestral intensity in a rock-and-roll song. That signature sound was bigger than life, hence Spector's nickname, "the Wagner of Rock and Roll." And when he no longer was in the forefront creatively, he still continued to live large, moving into a giant castle. Even his hair became supersized.

When Phil showed up for a court hearing in his murder case in May 2005, his hair caused a buzz of speculation. It was teased into a tall blond Afro that extended several inches above his head. It was as if his head had turned into a giant lightbulb. That, along with his trademark platform boots, made for quite a fashion statement. "He looks like a madman. I think it's part of his loss of touch with reality," said Dr. Kuriansky. In Phil's mind, hair could be a symbol of power and strength, as in the myth of Samson. The shoes and the hair would also make him appear taller. Even his tipping was grandiose. On the night of Lana's death, he reportedly left a tip of at least $450 on a $55 tab that he'd racked up at one of his stops.

But in the end, all that matters is the question of whether any of this relates to how Spector behaved that night inside his castle, alone with Lana Clarkson. Since nobody but the two of them was there, we can only deduce and theorize. Rest assured that since no cameras were rolling at the moment of death, both the prosecution and the defense have fashioned their cases out of the very same raw material: deduction and hypothesis, creatively designing theories to match up with the physical evidence and show their respective sides in the most favorable light. Psychology plays a major role in coming up with theories about motive. And when it comes to motive, the secrets of both the victim and the accused are key pieces in the puzzle of who did what to whom and why.

Dr. Kuriansky reminds us that all of us are unconsciously reworking our most significant childhood trauma by unconsciously reenacting it in many different ways: "You reenact the drama to try to heal it or undo it. It doesn't always take the form of a perfectly repeated act." In other words, you replay the drama but try to give it a happier ending or change it in some way to make it less agonizing, to puncture the festering sore of remembered pain.

If your beloved dog was given away when you were a child, as an adult you might become obsessed with rescuing stray dogs. If your father committed suicide, you might become obsessed with issues surrounding suicide and death. Dr. Kuriansky says that, unconsciously, Phil Spector would want to make the suicide of his father work out differently: "In the primitive mind, you undo the act of suicide by making it an act of life, i.e., kissing it. Kissing it puts it into such a bizarre opposite context. In the twisted mind, instead of being an act of death, it becomes an act of love or life or excitement." What exactly did Phil Spector mean when he said, "She kissed the gun"?

If Phil was acting out that evening, if he had fallen off the wagon, what would have triggered it at that point in his life? February 3 was not long after the holidays. According to Carlton Smith's book on the case, *Reckless,* Christmas was always a difficult time for Phil because his nine-year-old son, Phillip, had died of leukemia on Christmas Day in 1991: "His son's death was devastating, and Phil went into another steep depression." More than a decade later, the holidays could have triggered a repeat slide into melancholy.

There was also the issue of Spector's career. He had recently seen the Beatles' *Let It Be* album, which Spector had produced more than three decades earlier, re-released as *Let It Be . . . Naked.* The new version had very pointedly stripped away all of Spector's lush orchestral sounds, which Paul McCartney had so publicly disparaged. The *Los Angeles Times* reported that the music was returned "to the form it was in before producer Phil Spector took over the tapes and added massed choral voices, strings, and other touches characteristic of his wall-of-sound approach." It is possible that Spector might have felt terribly disrespected and, given his famous temper, may have been quite angry over that.

TICKET TO RIDE

In the wake of Lana's seemingly senseless death, other questions have arisen. Had Lana met Phil Spector before? There are some conflicting reports on that subject, given that they both traveled in a relatively small world. But Lana's confidante, Punkin, vehemently insists Lana never mentioned meeting Phil Spector to her.

So, then, the next question: Why on earth did she get into that limo and go home with a man she didn't know when it was almost three in the morning? "It made me feel really lucky, because I can't tell you how many times it could have been me," said a woman who knew Lana. This casual friend, who wanted to remain anonymous, likened their world to a college campus. "There's a real cliquey Hollywood crowd. Everybody knows each other. You go to any of these bars and you'll see people you know." That dynamic, said the friend, creates a false sense of security. "What's scary is we've all done it."

After the bars close at 2 a.m., this ultra-in crowd often ends up at an after party in the Hollywood Hills or somewhere else. "He could have said, Look, I'm having some people back, and come with me. It was a normal night in Hollywood. Wow, Phil Spector, how interesting and cool is that. He's going to talk about the Beatles!"

Several friends have also mentioned that Lana was very into music. "Hollywood was the place where all the musicians would show up and just jam. She was part of jam night," said the friend.

Punkin Pie, Lana's best buddy, actually ran the jam nights. "It's an all-star jam," Punkin explained. "It's usually a base of a house band and then on top of that lots of celebrity musicians drop by. . . . Back when Lana was alive, I had three nights going" regularly. And Lana would be right there with her friend Punkin on many of those nights.

"She knew the inside crowd, she knew the guitarists and the drummers that most people don't know. So to her, Phil Spector was like a Jimi Hendrix," said Lana's anonymous friend. And, of course, Lana was always looking out for her career: "He's a connection, because you're trying to get somewhere in the business."

But at three in the morning? "Absolutely," said Punkin. "Anytime you are out with a rock band, that's their hours, you know. The producers, that's when their night starts.

Because they have been in a studio all night or they have been at a gig all night. . . . So, for us, it was absolutely totally common to go anywhere at the end of the night with a band, or musician, or producer, or group. . . . That's their social hour." And, she added, who would think a legend could be dangerous?

Hollywood, say these friends, is not like anywhere else. The rest of the country just doesn't understand. Detroit is famous for cars. But Hollywood is famous for people who become famous. Everybody's always out selling themselves. In Hollywood, going to someone's home you've never met before is not like going home with a stranger. Everyone's running in the same circuit. Imagine a flock of people all flying toward what they each hope is stardom, a mass migration in which everyone knows someone that you know. Everyone is networking, trying to land that next gig or meet someone who will introduce them to a Hollywood player who might give them a shot. Everyone is desperate to be seen. Most of them are just flying in circles, but they can't see that.

Despite L.A.'s reputation as an early town, the real Hollywood continues all night long. The party girls "have an edge, they know the game and they know the ropes." One friend concludes, "She was a party girl, but she was one of the nice ones."

On the surface, Hollywood is a giant party with no last call. But the reality behind the curtain is quite the opposite. Hollywood is as tough and as cynical as a slaughterhouse. People are the product. They are worked until they are deemed too old or too lame, and then they are sent off to be turned into a by-product. The dream factory is a factory first. Show business is a business first. Since we're talking about clichés, let's use one: It's a tough town.

3
THE TEXAS CHILDREN MASSACRE

It's fair to say that everybody is walking around with at least a handful of secrets. There are sexual secrets, corporate secrets, financial secrets, and political secrets. In Texas, after a rash of child killings in which devout Christian mothers massacred their own flesh and blood, America became fascinated with secrets involving family, religion, and mental illness. Such monstrous violence is thankfully rare. But the suppressed rage behind it is privately felt by many wives who find themselves living in the same oppressive situations that apparently led these women to turn against their own families and become murderous mothers.

It would seem that all three of these Bible-belt ladies shared a secret. Despite, or perhaps because of, a strict framework of family and religion, they had become profoundly lost. Who paid the price? The eight children they killed.

In November 2004, in the small city of Plano, Texas, thirty-five-year-old Dena Schlosser severed the arms of her ten-month-old daughter, Maggie, leaving the baby to die. Police found the mother in her living room, covered in blood and still clutching a knife. Christian hymns were playing in the apartment. A Bible was open. According to Plano police, after Mrs. Schlosser's arrest she spent hours ceaselessly chanting, "Thank you, Jesus, thank you, Lord." One officer said he also heard Dena making guttural, growling sounds. Not long before the deadly slashing, she'd reportedly told her husband she wanted to give the baby to God.

In May 2003, in the small Texas town of New Chapel Hill, thirty-nine-year-old Deanna Laney went into the front yard of her home and bludgeoned her two young sons to death with rocks. Joshua was eight, Luke was six. It was eleven o'clock at night when Deanna woke up and took her boys, one by one, to the yard. She killed each in the same manner, telling him to lie down, then raising a large rock over his head and bringing it down repeatedly, aiming for the skull, with force. A third son, one-year-old Aaron, who was still in a crib, survived with severe head injuries. Deanna admitted muffling the youngest boy's cries so as to not wake up her husband. She called 911 and calmly told the operator, "I just killed my boys," adding that God had commanded her to do it. During trial testimony, it was revealed that Deanna Laney had experienced delusions on the day of the killings, seeing a child playing with a spear and a rock and squeezing a frog, and believed this was God telling her she should either stab, stone, or strangle her sons. She chose stoning.

Deanna's attorney told jurors that she was a very private person who kept the psychotic episodes that preceded the killings a secret. Testimony revealed that long before the killings, Deanna had begun hearing God's voice. According to a psychiatrist who testified at her trial, her delusions included reading signs from God into everyday events. For example, when her baby's bowel movements were abnormal, Deanna thought it was a sign that she was not properly digesting God's words. Several years earlier, Deanna reportedly had a hallucination in which she smelled sulfur and believed God was letting her know that the devil was near. Her husband testified he had no clue his wife was capable of killing her children and saw nothing to alarm him about his wife's mood prior to the attack.

But first, before Deanna and Dena, there was the mother of all baby killers, Andrea Yates, who massacred her five young children in June 2001 in the bathtub of the family's home in the suburbs of Houston, Texas.

BLOOD BATH

One morning, after her husband, Rusty, went to work at NASA, Andrea filled the tub until the water was three inches from the top. One of her children cheerfully asked, "Mommy, are we going to take a bath today?"

Instead, Andrea systematically drowned her kids, one by one. First she took three-year-old Paul and forced him into the bathwater facedown. The toddler struggled for approximately two minutes before going limp. Andrea then took the motionless Paul out of the tub and placed his body on the bed faceup, covering him completely with the bed sheet. She repeated this process with five-year-old John and two-year-old Luke. Each boy struggled violently, writhing, choking, and squirming for minutes on end until finally going limp. Their bodies then went onto the bed next to the others, under the cover. Next it was time to kill the baby, six-month-old Mary, who had been sitting on the bathroom floor wailing as her mother drowned three of her brothers just a few feet away. Andrea picked the little girl up and pushed her into the bathwater face-down.

Interrogation of Andrea Yates:
June 20, 2001
Sergeant: How long do you think she was able to struggle for?
Andrea: A couple of minutes.
Sergeant: Okay, and after Mary had died, what did you do with her body?
Andrea: I left it in there and called Noah in.

Finally, it was Noah's turn to die. The seven-year-old saw his baby sister's body in the tub. "Mommy, what's wrong with Mary?" he asked. She didn't answer his question. Noah was the most difficult to kill. He tried to run, but she tackled him, dragging him back to the tub and shoving him in. He put up a fierce struggle. By Andrea's own admission, the boy attempted to flip over and come up for air a couple of times over the course of the three minutes it took to drown him. After it was all over, Andrea took Mary's body out of the tub and put her in the bed with the three boys. Mary's little head rested on the arm of one of her brothers. Andrea left Noah's body floating in the bathwater. Andrea would later say Satan told her to do it.

THE COMMONALITIES

Andrea, Dena, and Deanna have an amazing amount in common. All three women lived in Texas. All were stay-at-home moms in their mid- to late thirties. All were coping with several young children. All were financially dependent on their husbands. All were extremely religious, deeply involved in movements that would fall under the Christian fundamentalist banner. That meant they were involved in worship that stressed living one's life according to a strict interpretation of the Bible. All three women read the Bible regularly, with intensity. Prosecutors say they found fourteen Bibles in Deanna Laney's home. Two of the moms, Andrea Yates and Deanna Laney, were homeschooling their children. Andrea Yates and Dena Schlosser were in relationships where their husbands, by virtue of their religious beliefs, acted as the leaders and bosses of their households. All of these women experienced a loss of independence and autonomy. As a result of being at home with the kids most of the time, they undoubtedly felt isolated and lonely.

While family and spirituality are certainly important, these women stressed those two aspects of their lives to the exclusion of almost all else. One wonders, Did they have any outside interests, hobbies, passions, or causes? Where was their curiosity about the rest of the world? Deanna Laney was particularly encircled by family. Her pastor at the Pentecostal church where she was a youth minister and sang in the choir was her brother-in-law. Another brother-in-law lived across the street.

ANY SECRET SIMILARITIES?

What's fascinating is that many of the living conditions that are considered normal and morally correct for extremely devout fundamentalist Christian women seem very similar to the conditions that are considered abusive by organizations that fight to protect women from domestic violence.

A well-known tool of women's advocacy groups is the Power and Control Wheel, which can be found in various adaptations by searching Internet sites on domestic violence prevention. I found one on the

Minnesota Center Against Violence and Abuse website. Think of a wheel with spokes, like an old wagon wheel, with eight spaces between the spokes. Each space contains a description of a form of oppression: intimidation, minimizing, blaming, using isolation, economic abuse, using coercion and threats, using children, and, finally, using male privilege. Under male privilege it lists: "treating her like a servant, making all the big decisions, defining men's and women's roles . . . put[ting] tradition and culture ahead of Western views. . . ." Under isolation, it lists: "using cultural expectations to control what she does, who she sees and what she reads . . ." Economic abuse is defined as: "not allowing her to have knowledge about finances, not letting her . . . earn money." Millions of women in America and around the world are controlled by these tactics, and — in some cases — that control is legitimized by a religious stamp of approval. Cultural expectations and church edicts can be interchangeable.

Many women who are not mentally unbalanced live with these dynamics and don't act out by killing their children or exhibiting any violence. They simply endure it. Still other women who believe they are modern, liberated, and evolved may recognize one or two of these dynamics in their relationship, and either remain in denial about it or put up with it. The secret is, while we gasp in horror at the actions of Andrea Yates, Deanna Laney, and Dena Schlosser, their predicaments are not totally foreign to us, nor are their rage and resentment.

BY REASON OF RELIGION?

One key difference between killer moms and the many merely unhappy wives in the world is simple: mental illness. These three deeply religious Christian women had a history of unstable, even psychotic behavior *before* they killed, and all used the insanity defense. Given the fact that Deanna said she was commanded by God to kill, that Dena thanked the Lord, and Andrea said she was under Satan's spell, people were asking: What's the secret link between their religious beliefs and their apparent madness? These cases illustrate how certain religious dogmas can make it harder to recognize and treat a mentally ill person.

Within extreme elements of the religious right are certain leaders who don't believe in psychiatry, don't believe in antidepressant drugs, and recommend that mentally ill people consult only God for a solution to their problems. Dr. Katherine Ramsland, a noted author who teaches forensic psychology at DeSales University in Pennsylvania, says that in fervently religious Christian communities, mental illness sometimes meets not with sympathy but with judgment: "There's this sense that mental illness is a punishment for not being correct in your religious behavior."

Dena Schlosser, the mom who sliced her daughter's arms off, was diagnosed with postpartum psychosis soon after that third daughter was born. In a terrible foreshadowing, Dena reportedly cut her own wrists the day after the baby's birth. The delivery may have been a traumatic experience for her. *The Dallas Morning News* reports she gave birth — without pain medication — in the family's Plano apartment. The paper adds that, a few days later, police were called when Dena was spotted running down the street screaming about demons. She'd left the baby alone in the room as she ran out. It should have been abundantly clear that she desperately needed help.

But Dena Schlosser and her husband attended the Water of Life Church. Their seventy-three-year-old pastor and self-described prophet, Doyle Davidson, is a controversial figure. He reportedly teaches that women possess a rebellious Jezebel spirit and need to submit to their husbands. On the witness stand in Dena's trial, Davidson addressed psychological health: "All mental problems, I'm convinced, are caused by demons. . . . I do not believe that any mental illness exists that is not manifestation of demonic activity." No wonder, then, that two members of his flock, Dena Schlosser and her husband, reportedly had qualms about the antipsychotic drugs prescribed for Dena and allegedly kept at least one of her psychotic episodes a secret from Child Protective Services, which had been monitoring her after she ran into the street, leaving her baby alone. Though she had seen a psychiatrist, the prosecutor in the case told jurors that both the system and Dena's husband had failed her. And what about the church doctrine of blaming mental problems on demons? One anonymous Texas psychologist warns it's time for these religious communities to educate themselves and police themselves with regard to mental illness.

Professor Ramsland thinks that is not likely to happen because "fundamentalism is not self-aware." Medical records indicate Andrea Yates also refused to take some of her antipsychotic drugs and sometimes flushed her meds down the toilet. The side effects of antipsychotics can be hard to endure, but Andrea may have thrown away her pills because she was reasoning that she had to get healthy on faith, that God would heal her mental anguish if she only prayed hard enough for it. Dr. Ramsland suspects Andrea may have also thought that taking the drugs was a sin. "Believe me, I have had clients who think, If I take a pill, then I'm changing what God made me and that's a sin."

Do some extreme religions essentially require that you reject medical science? Dena Schlosser's stepfather, Mick Macaulay, a mental health counselor, believes that Preacher Davidson's teachings, which shun psychological treatment for mental illness, pushed Dena toward a psychotic breakdown. "I'm not saying that anybody suggested 'Go cut your baby's arms off,'" Macaulay told the Associated Press. But, he added, "This diminishing of women, this diminishing of women's powers, women's importance, referring to women as Jezebels, I think, further undermines an already fragile ego state that Dena's experiencing." The Dallas paper also cites a psychiatric report that revealed that Dena had argued with her husband the day before she killed her baby daughter. She wanted to give the child to God or to Preacher Davidson. In response, Dena's husband allegedly "spanked his wife with a wooden spoon." Her husband, through his attorney, denied keeping Dena from getting proper care but added that in retrospect, he could have done some things differently. And Dena was said to be even more obsessed with Preacher Davidson and his beliefs than was her husband.

Dena's parents had long worried about their daughter's religious obsession, but they couldn't stop her. Professor Ramsland may have put it best: "Have you ever tried to talk someone out of their religion? It's not possible. You become the enemy. You are an instrument of the devil if you do that." Relatives ultimately give up trying to unconvert a loved one. But in the process, they can become co-conspirators in the silence that surrounds religiously fueled mental delusions. They enter the cone of silence and secrecy.

SPEAKING IN TONGUES

One of the other killer moms, Deanna Laney, was a lifelong Pentecostalist. In the year before she stoned her kids to death, she had reportedly told her East Texas congregation that the world was ending and she'd been instructed by God to get her house in order. Apparently, that provoked a big yawn among her fellow churchgoers, who were described as unconcerned by Deanna's pronouncements. Psychiatrists later concluded she was psychotic at the time. In fact, one psychiatrist testified Deanna thought she and Andrea Yates might somehow end up working together, "chosen" as God's only witnesses at the end of the world. The doctor testified that Deanna "thought they would be the ones to survive and preach."

Rusty Yates's aunt, Fairy Caroland, a Presbyterian minister, gave me an interesting explanation for why Deanna's congregation was so blasé about this devout mother's psychotic behavior and bizarre beliefs: "A Pentecostal church would make you really nervous if you haven't been in one. They tend to do what's called speaking in tongues. Their services tend to be highly emotional, much louder. . . . They do probably impress upon people a little more strongly the idea of Jesus is coming back soon and there's going to be a judgment against everybody for everything they've done."

According to the Associated Press, studies of women in the Midwest who killed their children showed a significant percentage of them had religious-themed delusions. Still, one social sciences professor cautions us not to read too much into that, noting, "Most of the people in nut houses are religious because most Americans are religious."

However, fringe faiths often attract mentally unstable people who crave strong leaders with immutable beliefs. People with fragile egos are lost. They want somebody to fill the void, to provide clear-cut directions, with no shades of gray. They're exhausted by life's endless choices. Following someone who tells you what to think narrows it all down. There's simplicity, relief. You might say there's a gravitational pull bringing people like Andrea, Dena, and Deanna into the orbit of charismatic preachers. But, on some level, isn't that relief what we all secretly want from our religions? We may say we're in search of God while we really may be trying to stop the chattering in our own heads.

PUT ON A HAPPY FACE

As these women became more and more involved in this restrictive and demanding religious world, their mental illness manifested itself and got worse. Depression is often caused by repressed anger. Is it possible that while these women *consciously* strove to submit to their husbands, on an *unconscious* level they were becoming very angry about it? Was that rage their biggest secret of all? What's striking is the compliance these women exhibited. Deanna Laney's husband testified that his wife never mentioned worries or problems, that "she'd most of the time smile at you." The father of the bludgeoned boys said, his voice cracking with grief, every day he asks, Why? "I don't understand it," he said, sighing, although he remained supportive of his wife throughout the trial.

Theirs was described as a model family. She was the perfect wife. Wow, is that stressful! Marriages are messy, difficult, long-term affairs that require awkward and painful communication and involve struggle and compromise. To try to avoid all that complication by putting on a happy face is to invite disaster. Does any of this ring a bell? These unhealthy, secret family dynamics that value appearances over honesty are all too common. Whenever married couples brag that they never fight, it's a red flag that they are way too invested in appearing perfect at the expense of personal growth and authenticity. Twelve-step programs have a catchy saying on this issue: you can save your face or you can save your ass.

We can never say for sure what is going on in somebody else's subconscious. But in the case of Andrea Yates, it's a very real possibility that she was furious at her husband, and the drownings of her children constituted a watery mutiny against her captain.

HUSBAND IN THE HEADLIGHTS?

When Rusty Yates got the ominous call from Andrea that morning to come home right away, the doe-eyed, clean-cut NASA engineer was seemingly astonished at the hideous surprise his wife of eight years had laid out for him. He reportedly collapsed on the lawn of his Houston-area home and lay there in the fetal position.

Was Rusty yet another victim? Or was he an emotional accessory?

It's easy to blame Rusty. Many have. But others point out that Andrea was an adult and was responsible for all her perplexing lifestyle choices — at least until the moment she went insane. So the question becomes, When did she go crazy? *Why* did she go crazy? Did she go crazy at all, or was it a cover for rage? At least one jury said she was not insane, although many psychiatrists condemned that verdict as nutty. After her

2002 conviction was overturned due to inaccurate testimony by a key witness, the issue of Andrea's mental state became a central theme in her 2006 retrial, as dueling experts fought over whether Andrea was really crazy or just an overwhelmed mother who knew right from wrong when she killed her kids. In the end, the second jury decided Andrea was not guilty by reason of insanity, allowing her to go to a mental institution instead of a prison.

FAMILY VALUES?

As Andrea's case gained national headlines, her family secrets emerged. Andrea had a history of mental illness. Her father also reportedly suffered from depression. Two years before Andrea killed her children, shortly after she had given birth to her fourth child, she was hospitalized for depression after trying to overdose with a fistful of pills. Not long after that, she was caught in another suicide attempt by her husband. She was clutching a knife that he is said to have pried out of her hands. Rusty's own mother was reportedly not told about these two suicide attempts, indicating that they were treated as shameful secrets and preemptively cutting off any help Rusty's mom and others could have given to Andrea at that earlier stage. This created even more isolation.

A psychiatric assessment around this time described Andrea as "depressed and anxious after the birth of her baby . . . She appears to be suicidal." The doctor's diagnostic impression? "Postpartum depression with psychosis."

At this point, Andrea had been married for about six years. She'd already had five pregnancies, including one miscarriage, for a total of four children. Still, Mr. and Mrs. Yates proceeded to conceive their fifth child, Mary.

In the media frenzy that followed the Yates killings, *Time* magazine asked the big question, "Having already endured one harrowing postpartum episode, why did she have another child?" It's a good question. Why did Rusty impregnate Andrea yet again, given her precarious mental state? At least one doctor who treated Andrea had warned both her and Rusty *not* to get pregnant again. The stats show women who have suffered from postpartum depression have a 50 percent chance of a reoccurrence as the result of another pregnancy.

Doctors warned that Andrea's sleeplessness and anxiety indicated that she was overwhelmed by the demands of daily life.

There was no way she could handle the children she already had, to say nothing of more kids. The warnings were ignored. According to Suzanne O'Malley's detailed book on the Yates case, *Are You There Alone? The Unspeakable Crime of Andrea Yates,* one doctor's report marveled that "Apparently patient and husband plan to have as many babies as nature will allow! This will surely guarantee future psychotic depression."

Why did Rusty want such a big family? What did that have to do with his religious beliefs? Many fundamentalist Christians are opposed to birth control. It seems possible or even likely that, in wanting to have as many children as nature would allow, Rusty and Andrea believed they were following the word of God, as they interpreted it in the Bible.

I was unable to talk to Rusty himself. Half a decade later, he's newly remarried and getting on with his life. But Rusty's aunt did respond to the criticism of her nephew's decision to impregnate Andrea again, resulting in the fifth child, Mary. She explained that "when they were told there was a fifty-fifty chance that she could have some similar symptoms, basically Rusty and Andrea both had the same kind of reaction. . . . They were both very optimistically naïve."

114

But Rusty's aunt doesn't think they were intentionally reckless, adding, "During the time that she was suicidal, she was on birth control." Why anyone would want to be intimate with a woman who is suicidal is another issue.

CULTURE CLASH

Dr. Katherine Ramsland says it's not fair to put all the blame on Rusty, that you cannot ignore the cultural factors at play when you're a Texan living in a conservative Christian world: "I think that he's in a culture that is about people doing for themselves. And mental illness is not okay. It's something to be ashamed of; it's something people should just get past." So somebody who is psychotic is supposed to just get over it and snap out of it? That sounds crazy to me.

One of Rusty Yates's lawyers, Edward Mallett, says the blame belongs not on his client but on the mental health community, charging they gave Andrea the "wrong diagnosis, wrong medications, wrong treatment, wrong instructions to Rusty." Mallett believes Andrea's diagnosis of postpartum depression was "a misdiagnosis. I think the diagnosis should be schizophrenia. . . . The one thing about schizophrenics, their schizophrenia gives them someone to talk to inside their head. And it is in the context of schizophrenia that we perhaps can understand her behavior better."

But Los Angeles psychoanalyst Dr. Bethany Marshall points out it's quite possible to be suffering from both. "You can be schizophrenic *and* have postpartum depression or postpartum psychosis."

ROCKET SCIENCE

Yates's attorney fiercely defends his client's life choices and intelligence, stressing, "Rusty isn't any kind of freak." He described Rusty as a popular guy who played high school football and started working for NASA when he was in college. "The old cliché You don't have to be a rocket scientist to do this or that — well, he's a rocket scientist. Extraordinarily intelligent."

But apparently the rocket scientist couldn't see what it doesn't take a rocket scientist to figure out. Clearly, his wife was in no condition to get pregnant again. Certainly, she was in no condition to watch over five young children. Absolutely not alone. Not to mention homeschooling them at the same time.

That's something that could stress out the most well-balanced mother on the planet, to say nothing of a woman who'd complained of visions and voices two years before the killings.

"She was too fragile . . . to have any children at all," says Dr. Marshall. "If you can't care for yourself, how are you going to care for a child?"

VOICES

All three of these killer moms heard secret voices or believed they were being sent supernatural messages or witnessing things that only their eyes could see. The fact that this didn't register as a family crisis demanding radical lifestyle changes is what makes these cases so frustrating.

According to *The Dallas Morning News*, Dena Schlosser had experienced numerous incidents that should have called for some drastic action by her immediate family or by the public mental health system. The paper reports that just days before baby Maggie's death, her troubled mom took her out for a walk in the middle of the night and thought the whir of a small engine was somebody building an ark.

It's natural for a spouse to hope that, somehow, a loved one will get better or move beyond a personal crisis. But the crucial lesson for anyone dealing with a troubled family member is *never* to assume the problem is just going to go away or to rely only on optimism or faith that things will just miraculously get better. That kind of magical thinking is dangerous. That non-confrontational approach is also known as denial. Don't *ever* keep a secret about a loved one's delusions or hallucinations, especially not from police, doctors, or child services. That's a secret that really can be deadly. Mental health experts say the sad truth is that delusions and hallucinations often get worse over time.

Case in point. Two years before Andrea killed her kids, a medical report quotes her as saying, "I had a fear I would hurt somebody. . . . I thought it better to end my own life and prevent it. . . . There was a voice, then an image of the knife. . . . I had a vision in my mind, get a knife, get a knife. . . . I had a vision of this person being stabbed. . . . the aftereffects."

This is what psychiatrists call "command hallucinations." Dr. Marshall theorizes the visions and voices Andrea was hearing two years before the murders were issuing commands that she successfully resisted; but "once the disease progressed, she stopped resisting the commands."

Schizophrenia is a biologically based disorder, but surroundings play a role. "We know the environment plays an important role in whether or not the schizophrenia is going to get activated. It can lie dormant," says Dr. Marshall. "I think the primary contributing factor is that she was overwhelmed by being placed in an environment where she didn't have enough support and the demands were too great on her."

Five kids, ages seven, five, three, two, and six months. A husband who works full time at NASA as a rocket scientist. A troubled, homeschooling mom. You do the math. It adds up to insanity.

KING-OF-THE-CASTLE SYNDROME

In the wake of these baby killings, other questions have arisen about the role of the husband/father when it comes to child-rearing in religious households where the man is deemed to be the spiritual leader. Does the woman do all the housework and the bulk of the child-rearing?

"He played with the kids a lot himself personally," Rusty's aunt told me. "He did and still does work at NASA during the day, and she was at home with the children. There's no doubt about that. That's not unlike a lot of families out there." But Andrea was not like the other mommies with five kids.

Andrea's best friend, Debbie Holmes, described Rusty's behavior this way: "I'm not saying he didn't play with them or enjoy them, but as far as care for them, he didn't," adding, "If the kids' faces or hands were dirty, he'd say, 'Wait till your mother comes.' " A therapist who saw Andrea for months testified that the one time she met Rusty, he referred to the Bible, saying wives must submit to their husbands. The therapist's notes read, "sense of [Andrea] being overwhelmed and trapped with no alternative."

I asked Rusty's attorney the question "Do you feel that he was practicing a patriarchal philosophy that required Andrea's subservience to him?" The attorney's response: "I think that's very unfair to Rusty and very unfair to Andrea. . . . Andrea was smart, strong, capable, independent-minded, and able to make her own choices as a young woman."

He's got a point. As a younger woman, Andrea was together enough to have become a nurse, a hospital career she excelled in for a number of years. That's a high-stress job that requires a certain amount of self-esteem and assertiveness. How did she go from that to this?

Psychiatrist's Interview of Andrea Yates

Doctor: What were you trying to accomplish, then, when you did take your children's lives?

Yates: They'd be in their innocent years. God would take them up.

Doctor: They'd be in their innocent years and God would take them up?

Yates: To be in heaven with him, yes . . .

Doctor: All right. And, if you had not taken their lives, what did you think would happen to them?

Yates: They would have continued stumbling.

Doctor: And where would they end up?

Yates: Hell.

Perhaps the most fascinating aspect of schizophrenia is that the voices these people hear are not speaking meaningless gibberish. In fact, the delusion can be the schizophrenic's way of giving voice to her unconscious desire. Dr. Marshall believes that if a schizophrenic is angry with her children because they overwhelm her and she simply cannot cope, then that suppressed rage can be incorporated into the delusion. Simply put, when you're schizo, the "voice" can start saying what you really want to hear.

TRAVELING PROPHET

Long before the 2001 tragedy, Andrea and Rusty had fallen under the sway of a controversial Christian preacher named Michael Woroniecki, who frequented college campuses. According to renowned Texas private investigator Bobbi Bacha, Woroniecki believed that "women should be subservient to men, and that if they do work then they are witches. He actually calls women at the campus 'working witches.' . . . All their function is to care for their husbands."

Some believe Rusty imitated the chauvinistic preacher. Both had large families and gave their kids biblical names and believed in homeschooling. The minister's family traveled in a bus, and Rusty even bought the bus from the preacher and moved his growing family into it. Picture this: a mentally disturbed mom, plus lots of kids, all living in a cramped bus! Then top it all off with another dangerous element . . . Satan!! In *Breaking Point,* Suzy Spencer's aptly titled book on Andrea Yates, the author quotes from the letters Mrs. Woroniecki reportedly wrote to Andrea urging her to get right with God before it was too late: "If you allow Satan to come in and 'steal the understanding' the consequences will be tragic." After Andrea killed her kids, Woroniecki said publicly he could not be held responsible for what anyone does with his preachings. By that time, Rusty had long soured on the preacher and traded in the bus for their Houston-area home. But it was too late.

WARNING: DO NOT MIX

Experts told me that for a budding schizo, teachings that even mention Satan can be very dangerous because they can stir up paranoia. A paranoid schizophrenic is someone who has a clear story line about someone or something being "out to get them." They have detailed plots in their heads and they'll tell you the story with the passion of a writer pitching a Hollywood script. The paranoid schizophrenic weaves real people and events into the delusion. The problem is, while you and I may be able to distinguish delusion from reality, a paranoid schizophrenic can't. Introducing Satan as a main character takes the plot to a whole other level. In trying to explain her mind-boggling crimes to police and psychiatrists, it seems even Andrea was a little confused about Satan's role. She told some she was saving her children from Satan — but she told others that she was secretly operating under Satan's will.

Andrea Yates Being Questioned by Interrogator,
November 7, 2001

Andrea: It's just something I was told to do.

Interrogator: Who told you to do that?

Andrea: Satan.

Interrogator: Satan told you to send the children to heaven?

Andrea: No, to kill them . . . I was pretty determined to do what . . . I was told to do, to drown the children.

What happens under the surface when a woman like Andrea Yates realizes she is literally, psychologically and financially, trapped? These women either veered off or failed to pursue a career path, gave away their independence as if it were worthless, accepted the responsibility of children, and then melded their family life around their religious beliefs, which require submission to their husbands. There's no way out. There is no room for their own individuality. Even Rusty noticed this back when Andrea tried to kill herself, reportedly telling a social worker, "Sometimes I feel like she lost her identity." Consciously, these women will never admit it. That's why they appear to become more obsessed with the religion. They don't want anyone, including themselves, to know what's roiling under the surface.

A lot of women are like this, and they come from all walks of life. Sometimes they are wealthy. Their manicured hands tap impatiently on the table. They've got everything but an identity. Their husbands provide and control. They feel powerless to walk away from the materially good life, and so they reek of stress and resentment and rage. They are locked into an affluent lifestyle, but one that doesn't let them express who they really are. These women may blow off steam by abusing the waiter and the parking valet. But that's usually as far as it goes. With the moms in Texas, mental illness took it to another level.

In the final analysis, Andrea, Dena, and Deanna may have been irritated at their children, but the ones they really hated were their husbands. Dr. Marshall illuminates the sick mind with this question: "What's the best way to get back at your husband? Kill the progenies." In one fell swoop, they have reclaimed all the power they've relinquished over the years. Or to put it in a way a rocket scientist might understand, every action has an *equal and opposite* reaction.

CHOICES

How many women out there feel similarly trapped and angry, but are well balanced enough that they would never act out their rage on a helpless child? What do these more well-adjusted women do with their rage and how is it connected to their dependency on their husbands? Being dependent on someone can make you feel helpless and powerless. Feeling powerless sparks rage. There are only two things you can do with rage: Express it or ignore it. These women may be stuffing their rage with anything from food to alcohol to . . . more religion.

So why are so many psychologically stable women signing up to be part of this fundamentalist culture that, at the very least, discourages female independence and individuality, potentially sparking feelings of powerlessness and rage? What's in it for these women?

Some experts feel it's a reaction to the postfeminist demands placed on women. At the height of the feminist movement, women felt they could just pursue their dreams and avoid marriage and childbearing entirely. Today many women interpret messages in the media as demanding they do it all: career, marriage and motherhood, perfect job, perfect home. That's not an easy trick. When a religion instructs a woman not to have a career, it's like a get-out-of-jail-free card. Until she finds herself in a new kind of prison.

Finally, some women simply fall in love with men who have an ultraconservative religious bent and go along with their husbands' wishes, no matter how demeaning. Says Professor Ramsland, "What people do to each other in the name of love and in the name of God is just horrendous."

PRESSURE TO PROCREATE

What happened psychologically to these killer moms has been described as an extreme example of what's happening in subtle ways in a lot of American marriages. One Texas psychologist tells me many of her female patients who are *not* fundamentalists feel depressed and stuck because they've put themselves into a traditional role within marriage. They bought into the fantasy of being stay-at-home moms. But they found out it's not like the movies.

"There's any number of women professing, in the privacy of my office, 'I thought this would be great, and boy, is this dull.' "

So why do we put ourselves under such pressure to create a traditional family? Why not stay single or adopt a child or take advantage of any number of other lifestyle alternatives out there? Think about it. America's population is skyrocketing; it's now at more than 300 million people.

RUSTY'S JOURNEY

If we look at Rusty's painful journey, supporters say he's long been moving in the direction of moderation. After suffering the mind-boggling agony of losing his five children, he finally remarried in March 2006 to a woman he met at his church. His aunt was at the wedding, and, she says, "I think he's in a very different place today" from where he was as a college student when he ran into Preacher Woroniecki on campus.

She said Rusty's personal evolution was reflected in his wedding ceremony. The pastor "talked about men and women together in marriage. And what he impressed upon both of them is that marriage involved a mutual subjection to one another. So he wasn't saying that one is over the other or any of that, and it was a beautiful ceremony." Rusty's aunt says she even got to say the closing prayer, which she says in this church is almost unheard of for a woman.

For a fascinating postscript to these tragedies, fast-forward to the North Texas state hospital where Andrea Yates and Dena Schlosser were committed after each was finally found not guilty by reason of insanity. According to an October 2006 story in *The Dallas Morning News,* Andrea and Dena, perhaps drawn together by their shared experience of psychotic religious delusions, have become close friends. Rusty Yates, who reportedly still visits Andrea regularly, told the paper he hopes the women can help each other through the long recovery process. Dena Schlosser was quoted as saying, "We talk about our past, we talk about our memories, our fun memories, the things that our kids did. . . ."

4
EXPENSIVE SECRETS

When it comes to keeping secrets, burying them under stacks of cash is one of the most efficient methods. But when rich people are forced to go to trial, all the money in the world can't stop their secrets from gushing out. If they don't spill out in court, they're served up to the media feeding frenzy outside.

And what astounding secrets the wealthy can accumulate! They say the rich aren't like you and me. Well, their secrets aren't like yours and mine either. Poor people can be weirdos. Middle-class people can be strange. Rich people are *eccentric.*

In the case of Robert Durst, eccentric doesn't even begin to describe it. He's carried so many secrets over so many decades that teams of investigators in three states still have not solved the puzzle of his life. The dark details revealed in his murder trial freaked out even seasoned reporters who'd thought they'd seen it all. Even the affidavit for his arrest warrant gave us the shivers.

Affidavit for Arrest Warrant
The State of Texas
County of Galveston

ROBERT DURST, DOB April 12, 1943; White male; 5'7"; 150 lbs.;

It is the belief of Affiant, and he hereby charges and accuses, that:

ROBERT DURST, in Galveston County, Texas, on or about the 30th day of September 2001, did then and there intentionally or knowingly cause the death of Morris Black by cutting off the arms, legs and head of the said Morris Black, using a knife, saw, or other sharp instrument. . . .

You might think Robert Durst would have hit bottom when he was arrested for killing and chopping up his seventy-one-year-old neighbor with a knife and a bow saw and dumping the old man's body parts in Galveston Bay. But his behavior was to get even weirder — oops, more eccentric.

Whether he was beheading a friend or cross-dressing, this heir to a multibillion-dollar fortune has always had to do every-thing his own way. Even in jail, awaiting trial, he did it in eccentric rich-man style.

NEW YORK POST
Naked Durst's Dirty Dancing
BY LESLIE T. SNADOWSKY

October 13, 2004 — GALVESTON, Texas

Cross-dressing millionaire Robert Durst continued his weird ways behind bars — doing nude jumping jacks in his cell, an ex-jailer said yesterday. The wacky wig wearer also jogged in place nude while watching TV, the former jailer said. When bemused guards looked in, the real estate heir didn't stop. He went on with his nude gyrations as though there was nothing strange about what he was doing.

To Morris Black's family, Durst is not a comedian but a slippery killer who is almost impossible to pin down.

At one point in Durst's long and twisted odyssey, a judge set his bail at $3 *billion.* Lawyers on either side marveled. It was the highest bail they'd ever heard of, anywhere in the country. The judge justified it by calling Durst "probably the wealthiest person in the criminal justice system in America." Naturally, since he was a wealthy guy, Durst's expensive lawyers appealed and got the bail reduced.

Robert Durst has gotten himself in and out of enough legal jams to fill a season of *CSI*. He's admitted to chopping up a body. He has long lived under a cloud of suspicion in the unsolved disappearance of his first wife in New York and the mysterious murder of his close friend in Los Angeles. Durst has been snagged for numerous lesser offenses: shoplifting, bond jumping, evidence tampering, and carrying weapons across state lines. And what has he gotten for all of it? How about a $65 million settlement from his family to cut all ties.

Money for Nothing

At birth, Robert Durst was already set for life. Heir to one of New York City's great real-estate fortunes, he had it all. His family owned a lot of very pricey real estate where a string of Manhattan skyscrapers now stand. The Durst Organization went on to commission the famous Condé Nast building in Times Square. The Dursts are among the royal families of real estate, and Robert was the first-born prince.

But his troubles started early. When he was seven, his mother plunged to her death from the roof of their mansion in Scarsdale, and little Bobby reportedly had the misfortune to witness it.

Matt Birkbeck wrote a fascinating book on the Durst saga, *A Deadly Secret: The Strange Disappearance of Kathie Durst*. Birkbeck told me that a few years after his mother died, the young Durst was sent to "a psychiatrist. And they gave a real startling analysis. He was a borderline schizophrenic with severe personality decomposition. He's already deteriorating psychologically. At ten years old, he's falling apart." Durst would testify that, growing up, he suffered from bulimia, did not have many friends, was addicted to pot, and often talked to himself.

Still, Robert Durst managed to grow up, graduate from Scarsdale High School and Lehigh University, attend graduate school at UCLA, and have a social life. He reportedly hung out with John Lennon, with whom he shared a fondness for primal scream therapy, and with Jacqueline Kennedy Onassis.

In 1971, Durst met a fresh-faced young woman who was renting an apartment in one of the buildings the Durst Organization owned on Manhattan's East Side. Kathleen McCormack wasn't part of the Manhattan elite. She came from a middle-class Catholic family. With big eyes, long hair, and classic features, she was an Irish-American beauty. She was also whip smart and determined to become a doctor. She and Durst married in 1973.

As the decade wore on, their marriage wore out. For one thing, Kathie Durst was determined to finish medical school. There was the pressure of their high-intensity social life, which involved stints at Studio 54 and trips to exotic locales. But there were other problems as well.

Kathie's brother Jim McCormack told me about an incident that occurred two or three years before Kathie disappeared. They were relaxing at his family's holiday dinner when, suddenly, Durst grabbed Kathie like a rag doll: "Bob had gone out to warm up the Mercedes. . . . [He] comes back in and encourages Kathie to go. She's trying to buy some time. He walks over and just grabs her by the hair and says, 'C'mon, we're leaving now.' Pulls her. It happened so fast, you know, I was in shock, I didn't believe what I was witnessing there." There were similar stories from other sources.

Ellen L. F. Strauss, an East Coast family-law attorney, told me she was going to law school while Kathie was going to med school, and they would have long talks about the problems in her marriage. Ellen told me that Kathie was afraid of Bob and flatly warned, " 'If anything ever happens to me, look to Bob. Bob did it, don't let him get away with it.' She said it to everybody who would listen."

By 1981, Kathie told friends she wanted a divorce and a decent settlement from her rich husband. "A lot of people, from what I understand, were urging Kathie to walk away from the relationship," says her brother. Kathie had already contacted a divorce attorney, according to family and friends.

"Kathie, leave. Do a settlement later. Get out of harm's way," Ellen begged.

There were still other problems, including Bob's alleged extramarital affairs. In Birkbeck's penetrating book, he quotes a friend of Kathie's as saying Kathie believed Bob was having an affair with actress Mia Farrow's sister Prudence, said to be the inspiration for the Beatles' song "Dear Prudence."

According to the book, the friend told detectives that Kathie had "had enough. She wanted out. But she wanted some money out of it and Bobby said no. She had nothing, not even a dime. She wanted a settlement, but he wouldn't give her money to live on. She's married to a millionaire and begging her friends for a few bucks. It was pathetic."

On the evening of January 31, 1982, Kathie, in sweatpants and sweatshirt, showed up at a friend's house for a small party. Jim believes his sister was drinking, and, given the era and the fast crowd, she may have been using cocaine. Jim told me Kathie left early, after arguing with her husband on the phone: "There was a series of phone calls. . . . He was insisting that she come home right away. He was basically being very controlling."

But was someone else secretly trying to control the situation, too? Ellen tells me a close friend of Kathie's pushed her to confront Bob. This female friend, says Ellen, was secretly in love with Kathie and wanted the marriage over so she could have a lesbian affair with Kathie, but Kathie was totally straight and simply not interested.

There's disagreement about who initiated the angry phone calls, and who was egging

137

whom on. But one thing is not in dispute. That night, Kathie left the party to meet up with Robert. Her friends never saw her again.

CONTROL ISSUES

Durst waited several days before strolling, with his dog, into a Manhattan police station and reporting his wife missing. Was this jet-setter couple so used to being apart that he failed to notice she'd fallen off the face of the earth? After all, she was cramming for med school and they regularly bounced between three high-priced residences. Or was this rich guy buying himself enough time to make sure she'd disappeared? That was the question that had detectives scratching their heads.

Durst told police his wife had arrived back at their quaint country home in South Salem, New York. She drank a bottle of wine, they argued, and he put her on a train back to the city.

Kathie's brother believes Durst was shaken by the impending divorce because Bob had control issues and "Kathie was the one thing in his life that he could control." Considering that Robert had watched his mother die, the issue of abandonment by the second most important woman in his life could have been tremendously destabilizing, provoking the grief and rage he may never have fully processed when he was a child. This rage could have been buried for decades.

Robert Durst, at about five foot seven, is not a big man. But he had a huge ego. Was he going to let his wife leap out of his life just like his mother did?

Still, despite the suspicions of Kathie's friends and family, Durst was never charged in the case. No one has ever been charged! Her brother believes police investigators "were not proactive. They were reactive, waiting for someone to call . . . waiting for a sighting . . . waiting for something else to happen." I asked Jim if he thought that had anything to do with Robert's influence as a Durst? "Absolutely," he said. "The Durst family was and still is one of the most powerful families in New York City. They are off the radar. They do not seek publicity like Donald Trump. They are a very controlling family in terms of business, in terms of relationships." This is not to suggest that the Durst Organization did anything untoward, but rather that power, by its very existence, intimidates those who perceive themselves as having less of it.

The case of Kathie Durst's disappearance

was a hot potato that got cold and went stale. But perhaps Bob paid a price for the bad publicity it brought him. In 1994, a dozen years after her disappearance, Bob felt his father's rejection when he was passed over to run the family's real estate empire in favor of his younger brother, Douglas. Given the scandal and Robert's pot-smoking ways, Douglas must have appeared to be better business material. Durst recoiled from his family after that. "He was hurt," says Strauss. "He stopped talking to his father." Later, he even skipped his dad's funeral.

Trust-Fund-Baby Blues

When you're a trust-fund baby growing up in Manhattan, you can face very stark and narrow choices.

Door #1: Live the straight and narrow, work hard, go to Ivy League schools, excel, follow in your father's footsteps, and you might — *might* — inherit the whole empire, instead of one of your siblings. But if you're not up for that monumental challenge, there's . . .

Door #2: Get passionate about a charity and use your wealth to make the world a better place, or . . .

Door #3: Focus on marrying well, having a family, and advancing in the high-society circuit, or . . .

Door #4: Take the money, do the drugs, do whatever you please, distract yourself with all the sycophants clamoring to be your friend or your lover, and degenerate into a jaded shell of a human being who has no moral compass and no purpose other than to explore the dark side and throw around your inherited weight.

Some suspect Durst miscalculated, assuming he could work some, party a lot, and still get the corporate brass ring. "He would have been very happy had he been allowed to take over the family business. He thought he was going to run the company," says attorney Ellen Strauss. Durst did middle-management work in the family business and reportedly met Kathie when he collected her rent.

But did he suffer from delusions of grandeur that led him to regard his own abilities and accomplishments as more than they actually were? Was he unrealistic in possibly assuming he would inherit the empire despite his troubles and idiosyncrasies, like his well-known habit of growling like an animal? "Obviously, they passed over him for a reason," says Strauss.

"He would sit at the table and belch and

think nothing of it. . . . Bob's attitude? The rules don't apply to me. I can buy my way out of everything because my family has got a lot of power . . . yadda, yadda, yadda," says Kathie's brother. When someone's idea of achievement is their ability to flaunt social convention, hoist the red flag.

Durst himself alluded to his handicaps. On the stand he said he favored a "hippie lifestyle" and that he felt out of place in the corporate world: "Everybody looked like they'd gone to Brooks Brothers and purchased the same things. . . . I could never get into dressing properly and taking the whole thing seriously." Durst testified that he felt "relieved" when his father turned the family business over to Douglas. But others say he was bitter and felt betrayed by his family.

COAST-TO-COAST CARNAGE

Fast-forward to December 2000. That's when *People* magazine reported that a New York State police investigator had reopened the Kathie Durst case. It was nearly two decades after her disappearance. According to *People,* investigators were reexamining evidence and repeatedly searching their country home, although Robert had already sold it. Authorities also dragged a nearby lake. The drama was about to take off and fly cross-country to Los Angeles.

Susan Berman, an author and friend of Robert Durst's, lived in L.A. She had served as his informal spokesperson after Kathie's disappearance. Three weeks after the *People* magazine article appeared, Susan Berman was murdered. She was writing a book about the Mafia, and some suspected a mob hit. Others had their doubts. Even though she was the daughter of Davie Berman, who was purportedly involved with the late, great mobsters Bugsy Siegel and Meyer Lansky, some suspected Susan only had historical tidbits to impart, as opposed to any current information that could provoke a hit.

Word spread that the reenergized investigators from New York may have been planning to fly to L.A. to interview Susan about Kathie's disappearance. Ellen Strauss says that a month before, she even sent New York investigators a map to Susan Berman's front door, believing Susan was Robert's confidante and could tell them something.

Soon it was too late to talk to Susan Berman. "She was shot in the back of the head, so whoever she let in was probably someone she knew and just pulled out a gun and just shot her," says Ellen. She added that the killer must have felt guilty, because he sent a note to cops. Written in green ink was Susan Berman's address and the word *cadaver*. Durst favored green ink, according to *The New York Times*.

Susan's murder was never solved. In March 2006, I called the Los Angeles County District Attorney's Office to find out what was happening with the Berman investigation. The spokeswoman told me the LAPD was handling the case. Repeated requests to the LAPD for an interview were fruitless, with the only comment being there were no updates. One law-enforcement source told me there was an L.A. detective assigned to Susan Berman's murder but claimed the case was sitting "in a shoebox under his desk."

Nancy Grace, CNN Headline News, July 15, 2005

Nancy Grace: When you take a look at Durst, I mean, whoever is around him better go hide under the bed. His wife went missing, never seen again, last known with him. Then his friend, a very dear friend of his wife's, Susan Berman, ends up murdered execution-style in her home. Wasn't he loaning her money?

Matt Birkbeck, Author: He had lent her money. I mean, they had been — they had been best friends for a very long time, and it's now believed that he had confided to her what happened to Kathie Durst. What's interesting is that Susan Berman died . . . four weeks after news of . . . the new investigation into . . . Kathie's disappearance had been publicized. That's when Durst, 3 days later, had gone to Galveston, then three weeks later from that, Susan Berman was found dead.

BUYING TIME?

What is one of the common denominators in criminal investigations involving the rich? They have a tendency to drag on and on and on. The wealthy can pick up and move, as Robert Durst did. They have the resources to hire the best lawyers, as Durst has been known to do. These are attorneys who use every legal trick in the book to postpone, litigate, obfuscate, intimidate, and avoid cooperation, often for decades on end. Meanwhile, evidence can deteriorate or disappear, key witnesses can go senile or die, and the public can lose interest. In my experience as a reporter, I have seen countless examples of murder cases that passed the coverage expiration date as viewers lost interest over months and years. As for evidence, authorities certainly would have

145

had a better chance of finding any proof of a crime in Kathie Durst's case had they torn apart the Durst home and dragged a nearby lake in the *weeks* after Kathie went missing, instead of some *eighteen years* later.

The same delay dynamic can be seen at work after a wealthy defendant is charged. The Sixth Amendment of the U.S. Constitution talks about a defendant's right to a speedy trial, a right designed to prevent undue incarceration and anxiety and to maximize the defendant's ability to mount a credible defense. But many wealthy defendants have figured out that biding their time and delaying a trial is more to their advantage. The murder case of Phil Spector, accused of killing actress Lana Clarkson in February 2003, is a perfect example. Spector switched attorneys several times, resulting in delays that pushed the start date of the trial into 2007, four years after the crime. As well-known author and Hollywood observer Dominick Dunne noted in *Vanity Fair* magazine, Spector "has not spent a night in jail." Over the years, the uproar that accompanied the initial news that this beloved woman had been shot in the mouth at Spector's estate died down. Lana's friends expressed outrage to me over the delays, calling them a blatant defense tactic. In a similar manner, Kathie Durst's friends and family expressed to me frustration with what they considered the glacial pace of the criminal investigations after Kathie's baffling disappearance.

Contrast all that with what I have seen so many times in criminal courts while sitting in the gallery waiting for a VIP case to come up. Before me would pass one accused person after the other, all represented by a public defender, as they were too poor to afford their own lawyers. In these cases, the system seemed to be flying on speed. It was often as if the judges, prosecutors, and even the defense attorneys couldn't get through these cases fast enough, talking fast, using shorthand, and making deals that they briefly described to the defendant in order to get their uninformed approval. Some of these defendants had language barriers. Although an interpreter was in place, the whole process was ping-ponging so fast that you could see that these confused and frightened defendants were being pressured to make decisions in a matter of seconds that could affect the rest of their lives. I remember sitting in those courtrooms, waiting for my "important" cases, and thinking, Justice is so *not* blind. It has 20-20 vision. A poor person caught selling drugs can end up doing a lot more time than a celebrity caught using drugs, or a wealthy man who admits not only to using drugs but to chopping up a body and scattering it in the sea, as we shall see.

Affidavit for Arrest Warrant (Galveston, Texas)

Affiant spoke with the owner and landlord of the building located at 2213 Avenue K. . . . Ms. Dorothy Ciner is the lessee on apartment number 2. Her rent is always paid early because she told him that she travels a lot. . . . He had not seen Ms. Ciner since the first of the year. . . .

Around the time Susan Berman was murdered, Ms. Dorothy Ciner, wearing a dress and glasses that were held together with tape, appeared in Galveston, Texas, and began renting an apartment for three hundred dollars a month in a low-income section of town. Sometimes a friend named Robert Durst would come visit Dorothy. They were never seen together at the same time.

As would later be revealed at trial, the person who claimed to be Dorothy Ciner was Robert Durst, secretly disguised as a woman. A mute woman at that, who claimed to have a voice ailment that kept her from speaking. The landlord, Klaus Dillmann, testified "Mr. Durst was very convincing dressing as Mrs. Ciner. . . . I can't even say 100 percent today it is the same person, but obviously it is." As for her style? "She looked like a middle-aged woman with a flat chest. I felt sorry for the poor thing."

Dorothy Ciner, it turns out, was an actual person who went to high school with Durst in Scarsdale. The real Dorothy has said publicly that she and Robert went on a few dates and he had a crush on her. As an adult, Durst chose to go back in time and borrow her identity. Why? Not for the usual reasons, that is for sure. Usually the motive behind stealing someone else's identity is money, one thing Durst did not lack.

According to the Department of Justice, in one six-month period in 2004, 3.6 million U.S. households learned they were victims of identity theft. Almost half of those cases involved the unauthorized use of a credit card. Only 15 percent of the victims experienced the misuse of personal information. That would probably be the category under which Durst's alleged name borrowing would fall. But his motive was unique.

On the stand, Durst said he went to Galveston to hide out after his "life became hell" when he learned, in the fall of 2000, that authorities had reopened the investigation into Kathie's disappearance eighteen years earlier. He specifically accused the Westchester County district attorney, Jeanine Pirro, of launching a witch hunt, "a new investigation of Robert Durst to further her political career. I believe she wanted to charge me and get publicity to further her political career."

MASQUERADE

People go underground in a lot of different ways. Why didn't Durst just dye his hair, grow a mustache, and don a cap? Why did he choose to disappear as a woman, even buying a woman's wig? Some feel his cross-dressing has no particular significance, that it was just a way for Durst to disappear from the prying eyes of law enforcement. Durst himself later claimed on the witness stand, "I hated wearing the wig. I don't know how women do it." He told jurors he once set fire to his wig while lighting a cigarette in a bar. He regaled jurors with the story of his trip to the library, when he forgot *he* was a *she* and walked into the men's room, stunning the other man at the urinal. Ha ha ha? Not so fast.

When it comes to analyzing a criminal's

behavior, everything is significant, everything is a clue to his psyche. Especially something as eccentric as cross-dressing.

DATING YOURSELF

The Renaissance Transgender Association puts forth various possible reasons that men choose to dress as women, from erotic arousal to fetishism, from tension relief to female envy, from "fooling the world" to "conscious alternative personality."

According to the association, "The alternative 'female' personality is a different person from the male. 'She' frequently has 'her' own name, makes 'her' own social niche, and 'her' own history. Many cross-dressers refer to their 'female' selves . . . with another third-person term when they are not in drag. . . . For some cross-dressers this alternative personality has a 'life of her own.' This is not, however, a split personality, because the cross-dresser knows that the 'female' character is an illusion, a character in a drama produced and directed by the cross-dresser himself. The cross-dresser, who has created an alternative personality, actually finds satisfaction in bringing that character to 'life' and in playing out episodes of the drama."

Could there be a better description of

Robert Durst, the ultimate drama queen, whose episodes were playing out coast-to-coast and as far south as Galveston Bay, where the body he chopped up would be discovered?

Says Kathie's brother, "I truly believe he was running from reality. And it was coming down on him very heavy." In court, Durst himself said, "It seemed like the problem was, I was Robert Durst. . . . I wanted not to be Robert Durst."

But why run as a woman? Why did he frequent drag clubs, as was reported in the *New York Post* in 2003, under the headline CLUB QUEEN DURST, a story that quoted a homeless man as describing Durst this way: "I remember seeing the ugliest blonde I've ever seen in my entire life. . . . He was wearing ripped-up stockings and looked like a cancer patient in his cheap blond wig."

Cross-dressing is not an indicator of sexual orientation. Many heterosexual American men are secret cross-dressers. I interviewed one heterosexual man who enjoys dressing up in sexy women's lingerie for evenings of autoerotica when circumstances give him time alone. This was kept a secret from his wife until she discovered some credit card charges for Victoria's Secret and confronted him, mistakenly believing he had a mistress. Turns out he was his own mistress. He told me his angry wife refused to believe his explanation until he offered proof. From a secret hiding place, the husband reluctantly pulled out a pair of very, very large women's high-heel shoes — which fit him perfectly.

I also spoke with a woman who has been married to a heterosexual transvestite for two decades. On the condition of anonymity, she explained that a young boy who has lost his mother commonly will hold his mother's clothes for comfort and "touch her underwear, smell her underwear, because she's gone. He's missing her and it's something to hold on to . . . and then it could evolve from there."

She theorized that the type of woman Durst chose to be, dowdy and middle-aged, suggests he was not acting out a sexual fetish: "Red lips, a tight miniskirt, stiletto heels, that would be more of a sexual maniac." Instead, this woman suspects, Robert's cross-dressing probably "made him feel safe. He associated that with closeness and warmth, a security blanket." She also noted that men who cross-dress are generally very self-absorbed and feel both anger and self-pity. "It's actually an egotistical narcissistic affair with themselves. . . .

153

It's me, myself, and I. . . . They're lonely and it becomes a big habit. They get an erection because of the silky stuff . . . masturbate. . . . It becomes an addiction. It's escapism into the female form. It's also a way of keeping himself company." Because they can't find anybody to relate to, in the end, "They're dating themselves." Of course, this woman correctly cautions that these are all just theories, that every person's sexuality is unique.

But why lay low in such a low-rent, transient area, when — with a trust fund of roughly $2 million a year — he could have hidden out and cross-dressed in style?

POOR LITTLE RICH BOY

Many have commented on Durst's eccentric spending habits. He could be wildly generous but was often extraordinarily cheap. For example, Durst, according to Kathie's brother, didn't like to buy new cars. A lot of very rich people are like that, especially people who've inherited money.

The nouveau riche love to show off their wealth, but the old-money crowd likes to hide it. Some psychologists say trust-fund babies know, deep down inside, they didn't earn the money themselves and subconsciously fear that if they lose it, they won't have a clue as to how to earn it back.

Nouveau or old, a lot of wealthy Americans like to keep their money a secret from others, be it the government, an ex-wife, or a business associate, in an attempt to reduce taxes, understate their assets, or protect themselves in the event of a lawsuit or divorce. One way to keep a stash of cash secret is to put it in an offshore account or a Swiss bank account. Some even opt to create privately held offshore companies based in obscure places like the Caribbean island of Nevis, so that the account doesn't bear the individual's name and therefore his or her transactions don't leave as much of a trail. Sometimes these financial games can mean trouble. In 2000 the Financial Action Task Force, which is part of the Organization for Economic Cooperation and Development, put out a blacklist of countries that were accused of being uncooperative in the war against tax evasion and money laundering. The Federation of Saint Kitts and Nevis were on the list. Saint Kitts and Nevis were later taken off the list, thanks to new regulations, although it's still easy to find ads encouraging the rich to set up there. While many share Durst's penchant for financial secrecy, Durst's motivation was quite uncommon.

Robert Durst had low self-esteem. He had been cast aside by his father and would never run the family empire. Reporter Leslie Snadowsky, who covered the Durst case for the *New York Post,* says Durst "was trying to shed this mantle of a billionaire . . . because he felt alienated from his family."

In Durst's case, living on the cheap was, at least in part, an unconscious reflection of a dark side, a poor self. The poverty mentality mirrored an inner poverty. To the world, Robert was rich, but inside he felt poor. Everyone remarks on his long-running addiction to marijuana. He was what people call a pothead.

And his biggest failure, in his unconscious mind? He'd failed to save his mother. Psychologists say when children witness traumatic events like the death of their mothers, they often blame themselves, no matter how irrational that self-blame is. The shabby surroundings Durst chose were a metaphor for how he felt about himself.

Durst may have found a way to integrate all those negative self-images with the major tragedies of his life. By creating a woman out of whole cloth, he brought Mommy back to life. He may have also psychologically reincarnated his missing wife. These females were wrapped up in his "Dorothy" persona and placed in a world that finally felt authentic. A poor world. A transient world. The sad, lonely little boy was hiding out in his secret clubhouse with all the most significant women in his life — his high school sweetheart, the wife he once loved, and the mother he adored.

Robert chose to make Dorothy mute. A dead mother is also mute. A missing wife is also mute. Dorothy was a name that harkened to his youth. There are no accidents in these choices. Each decision has meaning, even if the person who makes the decision has no conscious awareness of the meaning.

MOTION SICKNESS

Sometimes choices have double or triple meanings. "I believe he was just setting himself up to do no good in different cities," says Snadowsky, who has tried to track Durst's movements in the years following his 1994 alienation from his family. "What he would do is move from town to town, city to city, renting apartments . . . he would rent a lot of low-rent type of apartments . . . to blend in with the regular people," she adds. Snadowsky, who lived in Galveston for months while following the trial, told me her extensive research showed Durst had a fondness for renting places near the

Salvation Army or women's shelters.

Snadowsky explains, "In Galveston on K Street where he was, he was about a block away from the Salvation Army, where he used to go, and I have quotes from the . . . Salvation Army guy saying, 'Yeah, we had Robert Durst here.' And in his backyard, on the other end of the street, was a women's shelter. It was a pattern." And there were other patterns. Bobby was always running.

On September 30, 2001, trash bags containing severed arms and legs were found bobbing in Galveston Bay, along with sections of a newspaper with a mailing label. The address? 2213 Avenue K. Cops quickly focused on the apartment of seventy-one-year-old Morris Black. They saw blood and traced it to the apartment across the hall, Dorothy Ciner's unit. Inside Dorothy's apartment, investigators found bloody boots, a bloody knife, and blood on everything from the carpet to the kitchen walls. In his book, Matt Birkbeck described it as "a slaughterhouse, some sick scene from a slasher movie." The cops also heard from neighbors about Dorothy's friend Robert, who'd been spotted putting bags into a silver car.

Just over a week later, Durst's silver Honda was found and he was arrested. In his car, police reportedly found a saw. He had been staying at a hotel under the name Jim Truss, another name from his school days.

He was charged with murder. Bail was set at $300,000. Being the rich fellow he secretly was, he quickly made bail and then went on the run. His disappearance sparked a manhunt that lasted about six weeks. It ended pathetically on November 30, when Durst was caught shoplifting a single Band-Aid and a chicken salad sandwich from a supermarket in Pennsylvania and ultimately sent back to Texas for his murder trial. By that time, police had figured out that Durst was a wealthy man who reportedly had homes in New York and Northern California. "The reason he stole the sandwich is not because he is a petty thief. It's a trip to him. He likes to feel empowered by stealing things, getting away with things. . . . He feels like he can get away with everything," says Bobbi Bacha, a private investigator for Blue Moon Investigations, Security and Protection of Webster, Texas, who investigated Durst.

It was a strange game. "It looked like wherever Robert Durst went, he used other identities," Snadowsky told me. "When he was on the lam for those weeks after he killed Morris Black and went on that joyride across the country," he used "different social security numbers . . . different driver's licenses. He kept switching . . . and we found a time when he even used his missing . . . wife's social security number sometime down the road. Kathie disappeared in 1982, and years, years later he used her social security number."

"I don't think anyone is ever going to know the full extent of how many different identities this man's had, what property or vehicles he's owned or rented," says private eye Bacha.

Durst had yet another secret. After his arrest, another wife emerged into the spotlight. It turns out Durst had secretly married in December 2000, the same month Susan Berman was killed. The bride? A New York real-estate broker. *The New York Times* ran an article in November 2003 with claims of a battle between Durst's new wife and the Durst family "over who would control Mr. Durst's millions if Mr. Durst was found incompetent." Remember, even though Durst was estranged from his family, he was still reportedly getting nearly $2 million a year from the family trust. In the end, incompetence was a nonissue, at least on Durst's part.

DEFENDANT AS CELEBRITY

How does a jury find a man not guilty who admits he shot his neighbor, cut up the corpse, dumped the body parts in Galveston Bay, and then tried to hide from authorities?

— Ed Lavandera, CNN correspondent,
November 11, 2003

It was the question everyone was asking in the wake of Robert Durst's eventual acquittal on the charge of murdering his neighbor Morris. Durst himself appeared totally shocked when the not guilty verdict was read, his jaw visibly dropping.

But, again, follow the money. Durst had hired a dynamite defense team of top-flight lawyers. One of them, Dick DeGuerin, went on to defend former House majority leader Tom DeLay. Another of Durst's defense attorneys, Michael Ramsey, would later defend former Enron chairman Kenneth Lay, albeit unsuccessfully.

The local prosecutors were no match.

The D.A. called Durst a "cold, calculating" murderer who "carved up Morris Black like a side of beef," then put down a few cocktails and retreated to a resort hotel, where he ordered room service.

161

It was a strong start, but the state sputtered when it came to providing jurors with a clear-cut motive. The general consensus is that prosecutors were so confident of their case — given that Durst admitted to shooting Black and cutting up his body, putting it in garbage bags, and tossing it into the bay, and given that Durst had jumped bail and fled the state — that they underestimated the ability of this brilliantly creative defense team to come up with reasonable doubt as to premeditated murder.

DESCENT INTO MADNESS

Durst had filed a plea of not guilty by reason of accidental shooting or self-defense. On the stand, the kooky heir told a story that painted the victim as a buddy who was also a violence-prone old geezer who kept breaking into Durst's apartment to watch TV, since he didn't have one of his own. Durst claimed Black had gone into his apartment and grabbed a gun that Durst had hidden and then swiveled as if to point it at him. They struggled over the gun and it went off, accidentally killing Black.

In court, there were gasps as Durst and one of his lawyers did a full-on reenactment, playing out the alleged struggle they claimed led to an accidental shooting. The attorney

162

played Morris Black and fell to the floor during the demonstration.

For the pièce de résistance, Durst also managed to come up with an explanation as to why he carved up his former friend's body.

On the stand, the heir explained that, after the gun went off, he realized no one would believe it was an accident since he had rented the apartment posing as a woman and his wife had disappeared under suspicious circumstances. So he panicked and began what his attorney called "a descent into madness."

It took Durst twelve to eighteen hours to carve up Black's body, according to the medical examiner's estimate. Durst said he used saws and an ax. But first, he drank a fifth of Jack Daniel's. "You were drunk while cutting up Black?" the prosecutor asked. "I hope so, yes, sir," responded Durst. By Durst's own account, "I was swimming in blood and I kept spitting up and spitting up and I don't know what is real, I don't know what is not real. That is what I remember."

According to *Vanity Fair,* whose reporter Ned Zeman put out a comprehensive look at the case in February 2002, some of Kathie's friends saw a clue in Black's personal life that they felt pointed to something far more sinister than an accidental shooting. "Black was a mystery man. He lived an itinerant lifestyle. And yet, at the time of his death, he had $137,000 in a South Dakota bank," Zeman writes, adding that shortly before he was killed, Black told a neighbor "that he had 'a big secret' that he couldn't possibly discuss." Zeman's article says at least one of Kathie's close friends "promptly envisaged a history between Black and Durst."

Ted Streuli, then a reporter at the *Galveston County Daily News* who worked the case, told me, "I think our image of Morris was more of this kind of transient derelict type . . . and you didn't expect a guy living in a rent-by-the-month room on Avenue K to have 125 dollars, much less 125 thousand dollars, to his name. I think that really piqued everyone's curiosity. . . . How'd these guys know each other . . . and the speculation really ran wild."

But, says Streuli, in the end nobody ever came up with any long history between Morris Black and Robert Durst: "And I remember some of us looking at, you know, can we put Morris Black in L.A. at the time Susan Berman was killed, or can we put him in New York at the time Kathie disappeared. No! Nobody ever could. Nobody ever found a connection. Nobody ever found any evidence of any preexisting relationship. . . . Nobody ever connected the dots, and we tried."

Prosecutors didn't have any deep back story to explain why Durst might want Black dead, and implied that Durst wanted to assume Black's identity. That explanation of a motive for murder failed to impress the jury, so they came back with a verdict that stunned everyone.

GALVESTON, OH GALVESTON

Private eye Bobbi Bacha wasn't stunned. She saw another very clear explanation as to why the jury let Durst off. It's what she called the hillbilly mind.

"Galveston has never had anything like this. It's a small town. They've never really had any real celebrities. Here's a multimillionaire whose father built Times Square. They know he's very powerful. And here are these county residents, blue-collar workers. They know they're holding a get-out-of-jail-free card for this man. And I think they tried to find a way to get him off."

Those who grew up with Durst found his acquittal terrifying. His brother Thomas, a San Francisco–area developer, told the *New*

York Post, " 'I'm in shock. I'm just in shock. . . . He'll kill again, I have no doubt, the question is who is next?' " *The New York Times* also reported that Durst's brothers "remain concerned about Robert's intentions toward them." Douglas Durst, who took the helm of the family's multibillion-dollar business, hired security guards for his home after Robert jumped bail. "It did not help matters that while he was on the run he pulled into the driveway of Douglas Durst's estate with two loaded handguns in his car," said the *Times.* The paper reports that Prudence Farrow was said to be nervous as well, having told investigators that Durst became "furious with her when she tried to break off their relationship" just days before she found out Kathie had gone missing.

THE SCENE OF THE CRIME

After Durst's murder acquittal, he still had to face justice for bail jumping, evidence tampering, and transporting guns across state lines. After serving a few months in a New Jersey federal prison on the gun violation, he got out on supervised parole in July 2005. It is believed he was whisked away from prison in a limo with dark-tinted windows. Still, he managed to get in trouble by allegedly going back to the place where he shot and dismembered Morris Black. By visiting his old place on Avenue K, he violated his parole and rattled some of his former neighbors.

You'd think having beat a murder rap he'd play it safe. But no, no, Durst took an unauthorized trip back to the scene of the crime, the boarding house where he killed his neighbor and where some of the witnesses who testified against him still live. He also went to a nearby mall for some holiday shopping . . . and guess who he ran into? Who's the last person he'd want to see while violating his parole? The judge who presided over his murder case.
— *Dan Abrams,* The Abrams Report, *MSNBC, January 24, 2006*

I was walking down the mall and I saw this man walking toward me talking on the cell phone. As he got closer, my first thought was I know that guy, and then I realized, Oh my God, that's Durst.
— *Susan Criss, judge who presided over Durst murder case*

The judge told Dan Abrams that Durst was

so shocked to see her that he dropped his cell phone and it cracked apart. This, by the way, is the same judge who had set his bail at $3 billion, provoking his hostility and a legal battle. But in true blue-blood, stiff-upper-lip fashion, Bob chatted about how his lawyer was representing Tom DeLay. Meantime, the judge did her best to subtly back out of the conversation and away from Durst.

Durst was re-arrested for violating his restrictive parole, and thus began yet another legal saga. Behind bars once again, the heir sued the state of Texas, claiming he was being treated too harshly. He was released in the winter of 2006. The Texas Board of Pardons and Paroles ruled that he did not deserve to be under the state's highest level of supervision for parolees. They had to concede Durst was not a violent criminal since he had only pleaded guilty to federal charges of gun possession and state charges of bond jumping and evidence tampering — even though he had chopped a fellow to pieces! Finally in November 2006 his parole obligations ended and he was truly a free man.

In the end, Durst also managed to get his family to pay him $65 million in return for cutting all ties. While it's a lot more complicated than that, it must feel strange to be that wildly unpopular with your own family.

How does all this affect the investigations in Los Angeles and New York, which theoretically are still ongoing? Matt Birkbeck says money and power have a chilling effect. "You've got D.A.s in L.A. and in Westchester County who have to consider, Hey, he beat the rap on something that was so obvious. I mean, he admitted to carving this guy and killing him. And he was still acquitted. . . . So they're probably thinking, He's going to bring in his high-powered attorneys, we're going to have the Battle Royal, is this something we can win, is this something where we are going to waste taxpayers' money?" Police and prosecutors are people first. They react with the same basic human emotions that govern all of us. Wealth can inspire fear or, at the very least, make the authorities feel like they must tread very carefully, because they are guaranteed to pay dearly for any mistakes. Every crime goes through the system in the context of where it happened and who is involved. This is the secret truth of our criminal justice system.

Reporter Ted Streuli is one of many who remain perplexed by the puzzle of it all. "Certainly there seem to be a lot of coincidences here. If Robert Durst was responsible for whatever happened to Kathie *and* for Susan Berman's death, it's astounding that police departments of that size couldn't put the pieces together and bring him to trial." The fact is, even the snarkiest citizen deserves the presumption of innocence, especially when he hasn't even been charged. That includes Robert Durst. As it stands now, Morris Black's killing is the only one in which Durst has been shown to be involved.

As for those still trying to climb out of the wreckage of Durst's stupendously messy life — Kathie's brother, Jim McCormack, says, "You take the shoebox and put it up onto the top shelf of the closet, push it to the back, and close the door. When the door is shut, you don't feel the pain . . . but when I get a call like this today, or sometimes I'll be driving down the highway thinking, I'll just starting thinking again. . . . I'll start crying."

Jim is a law-abiding citizen. He might fantasize about revenge, but he's just joking. "I would love to see him face-to-face.

After all, I'm sixty-one years old. I'm still in reasonably good shape and I would probably be committing an act of self-defense — if you know what I mean."

5
SAVAGE SUBURB

What are the chances? From reporters to former prosecutors, all the TV pundits, including me, couldn't stop talking about the freakishly bizarre and tragic series of events involving prominent defense attorney Daniel Horowitz. This lawyer, whom many of us knew as a peaceful and generous man, seemed to have found himself trapped in a suburb of savagery.

At fifty, Horowitz was at the peak of his professional career. He was a familiar face on national cable TV shows, weighing in on the Scott Peterson and Michael Jackson trials as an expert legal analyst. But in one horrible instant, Dan Horowitz went from commenting on the news to *being* the news. This respected lawyer's life collapsed in tragedy when his wife was brutally murdered, just as he began to argue one of the biggest cases of his career. Suddenly the tables had turned. Dan Horowitz found himself spinning in the media spotlight, his privacy violated, his secrets revealed, his life subject to all sorts of scrutiny and conjecture.

This stunning turn of events happened just a few short months after Horowitz and his fellow court watchers had packed up and fled Neverland country. After Michael Jackson was found not guilty of molestation in June 2005, reporters and attorneys scattered every which way out of Santa Barbara County in central California. Horowitz headed up north to his home in the San Francisco Bay Area. There, he focused on his new high-profile case. This time, he was the lead defense attorney.

POLKING AROUND

Dan Horowitz was representing a slim suburban housewife named Susan Polk. Susan was accused of murdering her husband, Felix, with a paring knife during a confrontation in the pool house of their Northern California estate. The Polks had been a family at war. After a relationship that had spanned three decades and produced three sons, Susan and Felix were at the end of a very nasty divorce. Susan had moved out and was living in Montana, but she had recently moved back into the family home. Just a few days before the killing, sheriff's officers had reportedly been called to the house as husband and wife argued over who was entitled to sleep where.

Susan was reportedly livid after finding out a judge had slashed her monthly alimony payment, awarded their $2 million home to her estranged husband, *and* given him custody of their youngest son, Gabriel. Gabriel later testified that his mom had talked openly about various ways she was planning to kill his dad, including hitting him with her car, shooting him with a gun, or pushing him into the pool.

One of the reasons the Polk case had become such a big national news story was because the defendant looked like such a soccer mom, a dainty lady in her forties who seemed more likely to serve you a cup of tea than stab you with a paring knife. She and her husband had raised their boys in a wealthy, well-manicured suburban community about fifteen miles east of San Francisco. During the trial, a treasure trove of strange secrets poured out about this privileged and refined-looking couple and their three children, who had grown into handsome young men. Like many families entwined in crime, the Polks seemed perfectly well adjusted, almost a little too perfect, until you scratched beneath the surface.

Susan's defense involved accusations that her husband, a prominent psychologist, had physically and psychologically abused her for years. She claimed Felix had threatened to kill her, their children, and their dogs if she ever walked out on him. But two of her sons, Gabriel and the oldest, twenty-three-year-old Adam, sided against their mother. Gabriel called her delusional, saying she made up the abuse. Adam went further, describing her as "the embodiment of evil." On the witness stand, Adam confronted his mother directly, telling her, "You're bonkers! You're cuckoo for Cocoa Puffs!"

No one disputed the fact that the environment within the household had long been toxic and that the Polk marriage was falling apart. Almost two years before Felix's death, Susan says she tried to commit suicide by downing a bottle of aspirin. This was the loud warning siren. Many couples are in unhappy marriages, but suicide attempts are powerful statements that the ante is being upped and the possibility of death, in some way, shape, or form, has entered the equation. A threshold has been crossed.

They separated several months later, but the potential for danger was obviously still present. After the killing, Gabriel told the sheriff's officers that his mother had tried to buy a shotgun a couple of weeks earlier while she was in Montana.

So here were the warning signs *before* the killing: a suicide attempt, death threats, and the attempt to buy a gun. At this point, Dr. Polk should have packed up his sons and headed for the hills. Forget school, forget work, forget the house. Let a lawyer deal with that. Just get out of harm's way! But a neighbor and friend of Felix's said even though Felix feared for his life, he was treating Susan more like a troubled patient than a potential killer.

Dr. Polk's inaction was actually quite typical of how spouses behave in these kinds of domestic conflicts. We often fall victim to inertia in long-term relationships. The tendency, even for a psychologist who should know better, is to linger and engage in ever-sicker interactions as the relationship disintegrates. Why? Because human beings have an ingrained tendency to stick with what they know and have grown comfortable with. The alternative, even if it's a lot saner, seems scary just because it's new.

We see this all the time. How many friends do you know who have been breaking up for years? There are examples everywhere of abused spouses who stick with the relationship, despite beatings and/or humiliations, because it's what they know. Sticking around too long is self-destructive behavior. As they say on Wall Street, if you're going to panic, panic early and get out first.

Also, as we see in so many cases of family violence, the extended family was left in the dark. Susan's mother told *Dateline NBC* that Susan kept the extent of her marital troubles a secret from her. It raises the question, Who do we consult and confide in with our relationship troubles? If the response is nobody, that's a dangerous answer.

PECULIAR PARALLELS

Almost three years to the day after Felix Polk was killed, his wife's murder trial began. The prosecutor called Susan Polk nothing but a "cold, callous, calculating murderer" who was in a rage because she felt her husband had gotten the upper hand in their ongoing divorce battle. He said seventy-year-old Felix Polk suffered twenty-seven stab wounds and cuts as he fought for his life against the much younger Susan, even accumulating defensive wounds to his hands and feet. The doctor's body had been discovered in the pool house by the youngest boy, Gabriel, then fifteen years old. His father's corpse was covered in blood. The prosecutor noted that Susan initially denied any involvement in the killing. When told her husband's body had been found, she allegedly responded that they were getting a divorce anyway. Perhaps most chilling was a conversation Susan allegedly had with her son Gabriel, who asked where his dad was. "He's gone. Aren't you happy?" she replied, according to the prosecutor. "No," the boy said. "I am," Susan allegedly shot back.

Then it was time for the defense opening arguments. Susan's lead attorney, Dan Horowitz, addressed the jury. He insisted that his client had acted in self-defense when, during an argument, Felix went into a rage and slapped her. The defense attorney claimed Susan tried subduing Felix with pepper spray, but Felix came back at her wielding the paring knife. That's when Susan says she kicked Felix in the groin, grabbed the knife, and stabbed him repeatedly as he lay on top of her. The problem with that defense scenario is that Felix's injuries were far more extensive than Susan's.

Horowitz then took a controversial tack, lambasting the victim's character. While friends say Felix was a smart, sophisticated man with a great sense of humor and a love of books and classical music, Horowitz accused Felix of being narcissistic and controlling, and of inflicting decades of physical and emotional abuse on Susan.

Horowitz took his strategy even further, going back to the early 1970s, when Susan was a high school student and Felix was already an established psychologist, husband, and father more than twice her age. Susan had been sent to Dr. Polk for counseling because she was suffering from panic attacks. Horowitz claimed that Felix had raped his teenage patient under hypnosis, an alleged secret that Susan apparently brought to light after she was arrested for her husband's murder.

What has been widely reported is that some suspected the doctor and his teen patient were carrying on a secret affair. If true, this could have opened him up to charges of statutory rape and been a violation of his professional responsibilities. On *Dateline NBC,* Susan's mother said she became suspicious when Susan "said something about sitting on his lap . . . I said, 'Wait a minute, that doesn't sound right.' " But Susan's mom told *Dateline NBC* that at the time, she didn't feel she could question a psychologist about his practice. Susan Polk says that even after she stopped seeing

Felix professionally she kept seeing him romantically and that he would cry and threaten suicide when she tried to end the relationship. So, says Susan, they finally got married when she was twenty-five and he was a divorced dad of about fifty. That, Susan claims, is when Felix's controlling ways escalated.

Dan Horowitz told the jurors that Felix Polk had a history of mental illness that dated back to a suicide attempt and psychiatric hospitalization in the 1950s. Said Horowitz in court, "this man had a chronic, lifetime illness that led him to have outbursts of rage, violence, and anger."

Watching and listening attentively in the gallery was the tall, dark-haired, and elegant wife of Dan Horowitz, Pamela Vitale. She had every reason to be there. Pamela had helped Dan write his opening statement and often assisted his legal practice, managing the computer databases.

It had been quite a week. But neither Dan nor Pamela chose to forget about the Polk trial as the weekend got under way. On Saturday, October 15, 2005, Dan Horowitz left home early to spend the day catching up on the Polk case paperwork in his office. Pamela spent that morning at home. Computer records reportedly show she surfed the Internet, catching up on the Polk case news coverage and other items. She was on the computer, say investigators, until 10:12 a.m.

When Dan Horowitz returned home at about 6:00 that evening, he was perplexed to see his wife's car still there. She had tickets to the ballet and should have left already. Then he noticed blood on the front door. When Dan walked inside his world turned surreal. Near the front door, he found Pamela curled up on the floor in a pool of blood. Neighbors reported hearing Dan's screams: "Oh my God, no, no, no!"

Pamela Vitale had been bludgeoned to death, leaving her with twenty-six separate wounds to the head and face, along with injuries to her body. From the wreckage all around her, it looked as if it had been a fierce and desperate battle to the death between her and her assailant. Blood spattered the walls. Some of her teeth had been knocked out. A few of her fingers were broken. There were shards of pottery in her hair. Her skirt was hiked up near her waist. She had a gaping wound to her stomach that exposed her intestines. Most sinister of all, a strange symbol had been carved into her back. Some called it a goth-style cross. Later the prosecutor would describe it as an

H-shaped symbol with an extended horizontal line. "She fought back very hard," Horowitz told a reporter. "That was obvious from the scene."

DAN THE MAN

I had worked alongside Dan during the Michael Jackson case just a few months before. Along with more than two thousand other credentialed members of the media from around the world, Dan and I were in the mix, jostling and angling to get the latest tidbit on the ever-morphing case. Not a lawyer myself, I often asked attorneys in the press pool to explain nuances of the law as issues came up in the trial. Dan didn't know me at first, but he took my card and proceeded to e-mail me more information than I could have ever hoped for. He was very generous with his time and knowledge. He was also very well known for doing lots of pro bono legal work for people who couldn't afford a lawyer. Some of them virtually lived in his own backyard.

Like so many other journalists and lawyers who had covered the Jackson case with Dan, I was stunned by what happened on October 15. It was so odd to suddenly find myself reporting on somebody I knew personally, especially given the horrific nature of the crime. A couple of days after the murder, I found myself making one of the most difficult phone calls imaginable. I was filling in for Nancy Grace on her *CNN Headline News* show and needed to get some crucial details so that I knew what was going on in the case. I had to force myself to punch in the numbers. Dan picked up his cell phone. He was astoundingly gracious and took the time to answer my questions, even though he clearly seemed in deep distress and depression. I made the call as brief as I possibly could.

NEIGHBORHOOD NEXUS

Both the Horowitz and Polk families lived in Contra Costa County, a lush and leafy suburb that was an easy commute to and from San Francisco. Dan lived in the town of Lafayette. Susan lived only about five miles away, in Orinda. Both are small, affluent communities where the typical income is far above the national average. But in every affluent area, there are exceptions. Some of those exceptions lived in the shadows of the ornate home Dan Horowitz was building with Pamela. This was where they had hoped to grow old together. Little did they know of the trouble percolating just down the road.

Friends described Dan and Pam as long-time lovebirds. Each had been married before. Pamela had a son and a daughter from her previous marriage. She had an eclectic background. Prosecutors said she had been a flight attendant for Pan Am airlines, then worked in the high-tech industry in the Bay Area, ultimately reaching the executive level. According to Dan, Pamela was an independent movie producer when he first met her. He thought she might be interested in a screenplay he'd written based on one of his cases.

Dan said it was love at first sight. He forgot about the screenplay and ultimately married Pam. She had a dream: She envisioned an Italian villa on a hill. Dan worked many major cases and raised the money to help his wife fulfill her dream. They had spent the last couple of years building the seven-thousand-square-foot mansion. Pamela supervised nearly all of the work on the massive construction project, down to the last details. The home was three stories high, with a large flat rooftop that allowed for 360-degree views of the surrounding countryside. Dan Horowitz told the *San Francisco Chronicle* that the estate, home, and property were worth between $8 and

$10 million. From the air, the giant structure looked like a palace straight out of *Lifestyles of the Rich and Famous*. I remember the first time I saw it, I wondered if it was a luxury condo complex in which Dan owned a unit. But no, it was theirs alone.

Dan and Pam were about to celebrate their eleventh wedding anniversary. They were hoping to move in during the following few months. Instead, Dan Horowitz would come to find out that pieces of molding from the construction project were apparently used as weapons to bludgeon his wife.

As they were building their house, Dan and Pam were living in a mobile home a stone's throw from the mansion's front steps. They had an imposing gate at the entrance to their twelve-acre property. A Sheriff's Department spokesman described the area as extremely remote. It's a place you would be hard-pressed to find if you didn't live or work in the area. But with so many construction workers coming and going, there was reportedly a note at the entrance with instructions on exactly how to open the gates. Others said it was also easy to go around the gates, as there were countless ways to get onto the sprawling grounds.

By all accounts, it was a very accessible place — perhaps, in hindsight, too accessible, given its remoteness. This case raises the issue of how difficult it is to strike the perfect balance between reaching for our dreams and protecting ourselves in the here and now. While they were building their dream house, did the Horowitz family unwittingly underestimate the potential risks of living for an extended time in a mobile home in an isolated area with strangers coming and going? Their wealth was obvious, since they were building a mansion next door. I've known others who have done almost exactly the same thing, with the explanation that that is the most efficient way to supervise the workmen and it's very expensive to build one house while paying a mortgage on a second home or renting. But at what other costs? Sometimes life seems like one giant calculation in which we constantly weigh the cost of various options. This is not in any way, shape, or form to blame Dan Horowitz for the horror inflicted on Pamela Vitale. But if we can learn to spot the hallmarks of vulnerable situations, then we can boost our chances of staying out of harm's way. Was the assailant emboldened by this living arrangement to assume it would be easy for him to come and go

186

undetected? Most of us take unnecessary risks in our daily lives, relying on our optimism, assuming that others will do the right thing, even though we know from watching the news that it's so easy to become a victim.

We can also get a false sense of security from owning handguns. An associate said the Horowitz family owned a gun and other weapons. But on the day of the murder, if the weapons were in their trailer home, Pamela never got a chance to use one.

A Real Whodunit

Investigators had been handed a case that was teeming with possibilities. It turned out that several other men lived on the sprawling Horowitz property in various cottages, campers, and old dwellings.

At first, suspicions centered on an old friend of Dan's who had sold a few acres to the attorney. Dan says he agreed to let the fellow stay as a groundskeeper of sorts, so he wouldn't displace a pal who'd lived there for years. But Horowitz had recently sought a restraining order against the man, though he never actually served it. Dan complained that the tenant got drunk and high and became enraged and confrontational. When tracked down, the man admitted to reporters that he had been a real jerk in the past. But he said he was now clean and sober and insisted he had absolutely nothing to do with Pam's murder and was, in fact, very upset over it.

But I wasn't convinced. It struck me as odd that he refused to tell reporters how long he had been off drugs and alcohol. Clean and sober, in the world of recovery, starts with the first twenty-four hours. So, theoretically, this guy could technically be sober and still be hung over. And then there were the construction workers.

Others wondered if anyone in the small army of laborers might have developed a grudge against Pamela, who supervised with an eye for detail. There had been a dispute with one contractor, but they appeared to have put it behind them.

To add another wrinkle, Susan Polk's middle son, Eli, who was still living in his parents' home in nearby Orinda, had called cops saying someone had broken into his family's home that very weekend, knocking a screen door off its hinges. Was there a connection? we wondered.

Also, being an experienced defense attorney, Dan Horowitz was well aware that, as the victim's husband, he would automatically be investigated as a possible suspect, because — statistically — a significant percentage of women are killed by their husbands or lovers.

Finally, there was always the possibility that Dan, having handled more than a dozen death-penalty cases and other high-profile crimes, was the target of someone harboring a resentment from an old case. One of Dan's most famous clients was a former Ukrainian prime minister accused of money laundering and fraud in a convoluted case involving tens of millions of dollars. Dan's client insisted he was the target of false charges generated by political enemies in his homeland. Dan succeeded in getting some charges dismissed. His client was convicted on others, but some of those convictions were later thrown out. More significant, in researching the case Horowitz allegedly found his way onto the radar screen of some Eastern European thugs who had it in for his client. In all, there was a mind-boggling assortment of questionable characters whom investigators needed to cross off their lists.

With all the controversial legal wars he'd fought as a prominent defense attorney, it wasn't surprising that Dan owned a gun. In the first days, when his wife's murder case was wide open, Dan's associate Ivan Golde told the *San Francisco Chronicle* that Horowitz had been worried about his family's safety but hadn't mentioned anything specific. Golde added, "Any attorney has that in the back of their minds." Defense attorneys, in particular, lead risky lives because of the nature of their jobs and the people they represent.

TURNING THE TABLES

What was unique was that Dan, famous as a legal analyst who was frequently asked to appear on television to dissect well-known cases and look for motives, now saw his own life being dissected and his own motives questioned by other legal analysts on TV. Dan was in the same arena, but in a completely different role. For him, it had truly become an upside-down world. Later, Dan told me the experience made him "more sensitive. I apologized to Sharon Rocha [Laci Peterson's mother] and I apologized to some other people . . . for some of the things I said on the air."

Contrary to modern myth, most TV pundits don't go out of their way to be cruel in their commentary, nor do TV reporters relish the kind of assignment in which they risk being labeled vultures. For example, most of us dread having to interrupt someone's grieving process to try to get a sound bite. On the other hand, I've had many experiences in which a murder victim's relatives have welcomed the opportunity to express something about their loved one that they wanted the whole world to know. For some, a TV interview can be a chance to offer a public eulogy, to pay tribute, to praise the deceased, to have them remembered for their accomplishments, rather than for the way they died. Dan seemed to feel that way when it came to discussing his murdered wife.

Dan chose to speak to a number of reporters. He even gave Nancy Grace an exclusive tour of the murder scene. He told Nancy, who is his good friend, "The only thing I want from the media is what they've done, which is they put on her picture. They put on our friends, who talk about how beautiful she was. And that's it. Okay. They've done what I need them to do. What they do with me doesn't matter."

Clearly, Dan wanted the world to remember Pamela Vitale as the beautiful, vibrant woman she was in the photos he had of her, not as she appeared in the autopsy report. Dan told me his wife had saved a sick friend's life, correctly diagnosing a serious condition that doctors had failed to catch.

Even in his grief, he was also being typically giving, saying yes to colleagues he had worked with in the past. This is just the person Dan is. I got it. Some people didn't. Some wondered aloud why Dan was going on TV so soon after his wife's death. Some even thought his behavior was a tad suspicious.

There were all sorts of questions. A couple of days after the murder, on the *Today* show, Matt Lauer asked one of Dan's friends if Horowitz had an airtight alibi. The friend assured Matt that Dan Horowitz did. Dan said he had attended business meetings and run a couple of errands before going home.

NBC's Dan Abrams was also part of the conversation. Lauer asked Abrams if somebody might have been after Horowitz because "he's often appeared on television taking what may be unpopular positions on some key cases." Said Abrams, "He takes the position regularly on television, which is the defense side. And a lot of people don't like that. They say, typical lawyer making excuses for guilty people." It's a reasonable argument. But suddenly it seemed like the potential suspect pool had expanded to anyone with a TV set.

Without a suspect or a motive, speculation continued to run rampant as the cable TV shows offered saturation coverage and analysis in the days immediately following Pam Vitale's murder. Meanwhile, cops were zeroing in on a troubled teenager who was a neighbor of Dan and Pam's. Down the long, one-lane road leading from the Horowitz estate, sixteen-year-old Scott Dyleski, a thin, pale-faced young man with stringy dark hair, lived in a much smaller home that he reportedly shared with his mother and two other families. At times, up to a dozen people were said to sleep there.

Friends say the former Boy Scout was just a regular kid until the summer of 2002. That's when his older half-sister, Denika Dyleski, was killed in a car accident. Local news reports say the eighteen-year-old girl had been in the passenger seat of a friend's car, wearing her seat belt, when the driver lost control. She was pronounced dead at the scene.

Scott was never the same, according to those who knew him. He started turning into what they call a "goth." Like jocks or geeks, goths are a youth subculture. Goth cliques are often filled with alienated teens from dysfunctional families who find a com-

mon expression in black clothing, dark
music, and a morbid philosophy that seems
designed as much as anything to shock
outsiders. Goths seem to relish attention
even as they feign contempt for the mainstream culture around them. Sometimes
they like to wear a stylized cross somewhat
similar in design to the symbol found carved
into Pamela Vitale's back. Scott was often
seen in a black trench coat.

OVERKILL OVERLAP

Soon after Pamela Vitale's murder, the
judge in Susan Polk's murder case declared
a mistrial, citing the widespread publicity
over the murder of her attorney's wife.

Outside court, Ivan Golde, the co-counsel
with Horowitz, pointed to a slew of conflicts
that would seem to make it hard for Dan to
defend Susan in the same jurisdiction where
his wife's murder was being investigated.
He told the *San Francisco Chronicle,* "You've
got the same pathologist doing both investigations."

The same sheriff's department that concluded Felix Polk was murdered by his wife
was now trying to figure out who murdered
her lawyer's wife. Dan Horowitz had argued
that investigators botched the Polk case by
arresting Susan for murder. Ironically, that

same agency would soon be credited with making a swift arrest in his wife's murder.

To me, this is where professionalism comes in. All these players knew each other and had a history of conflict in court. Dan was defending someone the Sheriff's Department had arrested for murder, and it was his job to make it look like they didn't know what they were doing when they cuffed his client. His best case was their worst-case scenario. He would never have guessed those very investigators would soon become his best hope in solving his wife's brutal death.

Less than a week after Pamela's murder, police arrested Scott Dyleski. It seems neighbors and a friend had tipped cops off about the boy. Not only was he into sinister-looking black outfits, he was suspected of running a marijuana-growing scam and using his neighbors as pawns. When the media got their first good look at the teen, there was shock over how physically small he was, measuring only five foot six and weighing a scant 110 pounds. By contrast, Pamela Vitale was five foot nine and weighed 178 pounds. But she was fifty-two years old and he was sixteen. And the evidence indicates she was caught by surprise.

ANDROID MESSIAH?

Scott Dyleski reportedly had a rather sinister screen name: Android Messiah. According to a teenage friend who testified for the prosecution in exchange for immunity, the two boys had devised a scheme to use credit card information stolen from their neighbors to order hydroponic equipment online so they could grow marijuana. Prosecutors offered evidence linking the Horowitz address to defendant Scott Dyleski.

At the trial, the owner of a specialty-lights store testified that just a couple of nights before Pam's murder, the owner had received several online orders for an indoor growing system. But she says she became suspicious and refused the orders because they listed one billing address and another shipping address. The store owner then got an "odd" call from a polite young man who seemed to be disguising his voice. He asked if the equipment could be sent to the billing address. That address was the Horowitz/ Vitale residence.

Investigators theorized that Dyleski then went to the Horowitz home as part of the stolen-credit-card pot-growing scheme. It seemed an odd motive for murder, especially when you consider that the store owner testified she told the young man that his order was declined, meaning she would *not* be sending the equipment out to any address.

In a very complicated but crucial twist, there was also evidence to indicate that this crime could be a case of mistaken identity! Scott may have thought Pamela was actually *another* neighbor, who had recently hit his beloved family dog, Jazz, with her car. Records show Dyleski had used that other neighbor's stolen credit card number during his unsuccessful attempt to buy the pot equipment, incorrectly listing Pamela's address as that card's billing address. Dyleski was reportedly distraught and furious at that other neighbor for hitting his border collie, something that had happened just a couple of weeks before the murder.

The *Contra Costa Times* reported that the dog suffered for days before finally being put to sleep by a local vet. A woman who lived in the same home as Scott told the paper she believed the boy might have gotten confused over which neighbor hit the dog and mistakenly assumed Vitale did it. Or he may have simply thought Vitale *was* that other neighbor, confusing their addresses. Going over to the mobile home may have been his way of expressing both his anger over the death of his dog and his frustration over his inability to get the pot-growing equipment delivered.

In fact, toward the end of the trial, during closing arguments, the prosecutor said there was "only one rational explanation" for the crime, "and that is that Scott Dyleski thought" the woman, who had reportedly hit his dog, resided at the mobile home where Pamela Vitale actually lived. The prosecutor implied that mistaken identity, hate, and greed all combined, exploding in a homicidal rage.

Scott insisted he didn't kill Pamela Vitale and pleaded not guilty. His public defender argued that Scott had returned to his home from a walk at 9:26 a.m., more than half an hour before the estimated time of the murder. His lawyer also alleged a third DNA profile was found at the crime scene, implying someone else was there.

HOMICIDAL OBSESSION?

Authorities felt confident they had accumulated plenty of evidence against a teen whom schoolmates had called weird. When examined after his arrest, the boy allegedly had a scratch on his face, bruising on his arms, and abrasions on his right leg. If true, that would be consistent with a violent struggle.

A reserve sheriff's deputy testified he discovered key evidence in the form of a duffel bag in an abandoned van in the yard of Dyleski's home. It reportedly had Scott's name tag on it and contained a ski mask, a black glove, and a black trench coat. Prosecutors said clothing inside the bag contained traces of blood. DNA from both Pamela Vitale and Scott Dyleski was allegedly found on the ski mask and the bag, as well as on the shoes. A forensics expert said Pamela's DNA was found on the bag. A partial match-up of Dyleski's DNA was allegedly found on Vitale's right foot. It's intriguing that more substantial DNA wasn't found, given the extent of the violence. However, the prosecutor argued Dyleski was wearing a ski mask, trench coat, and gloves. That clothing could have covered most of his skin.

A sheriff's investigator talked about finding a CD boxed set for the band Velvet Acid Christ in Dyleski's room. Prosecutors implied that a symbol used in the liner notes was similar to the one carved into Vitale's back.

Dyleski's fifty-three-year-old mother, described in the *Contra Costa Times* as a "long-distance healer who believes that DNA strands can be activated to alleviate disease," testified against her son, admitting that she burned his journal and handwritten notes after his arrest. In return, the D.A. agreed to drop charges that she destroyed evidence.

An investigator said he found artwork and poetry that the teen had signed with the phrase "live for the kill" and "murder." His former schoolmates had also seen sadistically violent imagery in Dyleski's drawings. Investigators believed the boy who wanted to cultivate pot plants had instead cultivated a homicidal obsession.

A man who lived in the same home as Scott testified that when he moved into the bedroom left empty by Scott's arrest, he was shocked to discover a sinister "to do" list hidden in a dresser drawer. He said the list read:

Knock-out/kidnap
Question
Keep captive to confirm PINs
Dirty Work
Dispose of evidence
(Cut up and bury).

With cash and valuables left out in the open in Vitale's home, this crime was clearly about more than stealing lights to grow pot.

There were signs of rage that must have been accumulating for a long time. And there was also a coldness. Investigators say that after the murder, the perpetrator washed his bloody knife in the bathtub of the Horowitz mobile home and drank water out of the victim's water bottle.

Once again, I was in the position of having to call up Dan Horowitz. Once again, it was hard to dial the numbers. Once again, Dan picked up and graciously answered my questions. One of my first questions was whether he had given much thought to the level of violence in our society and what's to blame.

"I thought about this," Dan replied, giving me an extensive outline of where he thinks our culture has gone wrong. He talked about our changing value system. He bemoaned everything being a "commodity" these days, including sex, love, status, and even life. He condemned the false belief that kids will magically learn right from wrong without being taught values. He said the way some kids grow up, "It's just like *Lord of the Flies*," referring to the classic novel where children moored on an island engage in a sadistic game of survival of the fittest. "I believe we should have stronger families and rules and standards and values."

Dan also talked about the materialism that kids see on television, which they measure themselves against. I asked him if he thought jealousy was involved, thinking of how this boy lived in a cramped house while this mansion was going up before his eyes. "Obviously, that is going to be something people are going to think about. You know, I did free legal work for the kid's family. Who knows?" he replied. Reports are Dan had done a significant amount of free legal work in the past for some of the people who shared a home with Dyleski. That was his style.

THE GLORIA FACTOR

Sadly, I couldn't get into any specifics with Dan because an air-tight gag order had been issued in his wife's murder case, preventing anyone involved, as a witness or an attorney, from saying anything.

Given the massive publicity the case had garnered and the dynamics that were forming, both the prosecution and the defense were in favor of a gag order and they got one, reportedly the first one issued in that county in decades.

I personally hate gag orders and believe they usually have the reverse effect of what they're designed to achieve. If the courts hoped to stop all the wagging tongues on TV, they were to be bitterly disappointed. Immediately, commentators began speculating that the gag order was designed to muzzle famed attorney Gloria Allred. She was believed to be representing Scott Dyleski's girlfriend, although she wouldn't confirm it at the time. Allred had previously represented mistress/unwitting star-witness Amber Frey when Scott Peterson was tried and convicted of killing his wife.

In another distasteful tidbit that had emerged in the case, reports claimed Dyleski went to his girlfriend's house and had sex with her hours after the murder. After the young woman allegedly told detectives she couldn't talk unless she asked Gloria first, the prosecution fumed. "The prospect of private lawyers 'preparing' prosecution witnesses under the veil of attorney-client privilege runs the risk of interfering with both the People's, and the defendant's . . . Constitutional rights," the prosecutor wrote in support of the gag order.

But Allred's philosophy makes a lot of sense to me. She argues that these young women need someone to look out for their interests precisely because they're trapped in a media storm not of their own making. Allred told Fox's Greta Van Susteren that she wanted to be an advocate for her client so that her "reputation remains intact." Given the goth nature of the defendant's lifestyle and public talk of a dark relationship with a female friend, I can understand why Gloria felt she was needed.

While a jury of one's peers is supposed to hear all of the evidence before rendering a judgment in the court of law, when it comes to the court of public opinion, knee-jerk reactions and gossip rule. Many people have suddenly found themselves, with absolutely no forewarning and through no fault of their own, facing the scrutiny and judgment of their friends, neighbors, and the public at large, all because they happened to be associated in some way with a crime victim or suspect. The O. J. Simpson case was the ultimate example of peripheral characters, like Simpson's houseguest, Kato Kaelin, and Nicole Brown Simpson's best friend, Faye Resnick, becoming famous, and the subject of endless talk, because they happened to be around when key events were unfolding. While those two classic Hollywood characters seemed to thrive on all the attention, for many others the spotlight can be debilitating, even terrifying. Women, especially, can find that the gossip about them when there's any hint of a sexual component, can take on a life of its own and turn venomous. Gloria Allred may see her role as protecting those who can't navigate the treacherous legal and media shoals by themselves. I believe she has a legitimate place in the process and should not be silenced.

SURPRISE!

In the end, it was clear that Gloria had her work cut out for her. Early in the Dyleski trial, Gloria was right there when Scott's girlfriend, in a surprise move, showed up in court and took the stand. The testimony she delivered was chilling. She matter-of-factly described herself and Scott as masochists who experimented with pain by hurting themselves. She said she and Scott had conversations about torture, sadomasochism, and credit fraud. Perhaps most shocking, Scott's girlfriend testified that Scott was fascinated by Jack the Ripper, the serial killer known for removing the internal organs of some of his victims. Scott's girlfriend said she and Scott chatted about removing human organs, specifically the kidneys.

The courtroom was stunned by the secrets this teenager was spilling so casually. Of course, not lost on anyone was the creepy parallel to Pamela's injuries, specifically the fact that her intestines had been left exposed.

CRAZY LIKE A FOX?

Before Scott Dyleski was even arrested, the murder of Pamela Vitale was creating nasty ripple effects in Dan Horowitz's professional life. His client Susan Polk cried upon hearing that a mistrial had been declared in her case in the wake of the murder of Dan's wife. But she quickly recovered. Even as Dan was summoning inner strength, from God only knows where, to carry on, saying Susan Polk needed him, Polk was getting ready to dump Horowitz in a very cruel and public fashion. She had already fired three other lawyers, one reason her case had dragged on for more than three years.

Now she was going to fulfill her dream of representing herself in court, never a good idea. As they say, the defendant who represents herself has a fool for a client. Or as journalist Jim Moret put it, "It's like buying a sonogram machine and saying, Well, I read the instructions. You know, why do you have to go to medical school? It doesn't work like that."

In a neatly handwritten motion composed behind bars, with a pencil, Susan Polk asked that Dan be removed as her counsel, smearing his name in the process: "My attorney, Dan Horowitz, was suspected in the murder of his wife. I have asked him to withdraw as my counsel as he has failed to follow through with promises that he has made to me, ineffective assistance of counsel. . . . I also believe that there is a conflict of interest arrising [*sic*] out of the murder of Mr. Horowitz' wife which would preclude his continued representation of me, in addition to other conflicts which have recently come to my attention, which may explain why Mr. Horowitz failed to file a motion to recuse Judge Brady [her judge] for cause and the entire bench of Contra Costa County, although he had promised to do so."

Jim Moret, who is *Inside Edition*'s chief correspondent and a lawyer, spoke to me about his interviews with Susan Polk. "I've talked to her three times in jail. And she doesn't sound crazy when you talk to her. Although she makes some wacky decisions like representing herself and firing lawyer after lawyer after lawyer, and then claiming Dan Horowitz had something to do with the murder of his wife." She's crazy like a fox, trying to postpone the day of reckoning any way she can, including axing her attorneys, a favorite tactic of well-off, well-educated defendants.

I asked Dan Horowitz if he felt like he had been victimized three times. First he lost his wife. Then he was viewed with suspicion as police searched for a suspect. Then his high-profile client fired him, in a very insulting manner. He told me, "I don't get into that 'why me?' I understand that things happened . . . they just happen. . . . What am I going to take out of this experience? Am I going to be an angry, bitter, mean, self-loathing person, or am I going to be a better person?" It was certainly a remarkable attitude under the circumstances.

KOOKY IN COURT

As soon as Susan started acting as her own lawyer, she made a mockery of her trial, according to many who watched her in action day after day. One stunning example was the bizarre four-day cross-examination she conducted on her youngest son, Gabriel, who was by then about nineteen and a star prosecution witness, testifying against her.

On direct examination, Gabriel told the jury he thought his mother was delusional and made up the physical abuse stories. Then it came time for cross-examination — by mom. Court observers said the mother/

attorney often sobbed, tears trickling down her face, as she questioned her hostile witness/son. After trying to get Gabriel to confirm that Felix was abusive toward her, Gabriel finally made an admission, "He threw water in your face one time," he testified. "One time?" Polk shot back, incredulous. The judge complained Polk's grilling of her own son was "bordering on the abusive." But mostly her questioning of witnesses sounded plain crazy.

Polk provoked snickers from the gallery when she asked a detective, "Are you aware my husband believed he was a psychic?" He answered he was not aware of that. "Do you believe in psychic phenomena?" she followed up. "No, not really," the detective responded.

She also interrogated him on whether he had ever investigated her claims that her husband was an agent for the Mossad. The detective said no, he never checked into whether Felix Polk worked for the Israeli secret intelligence service. Susan wouldn't let up. "Normally, if there's some kind of treasonable activity, doesn't that get reported to police?" Polk asked. "Yes," replied the cop.

She then tried to question the detective about a letter she had purportedly written more than a year before the killing, a letter that was chock-full of claims that her husband hit her. Obtained by Court TV, it read, "Throughout our marriage, Felix has been psychologically and physically abusive. He has punched me on numerous occasions, and threatened to kill me if I ever left him." In another passage, it read, "During the course of our marriage, Felix has at times drugged me. Almost four years ago, when I talked of getting a divorce, Felix employed hallucinogens."

The judge warned Susan not to ask the witness about the letter, because the detective hadn't seen it, but Susan defied her repeatedly. "Did you investigate whether or not my husband did the things in that letter?" Polk demanded. "Did you investigate if my husband raped me when I was a patient in his care?"

The assistant district attorney prosecuting the case was fed up. "I'm at my wit's end. I'm trying not to get angry . . . it's becoming absurd," he complained, adding, "she won't follow the rules. She won't stop interrupting."

Former prosecutor Wendy Murphy believes Susan Polk should have been reined in. "We do bend over backward way too much for the ridiculous demands of defendants," Wendy fumed. "She's not the first defendant who was able to drag a case out into the ozone."

PSYCHO SECRETS?

At one point, Susan's trial went from farce to science fiction. The alleged secrets that were emerging about the Polk family were so incredibly strange that they almost defy description. Then again, Felix was not alive to explain himself or put anything in context. As part of Susan's campaign to paint her husband as a demented man, she played, in court, tape recordings of a voice she claimed was Felix's giving a speech in the 1980s about ritualistic child abuse. That voice made some shocking claims about groups of children being violently abused and murdered. "The children were raped on stage, raped in every form imaginable," said the voice that blared via a speaker through the courtroom.

I spoke about this strange development with Valerie Harris, Susan Polk's case manager. "There were four audio clips and that's essentially what we played in the courtroom. But that was enough to give you an idea of how nutty Felix was," Harris told me nonchalantly as I tried to make sense of the bizarre recordings. She told me Felix had claimed that when the Polks' oldest son, Adam, was just a toddler, he had been sexually abused after being left with a caregiver, that he was driven to a warehouse where people wore masks and raped and killed children on stage. In court, the voice said Adam remembered a "baby put in a plastic bag and hammered to death." Then the voice cried out, in a riff on revenge against those who would harm children in this way, "My rage is omnipresent. . . . My fantasy of course is to kill them."

Teams of Hollywood scriptwriters would be hard-pressed to invent weirder courtroom scenarios than what actually took place in the Susan Polk murder case, or for that matter in the Scott Dyleski case. Was there something in the water out there in the 'burbs of San Francisco turning normal people into nutjobs?

"It's his voice on the tape," Harris insisted about the satanic-themed tape recordings played in court by Susan Polk. Harris said the defense bought the tapes from a reputable company that records conferences, and that the name Felix Polk was clearly on the label and that his voice was recognizable.

So whatever happened with these wild and disturbing claims of ritualized child murder and abuse? "It never went anywhere because essentially it never happened," says Valerie. She believes Felix Polk used the accusations to keep his family off balance: "What better way to keep a young mother completely focused on 'your kid is being ritualistically abused by Satan worshipers' so as a result she's not focused on what she's getting or not getting. . . . It's a really good avenue for Felix to use to control her."

FRACTURED FAMILY

In the end, who would know better than the Polks' own sons what was really going on inside that household? But even the kids are split. The middle son, Eli, sided with his mom. "The family was fractured before the murder," says Jim Moret. "Sides were taken, lines were drawn, and heroes and villains were cast in each of these people's eyes *before* the murder. . . . It's so sad, because the legacy of this family is one of torment and despair and severance."

PERSECUTED OR PARANOID?

Eli even ended up in the same jail as his mother after a series of run-ins with authorities landed him behind bars as he was preparing to testify in his mother's defense.

Eli claimed he was being singled out and persecuted for standing up for his unpopular mother. Susan's handwritten motions claim that "there have been numerous attempts to intimidate me and Eli since my incarceration."

Independent journalist Virginia McCullough marveled at how all of this drama was happening within the confines of a very small community, where six degrees of separation is the unspoken rule. "There's a Hitchcockian connection," says McCullough, adding, "Every court is a very small clique, and if you look very closely at the individuals involved and their history and their background, you begin to find out just how small." All in all, this insular community had been sorely tested by Susan Polk's antics and had responded with amazing patience.

In June 2006, the circus ended. Susan Polk was found guilty of second-degree murder. One juror said nobody on the panel bought her self-defense claims. That trial was just wrapping up when the new courtroom drama, Scott Dyleski's murder trial on charges of killing Dan Horowitz's wife, got under way. That same relatively small community was still living in the vortex of violence. Scott was ultimately found guilty of the first-degree murder of his neighbor Pamela Vitale. He was also found guilty of the special circumstance of murder committed during a burglary. That means life in prison without parole.

To me, these two overlapping tragedies form a puzzle of extraordinary dimensions. Every time I turn a corner, I feel like I have fallen through a trap door into another, deeper layer of these cases. Mysteries abound. Each case has a sick flavor to it; one centered around the goth lifestyle and torture, the other involving sick stories of ritualistic child abuse. It's like a David Lynch movie, except it's a reality show. And it's all happening in the most all-American of suburbs.

VIOLENCE IS CRAZY

In the end, it's hard to make sense of these violent crimes. It's all — to a great extent — irrational behavior. Rage gives people enormous strength they usually wouldn't possess. Plots can exist in sick minds that make no sense to you or me. Why would anybody carve a symbol into someone else's back? Why would anybody bludgeon another human being with a piece of molding? "I never go for the argument that, 'Well, why would anybody in their right mind do this, because they knew they'd get caught?' " says Jim Moret. "Then half the crimes wouldn't have been committed."

It's the same nonsense that you hear about evidence left at the scene of the crime. Why would a criminal leave his blood and DNA at the scene? Why would he leave a duffel bag for cops to find? BECAUSE CRIMINALS ARE SELF-DESTRUCTIVE AND NOT RATIONAL! People who opt for these kinds of solutions are not just enraged. They're idiots. There is no perfect crime, and the perfect criminal is someone so smart that he or she probably would decide against committing the crime in the first place.

We may never be able to really understand why someone would turn to such furious violence. Dan Horowitz is right. We have to be a part of the solution, so that it doesn't happen again and again. It would be nice if we could encourage the next generation to come up with nonviolent solutions to their problems. Sadly, the adults of the world aren't providing a very good example. Everywhere we turn, violence is being used as a solution, on the international, national, and local levels. And at the end of the day, it's all very self-destructive and irrational. Just turn on the news.

6
THE BLOOD-SPATTER BOYS

Sex and lies. So many cases seem to boil down to these two volatile components. If you think your spouse is lying to you about his or her sex life, watch out! If you discover your spouse has a sexual obsession, and you're not the obsession, treat it like a fire and head for the nearest exit. Sex addiction, like alcohol or drug addiction, doesn't go away unless the addict gets help. Without that, all the "I won't do it again" promises in the world are an absolute joke — on you.

David Camm had been a decorated cop in Indiana. Neil Entwistle was a British computer whiz. While they were born and raised on opposite sides of the Atlantic, the accusations against these two men have unnerving similarities.

Both were accused of executing their families. Leading up to the murders, both withheld vital information about their personal lives from their wives. Both men appeared to have sex, sex, sex on the brain. In both cases, forensic evidence known as *blood spatter* and *blowback* played a critical role. Such evidence is literally the flesh and blood of their flesh and blood.

In one sense, their stories are very commonplace. A lot of married guys have wandering eyes, feel resentful of the demands of marriage and fatherhood, and are carrying around secrets they keep from their wives. But these two men are accused of trying to escape their predicaments by pointing pistols at family members and squeezing the triggers. These two tragedies offer extreme examples of family dysfunction. Examining these cases can help us recognize when a relationship is on a collision course. It's a lesson worth learning.

The Department of Justice offers some frightening statistics about recent crime trends. Here are a few: About *one-third* of all female murder victims were killed by an intimate partner or spouse! Female murder victims are much more likely than male murder victims to have been killed by an intimate partner or spouse. Spouses and family members made up about 15 percent of all murder victims in America.

David Camm

Prosecutors contend David Camm killed his family in September 2000 because he feared his wife was planning to leave him. They say she knew he had cheated on her in the past, but finally decided to leave him when she began to suspect he was now harboring an even more monstrous secret. Prosecutors argued the one-time state trooper meticulously plotted to kill his family. They say Camm cleverly set up an alibi by choosing the night of his pickup basketball game at a gym close to his home. Almost a dozen friends and relatives were at the gym, and almost all of them said David was there playing basketball and they never saw him leave or sneak back in. Prosecutors contended that, given the highly casual nature of the pickup games, it would have been easy for David to slip away, drive the less than five minutes home, murder his family, and then saunter back into the gym to continue playing, as if he had never left.

Prosecutors noted that David sat out one game and let his uncle step in right around the time the medical examiner estimates the family was killed. One of the players ultimately testified for the state saying he couldn't be sure of David's whereabouts the whole night and believed nobody would have noticed if David had disappeared for fifteen minutes or so.

Prosecutors believe David snuck home knowing his family would be arriving back at the house from swim and dance classes. David's thirty-six-year-old wife, Kim, pulled the family's Bronco into the garage. Although investigators are still not 100 percent sure of exactly what went on inside the garage that night, they believe Camm's wife was gunned down first. Kim's body was found sprawled out on the garage floor.

Authorities say David then got into the front seat of the Bronco, where his five-year-old daughter, Jill, and seven-year-old son, Bradley, sat in the backseat, and shot them at close range in the car.

Two jailhouse informants ultimately testified that Camm had confessed to them while behind bars. One said Camm mentioned "the marriage was not going well and the financial situation he'd be in" if Kim left him. Another inmate testified that a weeping David Camm revealed he kept hearing a nightmarish cry in his head. It was his son, crying, "Help me, Daddy, help me."

David Camm was convicted in 2002, but that conviction was overturned by a higher court that ruled he didn't get a fair trial.

When Camm was tried a second time, in 2006, it was clear the public's fascination with the morbid case had not faded.

Newsman Travis Kircher was in court during David Camm's most recent trial. Says Kircher, "If the prosecution is correct, then David Camm pointed the gun directly at his daughter's head, and . . . Bradley was looking directly at the muzzle of the gun when the trigger was pulled, and that made it difficult for people to take." Travis, along with everyone else in the courtroom, was nauseated by the graphic autopsy photos of the slaughtered children on a big screen. "The whole courtroom was basically a wreck," said Travis, describing how weeping broke out, with the victims' family and the defendant's family grouped in separate areas. He said Kim Camm's family seemed afraid to even look up at the images, bowing their heads when they sensed a new photo was about to be projected.

Despite the palpable discomfort, Travis was a journalist determined to remain objective about Camm's innocence or guilt. Sitting inside the courtroom, he furiously typed notes and quotes on his computer for an experimental project his TV station had okayed. As a "Web reporter" assigned to the case for WHAS 11 News, in Louisville,

Kentucky, Travis typed a blog of who was saying what about whom on the witness stand. Soon Travis got good enough to send his posts straight onto the Internet via the wireless transmission the courthouse had supplied. His gavel-to-gavel blogging in real time was a new-technology hit, racking up more than half a million views. People were obsessed by the horrific case and ravenous for every last sordid detail. Many, according to Travis, were just plain angry.

What was it about this case that got the people of Indiana and neighboring Kentucky so worked up? It was the fact that David Camm, up until a few months before the triple murder of his family, had been a decorated Indiana state trooper and was considered a hero in his community. The trial revealed law enforcement's seedy side, disgorging titillating secrets about state troopers and sex.

BADGE BUNNIES

"I don't want to put a black mark on the Indiana state police, but I think people hate to see authority abused," says Travis. He's right. It scares people to think that men sauntering around in uniforms with guns strapped to their hips might be cold-blooded killers themselves. After all, these are the men with the power to pull you over on a dark road and make you step out of your car.

As human beings, cops are subject to all the foibles of the flesh. Though one must go through a battery of psychological tests to be a trooper, those tests don't reveal everything. Everyone has an unconscious motivation for the vocation they choose in life. Some men who go into law enforcement "are suffering from some sense of masculine inadequacy, and they go into the profession to compensate for this secret feeling of inadequacy," says Dr. Carole Lieberman, a well-known Beverly Hills forensic psychiatrist who deals with sexual issues in her practice.

David Camm has been described as a cop who used his badge as a tool of seduction, luring in women who are turned on by a man in a uniform. Some troopers refer to these women as badge bunnies. "He was just this big flirt. He just flirted with . . . any woman, any female that came in his orbit," says author John Glatt, who wrote a book on the case called *One Deadly Night.* "To put that guy in a [squad] car . . . with badge bunnies, I think he must have thought he was a rock star, he could do nothing wrong."

In David Camm's first trial, we learned about his double life. Woman after woman took the stand and said she had had sexually charged encounters with him, while he was married to Kim. Two women said they had sexual intercourse with the trooper. Still others said they were just kissed or fondled by Camm. Finally, some women said Camm came on to them, but they turned him down. About a dozen women testified. Together, they made quite an impression. Prosecutors argued one motive for the murders was that Camm wanted to be free to pursue sex with other women.

In one case, a woman testified she had sex with Camm in his patrol car as it was parked on the median of a freeway while he was on duty! "A total disregard for the badge," declared Nick Stein, the attorney for the parents of Camm's murdered wife.

PISTOL AS PENIS?

Camm's playboy-on-patrol image was a 180-degree turn from what acquaintances say he was like as a younger man. They describe a quiet guy who was not all that popular. So says Marcy McLeod Mahurin, one of Kim's best friends, who set the two of them up on their first date: "I do think once he became a trooper, his personality totally changed. I do think he became cocky and it was all about David. When you were around him after that, his personality was totally different." Others say David Camm was trying to compensate for a massive inferiority complex that he brought from an undistinguished childhood, where he failed to excel in school. That complex could have been exacerbated by his marriage to Kim, a very bright and academically gifted woman whose career in accounting was taking off, reportedly making her the family's bigger breadwinner.

"Being a trooper, carrying a gun — a phallic symbol — was his way of compensating for his feelings of inadequacy as a man. And when that was taken away . . . he felt less of a man and had to compensate in other ways," theorizes Dr. Lieberman.

Camm left the state police force, reportedly somewhat disgruntled over an assignment he perceived as a demotion, in May 2000, less than six months before the murders. Even though Camm went on to a decent job as a salesman for a family-run business, Lieberman suspects that "his anger at feeling inadequate came out toward his family. If he were just able to continue as a trooper and . . . use his uniform and his confidence to have sex on the side . . .

but when that was taken away, he had to prove he was a man all over again . . . and then something probably happened."

THE WORST SECRET?

The prosecution's claim that something else happened is the subject of emotional debate because of its highly controversial nature. The prosecutors contended Camm molested his five-year-old daughter, Jill, something the defense vehemently denies. Camm was never officially charged with the allegation, but prosecutors theorized Camm killed little Jill, her older brother, Brad, and their mom to keep the molestation a secret.

David Camm has reportedly acknowledged to police that if his wife was up late doing the ironing, the kids would sometimes pile in bed with him. "There were a couple of times when Jill complained that it hurt down there and the grandma just thought it was a rash or something," says the grandmother's lawyer, adding that the five-year-old girl "was at a dance recital and was crying" that it hurt between her legs. In court, the medical examiner who conducted the girl's autopsy said there was injury to her genital region, which could have been caused by either molestation or a straddle fall.

I asked Dr. Lieberman about the bitterly disputed molestation aspect of the case and the larger issue for society. Can sex addicts cross that line, from a compulsion to have sex with partners their own age to wanting sex with a child? The psychiatrist and trial analyst said sex addiction, just like alcohol or drug addiction, is about wanting to escape and losing impulse control. She offered a theoretical scenario of a sex addict craving sex but in a situation where it would be difficult for him to just get up and walk out to have sex with a woman: "It is possible that the craving would be so strong that he would then have sex with what's nearest at hand. You can kind of compare it to an alcoholic who gets a craving in the middle of the night for alcohol . . . [and] is faced with stores being closed, but goes rummaging through the garage hoping that there is still some stash there."

As it happens, there was no evidence that Camm was involved in a sexual affair outside marriage at the time of the murders. However, just days before the killing, Camm had allegedly asked an old lover whether she'd be interested in having sex again, and she said no thanks.

But Camm's attorney, Katharine Liell, says it's preposterous for the state to try to have it both ways, painting Camm as a playboy and a pedophile: "Womanizers are not attracted to children. . . . In the studies that I have seen and in my . . . eighteen years as a criminal defense lawyer . . . you don't find pedophiles that have normal sexual relationships within their age group."

"The prosecution can't decide what his motive is," Camm's brother Donnie told the show *48 Hours.* "They've been bouncing around on different motives and they can't find one to stick."

Too Much Information

During the first trial, the evidence of Camm's womanizing, complete with the stories of on-duty sex, was so extensive that an appeals court overturned his conviction. The higher court noted, "Some of the women were asked during their testimony to divulge details of their relationships with Camm, such as when, where, and how they engaged in sexual activities, including such details as the shaving of pubic hair." The appeals court said the testimony was such an inflammatory attack on Camm's character that it could cause jurors to want to punish him on the basis of his sexual indiscretions alone. All three guilty verdicts were thrown out. But after that reversal and before the second trial, something really wild happened: Police discovered a second suspect. His name was Charles Boney. His nickname was Backbone.

BACKBONE: BACK IN TROUBLE

Charles Boney is a habitual offender with a long rap sheet. The tall, heavyset African American is a high school graduate who attended college and penned a handwritten autobiography while he was in jail awaiting his trial in the Camm family murders. Despite his terrible predicament, Boney's writings show a strange sense of humor: "I have been to court several times and most of the news stations use the same pictures and footage. . . . I resembled a Halloween pumpkin, dressed all in orange and weighing in at over 310 pounds."

But there was nothing to laugh about. Boney was in serious trouble. Prosecutors insist he was very involved in the murders of Kim, Jill, and Brad. Boney admits he was at the crime scene that night.

Boney says he first met David Camm in July 2000 when they played ball against each other, "and I lost the game," writes Boney, adding, "David Camm talked to me about Jesus and church." Boney goes on to describe a second chance encounter with

Camm at a food market in September, the month of the murders. Camm "seemed distracted" and "asked me to follow him to a secluded area." Boney then admits that he sold a gun to the ex-cop for a couple hundred bucks. He says he didn't have anything to wrap the weapon in, so he used his sweatshirt.

The DNA from Boney's sweatshirt, found at the crime scene, is how cops eventually found him. Boney insists Camm set him up to take the fall for the killings. His lawyer, Patrick Renn, acknowledges his client was at the Camm home on the night of the murders, but insists it was only to sell a second gun to David. The attorney says Boney "was there to see the family come in, heard David Camm shoot and kill his family, and . . . David Camm then turned the gun on Mr. Boney to try and kill him. Fortunately . . . the gun jammed."

Boney has always maintained that he had no idea Camm would use the gun to kill his family. But prosecutors brought in one of his girlfriends, who testified Boney "figured" Camm would use the gun he provided to kill his wife. Prosecutors speculated that, in return for furnishing the gun, Boney was counting on a larger payoff down the road, which he believed would come from Camm via insurance money. For his role in the murders, Boney was convicted and sentenced to 225 years in prison.

According to Indiana law, you don't have to pull the trigger to be convicted of murder. You can be found guilty if the jury decides you knowingly aided, induced, or caused another person to murder. Boney was also convicted of conspiracy, meaning his jury believed he and Camm had an agreement and took action to further their plan.

Charles Boney is in his mid-thirties, so unless he successfully appeals, he will die in prison. He writes about this. "I have made a ton of mistakes in my life and I regret them. Nevertheless, with all that I have done, I'm not a murderer and I do not deserve to be punished for the rest of my life for a crime I did not commit. I have received nearly 800 letters from perfect strangers who believe in my innocence."

Foot Fetish

But Camm's lawyers warn that Boney is a dangerously manipulative sexual deviant who knows how to put on an innocent act. "He is as brawny as Mike Tyson, as brainy as Ted Bundy, and as brutal as both," says attorney Liell.

That brings us to perhaps the weirdest

aspect of this hideous tale. Charles Boney has a foot fetish. His own lawyer admits he's obsessed with women's legs, in particular their feet, acknowledging "several of his convictions came about for robbery because he was taking women's shoes." If that makes it sound like Boney was a delicate shoe thief, authorities stress he has a history of violent crimes against women. In the late eighties, Boney was convicted of robbery and attempted robbery. In the early nineties, he was convicted of armed robbery and criminal confinement, racking up several felony counts.

One of the convictions involved assaulting three female roommates inside their home. Authorities say that Boney, disappointed because they had less than a hundred dollars in cash, tried to force the women at gunpoint into a car to go to their banks. A neighbor saw this and called the police.

Camm's attorney says Boney's previous attacks on women were creepy and bizarre, claiming "he would paint his face with white clown makeup to try to disguise his identity. . . . Another time he wore . . . a china doll mask in which the features are simply frozen . . . and he would attack these women . . . usually knocking them down from behind. They would have injuries to their knees and elbows and chin. Kim Camm had injuries to her knees, elbows, and chin, as if she was tackled from behind." Boney's crimes appeared to have been motivated by a desire for money combined with a need to act out a fetish while wearing outlandish disguises.

In a chilling similarity to some of Boney's previous attacks, Kim's feet were mutilated, described as badly bruised with severe trauma. Boney's own attorney told me, "Not only were Kim Camm's shoes off her feet, placed on top of the vehicle . . . Mr. Boney in his statements . . . to law enforcement admitted that he's the one who placed those shoes on top of the car." Could Boney have been acting out his strange and violent foot fetish with Kim Camm? That's certainly what David Camm wanted the world to believe, claiming in tears, "I am innocent. I did not murder my family. I did not molest my little girl. The reality is Charles Boney murdered my family because he is a perverted monster."

David Camm wanted to bring all of Boney's criminal and foot-fetish history into his second trial, but the judge wouldn't allow it. Camm's lawyer calls that a huge miscarriage of justice.

For David Camm, it all came down to a few tiny drops of blood found on his shirt. The prosecution experts called it *back spatter*. To understand its significance, I turned to the famous forensic expert Dr. Larry Kobilinsky, who gave me a brief tutorial on the three main types of blood-spatter patterns that investigators look for on everything from clothing to bed sheets to surrounding walls.

1. ***Low-Velocity Spatter:*** "That means you're walking with a bloody knife and the knife is dripping onto the floor. Usually, the droplets are pretty big and the force that is behind that droplet is gravity."

2. ***Medium-Velocity Spatter:*** "Let's say you bludgeoned somebody with a board . . . in the head. You pull back, you hit them again. There's blood that comes up on the . . . surface of the scalp. Then you pull back again and let's say you spatter that blood on a ceiling or on a wall. . . . There's some force behind it. . . . It's intermediate in size."

3. ***High-Velocity Spatter:*** "There's huge power when . . . ammunition

[from a gun] is discharged. And the tremendous energy from that explosion is converted to kinetic energy, the energy of motion. And that propels the bullet. When that bullet hits the victim, there's huge trauma and impact. It basically explodes into the victim. That victim is going to back spatter. Very tiny, tiny droplets . . . a fraction of a millimeter. They fly through the air, and they move in the direction that the bullet came from. So they're going to hit the shooter, basically. The closer the gun is to the victim, the more concentrated the back spatter pattern will be on the shooter."

To the naked eye, a bloody crime scene can resemble anything from a Jackson Pollock painting to a plate of spaghetti. But to the trained eye using a magnifying glass or a microscope, Dr. Kobilinsky says patterns and symmetry emerge. Prosecutors say the droplets on Camm's shirt were definitely blood spatter. Defense experts beg to differ. David Camm's legal team told reporters, "People can be wrong. This bloodstain pattern analysis, as you can see by how many analysts we have and how many analysts they have, is an extremely subjective inter-pretation."

But, in the end, the jury bought the blood-spatter evidence and decided David Camm was indeed the triggerman. Camm was convicted, for a second time, of killing his family. He was sentenced to life in prison.

SEX APPEAL

Camm's attorney, Katharine Liell, is a friendly and articulate lawyer who is fiercely passionate about this case. She's particularly livid over the molestation claim: "The state failed wholeheartedly to show any connection between Dave and those [genital] injuries, and yet the state was still permitted to . . . argue that Dave Camm molested his daughter. . . . If the state believes that Dave Camm was a child molester, they should have charged him with it." The molestation issue is just one of the reasons Liell is appealing Camm's convictions.

As for the Boney angle, she says she's absolutely convinced Boney is the real killer and that he never even met David Camm, insisting there are no phone records to show any contact between the two.

Boney complains 225 years for selling a gun is a long time. Of course, there's a lot more to it. What was he doing with Kim's shoes? Why the similarities to Boney's previous attacks on women? What else went on that night? We may never know. In a lot of murder cases, we *never* learn the whole truth. The only people who really know that are the criminals, who generally continue to proclaim their innocence long after their convictions.

The ripple effects of these cases are massive. Kim's family is forever devastated. Kim's sister has multiple sclerosis and her condition has been worsened by the stress of it all. Kim's friends are crushed. David's family, up until this tragedy a pillar of moral strength in the community, still holds to the belief that David didn't do it. Their lives will never be the same either. And then there's Charles Boney's family. His mother will have to live with the knowledge that her son now seems destined to die in prison. Every single one of these cases has similar ripple effects, traumatizing dozens and dozens of people who are connected by accidents of birth or geography.

Then there's the expense of these trials to the taxpayers. The estimated tab in the Camm murders? Almost $2 million. The Indiana region may have to scrub some community projects to make up the cost.

IF WE COULD TURN BACK TIME

In grasping for answers, it's always interesting to ponder: If we could turn back time, what would we do differently? "Honestly, I've thought about that a lot," says Kim's best friend, Marcy McLeod Mahurin. It was Marcy who got a call from Kim a few weeks before the murders and noticed her friend seemed different: "I knew something was really wrong . . . just her whole demeanor. It wasn't so much about what she said. She wanted to hang on the phone, which was really unlike her. . . . I said, 'How are you and David?' and she said, 'I think history is repeating itself.' " Marcy says she didn't get any details about Kim's somewhat cryptic pronouncement, and that's what haunts her. It would turn out to be the last time they ever spoke.

"The problem with Kim is that she was so quiet about things that it would really be hard to know exactly when things went really bad," Marcy says. "Hindsight being twenty-twenty," she would have pushed to know more: "You know, I called her a couple of times and didn't get any answers . . . and left messages." In retrospect? "I would have kept calling and calling and calling until I got her."

Kim was a devout churchgoer. She had

238

commitments at her church. Marcy says her dear friend wasn't one to argue or fight. She was civilized and forgiving. When Kim and David separated briefly early in their marriage, Kim was pregnant with Jill and David was, by all accounts, having an affair. Still, Kim readily took David back when he asked to come home. For the most part, she kept the separation to herself. "She played Bunko with all the girls and none of them knew that they were separated," says her friend.

Marcy believes Kim had no idea that her husband's one known affair was just the tip of his iceberg of indiscretion. How many couples sit at the dinner table, talking about how their kids are doing at school, when one or both of them are fantasizing about liaisons they've had in the past, sometimes in the past couple of hours?

Someone who lies and continuously gets away with it has no incentive to stop. People simply do not change their behavior, not unless they really want to or are forced to. After David came back, would an intervention or counseling have led to a more honest relationship? What about a twelve-step sex addiction program? Or should their marriage have ended right there? There are no easy answers, because many marriages have survived affairs and thrived. The key is getting to the truth of the marriage. You must risk losing your marriage for it to remain healthy. If you can't get to honesty, you really don't have much anyway.

In the end, Marcy says this nightmare of losing her best friend has made her reconsider her attitudes toward relationships: "After this happened . . . all of my friends . . . and we were all friends with Kim and played Bunco, we all kind of made a pact with each other and said . . . if anything is ever wrong with anybody, we need to confide in someone so that this doesn't happen to anybody else. It just kind of made you think, Oh my gosh, if something is the faintest bit wrong, all you have to do is call somebody."

Speak up! Be an open book. And let your friends read you, problems and all. There should be no insurmountable shame in your story, even if there are embarrassments. Everybody's got relationship problems if they have a relationship. None of those relationships are perfect and they never will be. Don't confuse hiding an ugly truth with loyalty to your partner. If you experience guilt over holding your partner accountable, recognize that as *irrational* guilt.

We all live in denial to some degree. If we tried to ponder all the horrors of life at once, we'd go mad. But selective blindness in a relationship can be dangerous. You need to remain observant. You need to listen to your inner voice. On some level, we all know when something isn't feeling right. We need to tune into that frequency and respond to it. It could save our lives.

Lots of men cheat. That doesn't mean that those men are all killers. The threat of violence or death usually becomes more acute when certain other thresholds are crossed. As we saw in the Camm case, the issue of incest — real or imagined — is so volatile and emotionally loaded that it invariably creates a crisis of immense magnitude. The moment that issue enters the equation, take your kids and get out fast. Offer no advance warnings to the family member who may want to silence you. Another issue that can be enormously destabilizing to a relationship is debt, which can produce panic, rage, and shame, as is evident in the case of Neil Entwistle.

SOMETHING IN COMMON: THE NEIL ENTWISTLE CASE

In March 2006, as David Camm was convicted of triple murder for the second time in Indiana, British citizen Neil Entwistle was sitting in a Massachusetts jail waiting for his day in court. The charges? That he gunned down his wife, Rachel, and baby girl, Lillian Rose, allegedly using his stepfather's pistol.

"The commonality is the fact that they both felt emasculated or inadequate as a man. In Neil's case . . . it had to do with money," says Dr. Lieberman. Yes, Neil's secrets were about sex and money. He was in a downward spiral, unemployed, with a new family and mounting debts. But he still found time to surf the Internet for escort services. Neil looked them up just days before he allegedly massacred his wife and baby.

Investigators who searched the twenty-seven-year-old's computer found that Neil used the Web to get the names and addresses of various escort services, including Eye Candy Entertainment, Exotic Express, and Sweet Temptations. He also visited a site called Adult Friend Finder. Authorities say this site helps people find sex partners through chat rooms and personal ads. Authorities say Entwistle had expressed "a dissatisfaction with his sex life." Did Rachel have an inkling of her husband's sexual frustrations or his X-rated Web surfing? We may never know. Here's what we do know.

When friends showed up at the Entwistle home in Hopkinton, Massachusetts, on Saturday, January 21, 2006, they were perplexed. They'd been invited to a little dinner party and the lights were on inside. So why was no one answering the door? It would take almost twenty-four hours for them to get the answer. Like something out of a dinner-theater murder mystery, the hostess was lying upstairs in bed, dead. Executed with a gunshot wound to the head, she was in the fetal position. Next to her was her nine-month-old daughter, Lillian Rose, also dead, shot in the belly.

Unaware of all this, the dinner guests, still on the outside of the locked home, were curious and concerned. One of them went to the local police station and asked them to check it out. A few minutes later, two officers arrived at the Entwistle home, jimmied open the front door, and went in. Food and plates were laid out on the table, as if someone was getting ready to eat. The large heap of a comforter and other linens was on top of the bed in the Entwistles' master bedroom, but they didn't look under the covers. "It wasn't really a search for a missing person, it was a well-being check, and a lot of police departments don't even go in the house for a well-being check. They'll knock on the door and look through the windows to make sure there's nothing . . . out of the ordinary," said reporter Norman Miller, who has covered this story from the beginning for *The MetroWest Daily News.* In this case, while no one was home, there seemed to be nothing amiss. There was no car in the garage, so maybe the family had gone out. The police left.

The next evening, Rachel's mom, Priscilla Matterazzo, who lived about an hour away, in Carver, Massachusetts, arrived at the Hopkinton Police Department to fill out a missing person's report. She told police she had gone into the home after Rachel's friends had gotten the garage code from a neighbor. They'd looked around again. Still nobody home. Priscilla was worried. She'd been trying to reach her daughter for three days but couldn't. The last time she had spoken with Rachel was Thursday night. It was now Sunday, January 22. Police decided to go back to the Entwistle home and have another look around.

This time, when they went inside they noticed that *smell,* the unmistakable sign of a rotting corpse. This time, they lifted the comforter. At first they saw a foot. Then a woman's body in the fetal position. Next to her chest was the baby, lying on her back.

But where was the husband, Neil Entwistle?

ACROSS THE POND

Word soon came that the Entwistles' leased BMW had been found at Boston's Logan Airport in a parking garage. It had been there since at least midnight on Friday night. Significantly, inside the car were keys to the home of Neil's in-laws. It was determined that Neil Entwistle had left American soil at 8:15 a.m. on Saturday, January 21, the morning of the dinner party. He had purchased a one-way ticket using a Visa debit card and did not check any luggage.

Then came the transatlantic phone calls. Rachel's stepfather told police he got a call from Neil's dad offering a convoluted explanation of why Neil fled to England. A few minutes later, Neil himself called him to offer an explanation. So Massachusetts investigators decided to talk to Neil themselves.

Authorities phoned the recent widower on Monday, January 23, and had a long chat — two hours long. Here's how the search warrant affidavit describes Neil's version of events: "Neil said he woke up on [Friday] January 20, at about 7:00 a.m., fed his daughter Lillian, and then left house at about 9:00 a.m. to do some errands . . . then got back home at about 11:00 a.m." Neil says he went upstairs, looked for his family, and found them dead under the covers: "Neil said he pulled the covers back over his wife and daughter, went downstairs, grabbed a knife from the kitchen and considered killing himself, but then put it down because it would hurt too much." He then drove to Carver to tell his in-laws and to get a gun with which to shoot himself from his father-in-law's collection. Neil claims when he got there nobody was home and he couldn't get into the house. So, he said, he drove to the airport and left for England to be with his parents. A big problem with his story? Neil maintained he couldn't get into the in-laws' house. But cops found the keys to that very house inside Neil's car.

Word that this boyishly handsome husband was at first "a person of interest" and soon the obvious suspect in the gruesome executions of his wholesome wife and precious nine-month-old daughter created a media frenzy on both sides of the Atlantic. Once back in his native England, Neil hid behind drawn curtains at his parents' house in an old mining town a few hours' drive outside London. He missed the funeral.

After much international legal wrangling, Neil was finally arrested in a London tube station on February 9. He waived an extradition fight and was returned to American soil a few days later. It was as if the entire media establishment of the Western world had gathered to greet him. "Insane" is how journalist Norman Miller described it: "When he . . . landed . . . they had helicopters from every single news station following him. And . . . a lot of British media, TV and print." And on TV sets across America, his arrival got play-by-play coverage.

Shrubs were trampled as the media formed a gauntlet of cameras leading to the local jail in Hopkinton, Massachusetts. The small town is best known as the starting point of the Boston Marathon. Thanks to Neil Entwistle, Hopkinton now had another, far more dubious claim to fame.

Entwistle was arraigned, and once again, Norman Miller was on hand for the *Metro-West Daily News.* Norman described the courtroom as jam-packed with journalists, curious attorneys, and court personnel, and buzzing like a barroom without the alcohol. People were just talking, "waiting for something to happen. And then the family members of Rachel Entwistle walked in and there was instant silence . . . everybody's just looking at them. Nobody's saying a word. You could hear someone turning the page of a noteook. All the women were carrying lilies and roses for Lillian Rose. And there was not one noise until you heard the clank, clank, clank of Neil Entwistle's leg irons coming up from the holding area into the courtroom." Neil pleaded not guilty.

FROM COURTSHIP TO COURTHOUSE

Back to the beginning. The attractive couple who created little Lillian Rose Entwistle delighted in taking baby pictures showing their angelic child, apparently much loved, decked out in cute little outfits, or dressed up as a skunk on Halloween. What a pretty baby. What a terrible way to go.

Neil and Rachel met when Rachel took her junior year of college in England at the University of York. Friends say they seemed smitten with each other. In August 2003 they got married, and in April 2005, they had Lillian Rose. They were living in England. She taught school. He worked for a military research company. Then in the summer of 2005, Neil quit his job, reportedly for "domestic reasons." In September 2005, Rachel and Neil moved with their baby to Carver, Massachusetts, where they lived with Rachel's mother and stepfather. In the search warrant affidavit, authorities say Neil told them that he "wanted to try to live in both countries, but Rachel wanted to live in the United States where she could be closer to her mother. . . . Neil said that Rachel was more family oriented than he was."

With hindsight, some might wonder, Was this when Neil first began to feel resentful? Of course! In England, he had a job and was living in his native land, relatively close to *his* family. Now he was in a new country, jobless, not a citizen, with a new baby, and living for several months in the home of his in-laws. On top of this, Rachel had recently announced she wanted to be a stay-at-home mom.

Her close friend Lara Jehle told CNN, "She was very happy. And I think that was Rachel's — that was her element. That was who she wanted to be. She was a great stay-at-home mom. She loved what she did, in taking care of her family. And I think that was where Rachel shined the most." But was this a blinding responsibility for Neil, who did not appear prepared to support the family himself?

"She was working as a teacher. And then she said: Geez, I actually like being just a mom," muses Massachusetts private investigator Tom Shamshak, who is also a former police chief. Neil "was just immature, stressed out, no friends, no family, no job. Those are very strong stressors. The inability to provide for your family."

In a lot of domestic crimes, one also gets the sense that an imbalance within the marriage has sparked resentment. One of the most common imbalances is when a couple spends a lot more time with one side of the family than the other. We know that Rachel wanted her daughter to be raised as an American near the baby's maternal grandmother. How did Neil feel about this? There are also reports that it was especially difficult for him to find employment due to his status as a British citizen. If he was angry over losing his employment, leaving his native land, and living with strangers called in-laws, did he stuff it and pretend that everything was fine?

Dr. Lieberman adds another interesting psychological insight by asking why some married women feel the strong urge to be near their parents. Are they seeking protection? "Perhaps these women are reacting to their unconscious unease of being with this man. . . . They're feeling like something is not quite right. They're feeling a little fearful and want the protection of their family, although this is probably all unconscious." Unfortunately, she adds, that might serve to further antagonize the husband, sending the message that he's not a good enough protector and making him feel even more emasculated.

Indeed, many would later note that while Neil seemed perfectly ordinary on the surface, he was not. Perhaps Rachel wanted to be near her mom and stepdad to compensate for her unconscious fears about her partner.

CYBER PAST

Evidence of Neil Entwistle's obsession with cyber porn dates back to several months *before* he married Rachel, to spring 2003. The *Boston Herald* reported that Entwistle's British Internet company offered free sex, discreet sex contacts, and "free 7-day access to an XXX site containing movies and pictures."

Neil reportedly went on to try to market the *Big Penis Manual,* which offered to help men get larger penises without the use of drugs. *People* magazine reported on another now-defunct Entwistle site called Million-maker.co.uk, which promised a sizable monthly income to those who used their own websites to promote hard-core porn sites.

There were also reports that Neil plagiarized another engineer's technical papers to advertise his computer design services on the Internet. This Web scam seems to have been established in America. The ad reportedly listed the business phone number of Entwistle's father-in-law. At this point, Neil may have already been losing his grip on reality. According to the *MetroWest Daily News,* the engineer whose work was allegedly pirated took a look at Neil's sales pitch and couldn't figure out exactly what Entwistle was selling. It appears Neil was trying to impress potential customers with his technical knowledge but didn't really know what he was talking about. Some of Neil's postings have been described as sloppy cut-and-paste jobs. Neil might have been trying to cut and paste his way out of a serious financial problem.

And then there was eBay. EBay shut down Entwistle's account after numerous complaints came in, complaints about his failure to deliver software that had been paid for, complaints that seemed to crescendo in the week before the murders. More than a dozen popped up between January 7 and 9. Here's a sampling: "***WARNING***

Never received item." "Complete Scam,
eBay users beware!" "Do not do business
with this individual as he does not
exist!!!!!!!!!!!!!!(THIEF)."

And apparently some complaints were
directed not at Neil but at Rachel. Did Neil
decide to use his wife's name, without her
knowledge, to perpetrate an online scam?

Private eye Tom Shamshak has a theory:
"I think she learned that there was fraud
being perpetrated. . . . And maybe there was
a confrontation: 'What the hell are you doing? What's really going on here?' "

IT GROWS ON TREES?

Certainly Rachel had to have suspicions
about how they were affording their rather
luxurious lifestyle, considering neither one
of them had worked in months. They drove
a leased BMW, which cost them $498 a
month. Ten days before the murders, they'd
moved into a house worth almost half a million dollars. They'd signed a short-term
lease, handing over certified checks for
$5,400, presumably as a security deposit,
and $2,700, which was the monthly rent.
And, say authorities, just a few days before
the murders, the Entwistles bought a load
of new furniture to the tune of $6,000.

"He came to America and he sort of got

caught up in the American Dream or the American extravagance, and he wanted to live that life . . . BMW and all," says Dr. Lieberman, adding that when he couldn't sustain it, he felt emasculated and angry.

Neil must have known they didn't have the money to live like this. Why didn't they just rent a cheaper place, get an old jalopy, and eat Top Ramen, like so many struggling young couples do? Because, apparently, Neil hadn't told his wife they were broke.

According to the affidavit, Rachel's mother told police her daughter was "unsure of the condition of her and her husband's finances. Rachel would tell her mother that she would ask Neil questions about their finances, but Neil would not divulge any information, and this caused some conflict between Neil and Rachel." Rachel admitted to her mom that when she tried to use one of Neil's English credit cards, she learned the account had been frozen. Still, Rachel assured her mom that she believed they had enough money to buy a home outright, or make a big down payment, except that their money "had been tied up in 'offshore accounts' that Neil would not talk about." All he would say was that everything was under control.

As we try to understand what goes murderously wrong in some relationships and how to prevent it from happening again, we must look at the role of both the wife and the husband. Intimate-partner crime begins to unfold long before it's actually committed. Along the way, there are hints and clues of what's ahead. When a spouse stonewalls you repeatedly on money issues, it's a big flashing neon sign of trouble around the bend. Yet so many people put up with lack of accountability in relationships. The withholding husband becomes angry and the spouse is afraid to press. That's when you have to say, Level with me or I'm out of here. This lack of transparency about your financial situation is a deal breaker. If you are not in financial trouble, then your spouse should have nothing to hide and should be able to show you everything: bank and credit card statements, etc. As a spouse you have the right to know, down to the last penny, how much your partner has in savings and how much debt he has accumulated. That's what it means to be a family.

Rachel was ostensibly trying to determine their financial situation, but on a deeper level she must have been aware that something was terribly wrong. How could she not? Neil's explanations about their money being in "offshore accounts" are ridiculous. He didn't come from a wealthy family. He had never been that successful in business. She'd dated him since they were in college. Where did she think the money in that "offshore account" came from?

Sometimes we prefer to buy into something that we know is nonsense because it's easier than facing the truth. There are many women who intentionally stay in the dark about their husbands' livelihoods because it suits them. This phenomenon is brilliantly laid out in *The Sopranos*. A constant theme in the highly praised TV series is the many ways that mob boss Tony Soprano's wife, Carmela, lives in denial, pretending she's a good Catholic, all the while knowing the money that keeps her dripping in jewelry and luxury cars is blood money. But she just acts like she has no idea, so she can pretend she's one of the "good people." In one very poignant scene, when she goes to an elderly male psychiatrist, he refuses to take her check, calling it what it is, blood money. At that moment, she's forced to face the truth about herself. But she quickly descends back into denial because she doesn't want to sacrifice her opulent lifestyle.

In fact, Neil and Rachel were deeply in debt, from credit cards, student loans, and their overall manner of living. Neil must ultimately be blamed for keeping the dire nature of their financial situation secret. But why? The reason is always the same — shame and inadequacy. "Sex is what men turn to when they are feeling less like men. That's why [Neil] was increasingly looking for escorts and all of that . . . looking to have sexual liaisons so that he could restore his feelings of being a man, even though he . . . couldn't pay for all these things he was buying," says Dr. Lieberman. But what was the underlying shame that was causing him to overcompensate by living beyond his means in the first place?

SIR NEIL?

When we're in a relationship, each of us brings our baggage: our families, our personal traumas, our national identities. Did Neil feel he had to play the role of a successful British yuppie to be accepted in America? Was he trying to reinvent himself as more upper class than he actually was to impress those around him? To get a fresh start? This happens with a lot of Europeans. They come to America and quickly realize that the Yanks can't distinguish accents the way the folks back home can. It's very common for expatriates from Europe, whether from Russia, Italy, England, or elsewhere, to exaggerate their social standing and promote themselves as being from a higher class than they actually are. There are even quite a few phony aristocrats roaming the cocktail-party circuit trying to capitalize on a fictional lineage. This kind of thing is not new. A century ago, author Henry James wrote about head games between people who represent the Old World versus those who represent the New World.

Personally, I think it's all rubbish, and class distinctions are right up there with racism. But, sadly, both are still alive and well. I only mention this because of a telling comment that the search warrant affidavit attributed to Rachel's mom, Priscilla. She told the cops that "Rachel and Neil came back to the U.S. because Neil Entwistle would never amount to anything in England because of his accent: He was obviously a coal miner's son from a working-class background." Where did Priscilla come up with that, and what's the significance?

Did Rachel's infatuation with her British boyfriend diminish over time, as she realized he wasn't the aristocratic Prince Charming she may have first taken him for? They met at their British university's rowing club, and he was quoted on a website as boasting, "She was my cox, I her stroke!" Sounds very upper crust! In fact, *The Boston Globe* quotes Rachel's friend Lara Jehle as saying Rachel saw Neil as her "knight in shining armor." It hardly gets more princely than that.

Over time, living in England, did Rachel learn to distinguish the accents the way the British do? Accents are exotic and therefore often attractive and charming. But one day you wake up and you can't hear your lover's accent anymore. You just see the person. Neil grew up in a working-class neighborhood in a former mining town in central England. His mother was reportedly a school cook.

By the same token, was Neil initially swept away by the "Americanness" of his girlfriend? Many Europeans find Americans to be dynamic, exciting, and powerful, and buy into the myths that come with our nationality. Was he, in turn, disillusioned by his stint of several months at the home of his decidedly middle-class in-laws? His father-in-law was a contractor, not a captain of industry.

These kinds of disillusionments can be avoided by not buying into them in the first place. If class distinctions are irrelevant to you, then there's no disappointment down the road. Ditto for race, ethnicity, and financial status. We need to stay focused on what's inside, on our partner's spirit. Other expectations can lead to disappointment and then to hate.

THE GUN

Perhaps the most shocking aspect of this case concerns the gun used to kill Rachel and Lillian Rose. Authorities have determined it came from the gun collection of Rachel's stepfather, Joe Matterazzo. While Neil was living with Rachel's parents, he and his father-in-law liked to break out the guns in Joe's collection for target practice. Neil knew where the weapons were kept and where the key to the gun collection was.

According to Martha Coakley, the Middlesex County district attorney, Neil had access to his in-laws' house. "And so, without much difficulty, he could have easily let himself into the home. . . . We are not sure when he took the firearm, because Rachel's family never knew it was missing. But it would have been a fairly easy matter for him to go back down Friday, enter the house, and replace the gun from where he had taken it."

Authorities suspect Neil shot his family,

then drove to his in-laws' home an hour away, replaced the gun, and then drove to the airport to head for England.

> You know, he must have really hated this family, just hated them, to go get the gun from their home, kill their daughter, and put the gun back. You know what? If those facts are true, that's dangerously close to framing the stepfather for a murder. We all know DNA allegedly has been found on that gun. I'm talking about human matter . . . blowback from the shooting!
>
> — Nancy Grace, *CNN Headline News,*
> February 16, 2006

As soon as authorities learned that the father-in-law had a gun collection that Neil had access to, they tested his weapons, with Joe's full cooperation, focusing in on one .22-caliber revolver. According to the affidavit in support of the criminal complaint, "DNA matching Neil Entwistle was found on the grip of the firearm, and DNA matching Rachel Entwistle was found on the muzzle end of the firearm."

Forensic scientist Dr. Larry Kobilinsky put that evidence into perspective for me: "DNA is the gold standard of all forensic testing. It's got the most credibility. And so, when you find Entwistle's DNA on the handgrip, it simply means that he held the gun."

But, police acknowledge, Neil had used that gun before during target practice with his father-in-law. They also acknowledge that on Saturday, the morning of the dinner party, before Joe Matterazzo knew that his stepdaughter, Rachel, and her daughter, Lillian, had been murdered, Joe used the gun for target practice on his own. That is an exceptionally morbid detail. It would appear Rachel's stepfather was handling the murder weapon but didn't know it. All the while, Rachel's DNA was clinging to the muzzle. Authorities say that target practice did not wipe out the DNA from either Rachel or Neil: "On a handgrip, it's a very rough surface . . . you do find cells that slough off your hand that are deposited on the grip. If you take a swab and you rub the grip down and then you test that swab, you'll find DNA," Dr. Kobilinsky told me.

But couldn't Neil argue that since he had used that gun in the past, his DNA was not from the murder but from his earlier target practice, and whoever killed Rachel simply used the same gun that he had once handled? Dr. Kobilinsky calls that a hard sell, noting the defense would have to explain how and why a killer would go to his father-in-law's house and pick precisely that weapon. Also, that phantom individual would have to have been wearing gloves for his DNA not to show up, while Neil's did: "You can come up with a convoluted concept as to how his DNA got on that gun and how the victim's DNA got on that gun. But the simplest explanation is usually the correct one. And that is that he took that gun and used it to kill his wife."

KEY WORDS

Neil Entwistle's attorney is highly regarded in the Massachusetts legal world. He vowed not to try this case in the press and questioned whether Neil could get a fair trial, given the intense media scrutiny.

Among the most damning evidence against his client is that authorities say that on January 16 and 17, just a few short days before the murders, Neil Entwistle was on a computer reading about "how to kill people by various methods." Investigators have evidence that Neil Entwistle actually typed in Internet searches regarding "suicide, how to kill someone with a knife, and euthanasia."

We all may wonder why anyone would leave such incriminating evidence behind on their computer, since it's pretty common knowledge that police invariably go in and study the words that a suspect has searched for. The likely explanation is that at the time those words were typed in, whatever Neil was cooking up was still a vague concept, mostly fantasy. By the time it crystallized into an alleged plan, he'd long forgotten the words he'd typed into that search engine. Think of your own Internet searches. Can you precisely list all the keywords you've typed into Google or some other search engine over the last week? I couldn't. I Google more than a hundred words every week.

Prosecutors have concluded that while Neil may have contemplated murder/ suicide, in the end, say authorities, he could only go through with the first half of that plot.

Whether you believe they're guilty or not, the stories of Neil Entwistle and David Camm dramatically illustrate how dishonesty about sex within marriage can be a sign of impending disaster. The moral lesson is: Demand total honesty from your spouse about everything, *especially sex,* or get out of the marriage. Sex plus honesty can equal love. Sex plus lies can equal loathing. Be very observant. Learn how to spot signs and listen to your instincts. If your spouse is making you feel crazy because you sense something's wrong but can't prove it, chances are your intuition is right.

7
MOTHERS WITHOUT
BORDERS

Scott Peterson and Laci Rocha. Two beautiful kids who grew up in sunny California, connected first by romance, marriage, and pregnancy — then by murder. Study their long and convoluted dance toward death. Laci, gregarious and pretty but naïve, waltzed through life blissfully unaware of the deviousness of her charming partner, until Scott tripped her on Christmas Eve 2002. Where did they learn their moves? From their parents, of course. Laci's doting mother, Sharon, and Scott's sickly mother, Jackie, were the choreographers of their children's lives. Jackie in particular was tap dancing around secrets galore. Scott unconsciously learned to imitate those steps. It goes a long way toward explaining what drove him to slaughter his wife and their unborn son, Connor.

Jackie not only inherited her family's dark secret, but also spawned some family secrets of her own. She passed all these toxic heirlooms down to Scott, who carried them until he exploded in rage, exposing the secrets metaphorically through the vicious and violent murder of his wife and unborn child. This is certainly not to suggest, in any way, that Jackie is somehow responsible for the crime of which her son was convicted. She bears absolutely no blame for Laci's murder! But her life experience does allow us to analyze the potential intergenerational impact of one specific type of secret, a classic secret that's been around as long as man, a secret that always seems to wreak havoc.

Notwithstanding Scott's toothy grin, his family history is bizarre and filled with tragedy. Scott's grandfather on his mother's side was murdered in 1945, his head split open by a disgruntled ex-employee wielding a metal pipe. This caused Scott's fragile grandmother to fall apart. The family was essentially destroyed. Scott's mother was virtually given away at a young age, sent to an orphanage run by strict Catholic nuns, where food rations were reportedly miserly. Jackie soon became ill, suffering from respiratory ailments that would plague her for her entire life. By many accounts, it was a brutal existence. Jackie's tough childhood can help us understand her adult choices, which, in turn, affected her son, Scott.

Little Jackie grew up and had her first child in 1963, but the father left her, and she gave the baby boy up for adoption. Two years later, a second man impregnated Jackie, and she gave that infant girl up for adoption too. That girl grew up to be a woman named Anne Bird, and she wrote a book called *Blood Brother: 33 Reasons My Brother Scott Peterson Is Guilty*. In it Anne describes meeting Jackie for the first time and Jackie's odd explanation of why she put Anne up for adoption. "I asked her to describe the circumstances of my birth. 'You were conceived on a boat in the San Diego Bay,' she said. 'As soon as I found out I was pregnant, I went to a friend's house in Los Angeles and hid there for the duration.' . . . For a moment I wondered why it was such a horrible, ugly secret. But thirty years ago, I knew, there was still more of a stigma attached to unwed motherhood than there is today." Anne goes on to write that Jackie said Anne's biological father had offered to marry her, but she wasn't interested.

A third man came along, and a third child. Jackie kept that third baby and later married Lee Peterson, with whom she then had Scott. Dr. Keith R. Ablow, author of *Inside the Mind of Scott Peterson,* cites this history in his persuasive argument that the Petersons' dysfunctional family history turned Scott into the killer he became. He's right on target. The secret history of Scott's fractured family tells the story of Laci's murder.

In his groundbreaking pop-psychology book *Family Secrets,* John Bradshaw puts a complex psychological theory into people terms by explaining that families pass down family secrets from generation to generation, unless and until the shameful, toxic secrets are exposed and worked through to a psychologically healthy conclusion.

Who Knew?

Of all the things about the Scott Peterson case, the most shocking to me was this: Jackie reportedly kept the existence of the two children she'd given away at birth a secret from the children she later had, including Scott. The reason? Shame is always the number one suspect.

When Jackie's dad was murdered more than half a century ago and her devastated mother lost her ability to cope, shame entered Jackie's world. Being sent to an orphanage, whether run by nuns or not, is an extremely shame-producing situation, which also fosters rage, resentment, and a sense of alienation and abandonment. Jackie was discarded, sent away, by her mother. Her mom couldn't deal. She did the unthinkable.

Small wonder, then, that when Jackie became a woman, she *repeated the pattern* and ended up giving up her first two children for adoption. Jackie has been quoted as saying that she was naïve and not raised with the knowledge of how to cope with men. That may be true, but the world is packed with very ignorant women who hang on to their children through any and all struggles. Jackie's explanation might stand had only one child been given away for adoption, but two, by two different fathers, shows that — on a subconscious level — something else is at work. It's too similar to what happened to her.

This shameful secret burst into the light of day when the first child, Don Chapman, tracked Jackie down and wrote her a certified letter. In *A Deadly Game,* Catherine Crier and Cole Thompson's in-depth book on the case, she explains, "Jackie reportedly opened the letter in front of her family, and then 'freaked out' because no one else, including Lee, had ever heard about Don and Anne. . . ." If this is true, then Jackie is a woman who hid the central fact of her life from her own husband and her two sons for their whole life together.

I spoke with Anne Bird, who became a mother herself. She told me she believed that Jackie had indeed kept her existence, and that of Don, secret until the letter arrived. Anne told me, "I think she was going to take this to the grave, and then when she received the letter she had to tell everyone. So that was my understanding."

It would appear that Scott was in his twenties when he had to absorb this bombshell. This happened around 1996 or 1997, just as Scott and Laci's relationship was getting into full swing.

In his book, John Bradshaw writes, "In past generations, marriage when pregnant, illegitimacy, and adoption were all grounds for dark secrets. Had any of your grandparents had a child out of wedlock or by a previous marriage — perhaps a child that they secretly put up for adoption? I have had several clients who found out that they had a half-brother or -sister after one of their parents died. Some found out while their parents were still alive. They felt angry and betrayed and no longer trusted their parents. 'If they could lie about my brother or sister, what else would they lie about?' they thought."

But Scott seemed to suffer absolutely no trauma from this news. Instead of confronting his mom and demanding explanations and expressing his sense of betrayal at being lied to about something so important, Scott merely seemed cheerfully interested in meeting his new siblings. Shortly before her wedding, Laci told her mother she was stunned by the news of this secret backstory, but she noted that Scott handled it well. He didn't kick over a chair. There are no reports of him going into therapy or organizing family powwows to talk it through. Of all the signs of the approaching horror, Scott's eerily calm response to this mind-boggling news is the most telling.

Jackie had long been sickly. We all remember the video of her coming and going to court with tubes in her nose because of persistent health problems. Interestingly enough, her own mother also suffered health problems. Under the best of circumstances, it's extraordinarily hard to confront a mother about a hot-button issue like this one. We as Americans are trained to "buck up," "get a grip," and "move on." It's part of the whole "get over it" and "snap out of it" syndrome. It's especially difficult to confront a chronically ill mother about such an emotionally loaded subject as secret siblings. So what's a stunned son to do? Put the old blinders on. Stuff it down and hope nothing, like his own impending fatherhood, causes it to come up.

We like to think we're in charge of our lives. But our subconscious guides and controls much of our behavior. If only we as a society could once and for all acknowledge that all these secrets will ultimately come out in the wash. And if you don't want a secret to wash up as a horrific act of violence, you must deal with it when it's merely in the discomfort zone. Scott never dealt with his own discomfort. The Peterson family system, operating on a subliminal level, would have frowned on that.

UNCONSCIOUS KNOWLEDGE

There is a fascinating twist to the theory that people carry their parents' secrets and act them out. In his book, John Bradshaw says he has seen evidence in many cases he's worked on that unconsciously, the child *knows* the parents' secret long before being told. The child in some way acts the secret out as a way of bringing the festering sore

273

of shame into the sunlight.

Bradshaw offers a case study: A young woman marries a philanderer and goes to counseling to seek help in coping with her husband's numerous affairs. In a group session with her parents, the patient discovers that her proper, conservative father is really a closet sexaholic who has cheated on his wife for eons. On an unconscious level, the daughter has always sensed her father's secret and was driven to repeat the family pattern, because of a need to express the truth.

Taking it one step further, you could say that the young woman's nonverbal, unconscious message to the father she could not confront directly is: I've got your number. And now you know what it feels like to have to put up with somebody like yourself, in the form of a son-in-law.

This theory fits Scott like a glove. Scott had always lived a double life. He is said to have dated two girls simultaneously in high school. He often lied when he didn't have to. Scott was perpetually acting out the double life he unconsciously sensed was his mother's unspoken truth. And it turns out his subconscious was right. Once he learned of his mother's secret past, he didn't deal with his emotions, he buried them even more, which caused even more shame, sparking even more acting out through duality.

BREAKING POINT

Scott lived two lives when he was married to Laci, hooking up with Amber Frey as Laci's pregnancy advanced into its final few months. The reality of what was happening was too loaded for Scott. He needed to switch to an alternate reality, which took the form of a secret lover, with whom he could be emotional and needy and let out all the feelings that he otherwise stuffed inside. Amber represented the other world Scott could escape to and where he increasingly preferred to live.

With every week, the stress of the approaching birth of his son increased his desire to escape, because it reactivated the rage, confusion, and depression Scott had stuffed down upon learning his mother's secret. All of this was a psychological pressure cooker, and Scott, unanalyzed and lacking any self-awareness, was steering blindly through this tornado of emotional triggers, and acting happy.

Think about it. Jackie's secret concerns the exact same issue as Scott's: parenthood. She got rid of her first two children; one might conclude she didn't want them. The facts reveal that Scott didn't want children either, and he got rid of his too.

Ultimately, Scott went to the dark side, where he would reenact the traumas from his family's past. Scott's murder of Laci was a remix of his grandfather's violent murder combined with a seething acting-out of his mother's secret. In his subconscious, the murder was like making a collage, taking all the most painful and dysfunctional aspects of his life and wrapping them into one bloody canvas to express his truth.

DATE WITH DEATH

The dates of the crimes are remarkably close. Scott's grandfather and Laci were both killed in late December. Scott's grandfather died around Christmas week in 1945, while Laci went missing on Christmas Eve 2002. The last time Laci ever spoke with her mom was the evening of December 23, 2002, just before she vanished — with Scott's help. That is no coincidence. Anniversaries, even ones that are not acknowledged outwardly, often serve as triggers, and the potential for depression or violence rises. That is especially true if the loaded date also falls on an emotionally saturated holiday, like Christmas. One wonders what

Jackie's mood was over the years on Christmas, knowing its secret significance, knowing it was the time of year her life forever changed. After years of feeling an unspoken undercurrent on that anniversary, Scott must have sensed a symbolic significance in the timing. It's a way of ritualizing the killing, providing a context that gives meaning, at least in the killer's sick psyche.

THE PEOPLE PLEASER

Many have commented on how Jackie referred to Scott as her "golden boy." To me, this indicates that Jackie's subconscious message to Scott was: You should be thrilled that you are fortunate enough not to have been given away. You're the lucky child! Even though baby Scott was reportedly pampered, the lucky golden child still had the very same mother who was capable of giving away her first two children. So there was an unspoken, unconscious threat to the mother's message. That threat is: Hey, this is what I'm capable of. Don't cause me any trouble. And Scott didn't cause trouble. He was continuously described as a "perfect child."

The perfect child is really a people-pleasing child. Scott was raised to be a *people pleaser,* someone who feels a compulsion to please others at his own expense, telling people what they want to hear, being what they feel the other person wants them to be. Scott did this with his father and many girlfriends, imitating them, adopting their hobbies. Of course, since Scott's behavior was not grounded in any real beliefs of his own, it was all over the map. The same person who said he loved to hunt with his dad also claimed to shun meat while he was dating a vegetarian.

Any shrink will tell you that, underneath the façade, people pleasers are very angry people. A lifetime of pretense and wondering who the hell you really are. The people pleaser certainly has no idea. A big part of him resents his dependence on the approval of others and chafes at his own certainty that he must be perfect for anyone to accept him. The approval-seeking invariably comes at the expense of the authentic self, which feels increasingly hollow, spiritually bankrupt, and depressed. The authentic self, angry and empty, becomes the dark secret self. As in the classic novel *The Picture of Dorian Gray,* the more the outer shell shines, the more shriveled the inner portrait becomes. This is where the split occurs. The hidden persona is the one that ultimately fights to break out and express its repressed being, in Scott's case through murder. Think of this explosion of violence as one person's bloody revolution, in which the murder victim personifies the whole world the murderer is waging war against in his mind.

All the descriptions of Scott the child and Scott the man pretty much fall into the same category. On the surface he was perfect. This word comes up over and over. In her book *Blood Brother,* Anne Bird describes the first time she met Scott: "He walked in, already smiling, and it was a perfect smile. Right away I saw it. He really was the golden boy: handsome, athletic and tall." Wait a second, he's about to meet his formerly secret sister, a full-fledged adult about whom he only recently learned, and he's already smiling? Why? Is he campaigning for something? In a way, people pleasers are always campaigning, as if they need to be elected by you to be okay. It's as if they need your vote to feel good about themselves. And it's always election time. You are urged to vote early and often. They desperately need this reaffirmation. So any relationship with them becomes exhausting and ultimately unfulfilling for both parties. After a lifetime of acting perfect, Scott suddenly learns the reason he's been asked to act.

Pretty explosive stuff. Yet he is grinning. That's his only authorized response, at least according to his family's subliminal playbook and the role he's been assigned in it. Again, this is not noted in order to judge. Every family assigns roles! The aim is to become aware of these roles, so you can opt out.

Was the violence Scott later inflicted a reaction to the suppression of his negative emotions about his secret siblings? Anne Bird told me she has pondered these issues: "At one point, I did think that, with Jackie giving away children, it kind of . . . makes it seem that children are worthless." And then Anne added a fascinating aside: "The fact that Laci's and Connor's bodies were found virtually in my own backyard made me wonder: What does Scott think of me? . . . It made me kind of think that I was used as a dumping ground." Anne is referring to the fact that the bodies were found in San Francisco Bay, which can be seen from Anne's Berkeley home. In fact, during the search for Laci, Anne graciously allowed Scott to live there with her family to avoid the media glare back in Modesto. Scott stayed in a loft bedroom in Anne's house, a room that had a very nice view of the bay.

Scott must have been very taken with

Anne's social status, given what we know about him. Here they are, siblings by blood, but he's selling manure and living a marginally middle-class life. Meanwhile, his newly discovered sister had been adopted by wealthy, refined parents. Anne had attended finishing school and, for a summer, Oxford University. She had traveled extensively as a youngster, at one point living with her family in an English manor house. Scott traveled to exotic locales — in his mind.

There may well have been an unconscious jealousy of his sister on top of all of the other emotions fueling Scott's rage. Up until meeting Anne, he was the "golden child." But suddenly he found himself trumped. On the surface, he was initially charming to Anne. Was he so shut down that he had no clue as to how he really felt?

Scott has been called a lot more than a people pleaser. He's also been labeled a sociopath. He's certainly got qualities of both. The classic sociopath is a charming, manipulative individual, which Scott was. "The sociopath has a disorder of attachment. He cannot feel close or attached to the people around him. So it doesn't bother him to hurt others or cause them pain," says noted Los Angeles psychoanalyst Bethany Marshall, adding that the inability to form real emotional attachments starts very young, with "maternal rejection. That's the number-one developmental underpinning. It's not even the mother's negligence or depriving. . . . If Scott's mother could give up two babies, how did she treat him? Was she really as attached as she pretended to be?" In other words, despite everything looking golden on the surface, even a well-fed, middle-class boy can feel detached and alienated from Mommy if Mommy's neurosis prevents her from delivering the uncomplicated affection a child craves. As in any relationship, the devil is in the intimate details.

APPEARANCES OVER REALITY

Like so many parents who conveniently forget to tell their children the things about their past they are least proud of, it would seem Jackie Peterson withheld some of the most unpleasant details of her youth from Scott as he was growing up. Did Scott unconsciously share this tendency, valuing appearances over reality? Again, this is not to judge Jackie. It would be fair to say that in many, if not most, American homes, neat appearances are winning the battle over messy truths, which is the reason we're looking at this issue.

In homes where presenting a respectable public front trumps dealing with a really inconvenient truth, the line between fiction and reality can become blurred. Truth can become a dead issue, overshadowed by the more immediate need to look good. Scott, like so many people we all know — including some politicians and corporate titans — learned to say whatever worked to achieve his goals, lacing his stories with enough fact to make them close enough for comfort. Scott, like all good liars before him, wove truth into every fabrication.

Anne Bird told me that she has learned a tremendous life lesson from all of this: "I've always been very trusting of people. Abnormally so . . . I was raised to take people's word at face value. All of that has changed. I'm . . . more aware. Not so naïve." And she says that she has instilled in her children the utmost respect for the truth: "Honesty is just about the most important value in our house. . . . We don't have any secrets."

BAD SIGNS

Then there's the gun factor. Scott had a loaded .22-caliber handgun in his glove compartment. He said he used it to hunt. He also reportedly owned several other weapons. Whatever your position on gun control or hunting, please know one thing: People don't have guns by accident. And they don't go hunting by accident. It says something about their values, their propensities, and what turns them on. They call it blood sport for a reason.

There was another really bad sign. Michael Fleeman, in his book *Laci, Inside the Laci Peterson Murder,* describes how less than a month after Laci's disappearance, the Rocha family was informed by police that not only was Scott having an affair with Amber Frey, but he had, "prior to Laci's disappearance, taken out a 250-thousand-dollar life insurance policy on her." According to *The Modesto Bee,* "The Petersons took out life insurance policies on each other on June 25, 2001, a year and a half before" Laci's disappearance. Obviously, this was well before Laci was pregnant. But according to Catherine Crier's book, it's the very same month Laci made her first visit to a Modesto obstetrics clinic for her annual exam, where she reportedly expressed her intention to get pregnant by the end of the year. If indeed acts of violence begin to percolate in the unconscious long before they manifest themselves in the open, in what way was the timing of these two developments connected? Was this the innocent and prudent estate planning of a couple contemplating starting a family? Or was there something else at work? One would have to be inside Scott Peterson's head to know for sure. Even he might not have known his subconscious motivations for getting life insurance at that particular juncture.

Dangerous Cocktail

These are the main ingredients in the Scott Peterson Cocktail. But now we must look at how Laci's family flavors the mix, particularly the role of her mother, Sharon, in Scott and Laci's marriage and her interactions with Scott. These observations are made in the spirit of honoring Laci's life by learning from it, and with the understanding that Laci was blessed to have a mother as loving and caring as Sharon Rocha.

Nancy Grace, **CNN Headline News,**
January 10, 2006
Sharon Rocha: The person I was looking at after December 24, I just — I didn't know that person.
Nancy Grace: Sharon, when you look back on it, do you think you ever knew him?
Sharon Rocha: When I look back on it, no. I mean, I thought I did. But after listening

285

to so many of his lies during the trial, I was just shocked at what I had learned about him.

So said Sharon Rocha of her son-in-law, long after he was convicted of killing her daughter and the couple's unborn child, Connor. Three years after the crime, as Scott continued to sit behind bars, Sharon talked to Nancy Grace on *CNN Headline News.* Nancy's question, as usual, went straight to the heart of the matter. Sharon did not really know Scott.

How many other mother-in-laws are living in fantasyland, with absolutely no clue as to the real person who married their beloved daughter? We can dismiss Scott Peterson as a sociopath and an aberration, and wipe our hands clean of him. But are we doing ourselves justice?

THE DANGER ZONE

It has become accepted wisdom that a leading cause of death among pregnant women is murder — by the father of the child.

A study found that between 1993 and 1998, the leading cause of death among pregnant women in one state, Maryland, was homicide. Of the 247 women who died, murder was the *leading* cause, accounting for about 20 percent of the deaths. And there is nothing particularly sinister about Maryland. This is a frightening snapshot of a national behavior pattern.

A 2002 study of pregnancy-associated deaths in Massachusetts in the nineties indicated homicide was the leading cause of death overall, followed by cancer, acute and chronic respiratory conditions, car crashes, drug overdoses, pregnancy-related heart problems, and suicide. Those statistics include women who died in the year after the birth of the child, which means the pregnancy danger zone extends past child-birth into the postpartum period, where the stress of caring for a newborn can be acute.

Experts say a dangerous time for a pregnant woman is when she learns she is pregnant and informs her intimate partner she is with child, leading to confrontations over how to deal with it. Angela Nannini, a Ph.D. and an assistant professor at the school of nursing at Northeastern University, is an expert in pregnancy and mortality who is urging that more attention be paid to violence against women in early pregnancy, before the woman is even showing: "I would suggest that when autopsies are done that medical examiners . . . look for pregnancy in women, especially if it's murder or suspicious causes." This should be required, she says, even when there's no visible indication the victim was pregnant or that pregnancy was a factor in the crime.

"People wonder, where is this coming from?" one of the doctors who conducted the Maryland study told Court TV. Dr. Diana Cheng added, "The reality is there are a lot more of these cases that either aren't reported in the news or we just don't know about." Dr. Cheng also made an observation that is scary in its insight. She says, "Women tend to think pregnancy is a safety zone, especially if they are already in an abusive relationship. But what we're seeing is that no woman is safe from domestic violence or its most severe consequences."

PICKLES AND ICE CREAM

In reality, when women get pregnant they enter a danger zone. Many women fly completely blind into this turbulent airspace. The average pregnant woman is blissfully unaware of the forces of nature that have been unleashed in the man who impregnated her. In fact, the mother-to-be feels particularly entitled, due to her ongoing transformation, to behave in a self-involved way.

Family therapists say it's not uncommon for women to use their pregnancy as leverage to make demands in their marriage that wouldn't fly under other circumstances. They know, because they're "with child," that their extended family and friends will back them up. During pregnancy, the husband becomes easily overruled, which can irritate him and cause him to resent his wife.

But psychoanalyst Dr. Bethany Marshall says men don't kill over pickles-and-ice-cream errands. A husband who kills is responding to much more primal emotions: "These husbands are usually very primitive. They're developmentally arrested and they think like overgrown babies; they're infantile. So when the wife gets pregnant and there's another baby on the way, they get jealous of the baby. It's a complicated form of sibling rivalry and they want to knock the other sibling out of existence because they don't want to share Mommy with the other baby." That accounts for why they kill the babies, but why do they kill the mothers whose attention they seek? Says Dr. Marshall, "The other thing is they're mad at Mommy for being preoccupied with the new baby that's on the way."

Warning: As your belly swells, your mate's psyche may be swelling with financial fears, anxiety over the loss of his personal freedom, and — in some cases — discomfort over your expanding body and the special demands it brings. Laci, according to the poster used to search for her, was five foot one and as much as 140 pounds when she went missing. According to Catherine Crier's book, Laci was a fit 125 pounds at the time of a prepregnancy medical checkup and 153 pounds when she vanished. A weight gain of twenty-eight pounds was certainly nothing that out of the ordinary for a pregnant woman. But it could have set off the superficial Scott, who became obsessed with the rail-thin Amber Frey.

THE EDDIE HASKELL SYNDROME

Eddie Haskell, the sickly sweet goody-goody on the classic TV show *Leave It to Beaver*, thought he was manipulating the adults around him with his phony good manners. If only Laci's mother could have been as skeptical as Mrs. Cleaver.

Scott called Sharon "Mrs. Rocha" from the day he met her until his wedding day. From that moment on, he called her Mom. Is that being perfect, or perfectly psycho?

What Sharon may have taken for good manners and love was evidence of Scott's utter superficiality and phoniness, his cartoonish way of interacting with the world. But when you live in a superficial world, and most of us do, it's hard to notice when someone is being artificial.

On both sides of this case, the word that keeps popping up more than any other is "perfect." That is a major red flag. People are never perfect. Perfection does not exist in a relationship and is a goal so flawed as to border on madness itself. This sounds obvious. So why do so many people aim for it?

The story of Scott and Laci is a cautionary tale about the dangers of trying to live out a theoretical marital ideal, as defined by the American dream. Laci spent months organizing the perfect wedding. She seemed obsessed with having the perfect home. She thought she had divined the perfect time to have the perfect kids. It's clear Laci was very invested in living up to some kind of ideal. She loved Martha Stewart, made recipes from her books, and studied her show. She threw dinner parties where the emphasis was on perfection, right down to the place settings. In her book, Catherine Crier says, "Laci kept a running list of new objects the couple had agreed to buy for their home." She was reportedly intent on moving up to a better house and getting a more luxurious car. This is not to blame Laci. She was merely playing the part our culture teaches a new wife to play.

Both Laci and Scott were in a materialistic phase. All this is a fancy red flag, not just for the financial strain it can put on a young couple. Acquisitiveness and a focus on possessions can also be desexualizing. Suddenly, you're in the shipping-and-receiving business. That takes the emphasis away from what was originally the primary draw, the intimate romantic relationship. Laci was planning on becoming a stay-at-home mom, a decision Scott may have resented for financial reasons, as so many husbands do. It seems clear Scott had a different agenda, especially when it came to kids.

THE SHARON FACTOR

Laci Peterson's mother partially revealed the "why" of this most infamous of crimes on national television. She explained that Scott had told Laci before she got pregnant that he didn't want to have kids, causing a tearful Laci to call her mother. Here's exactly what Sharon told Larry King about Laci and Scott.

Larry King Live,
January 9, 2006

Larry King: When she got pregnant, this was joy?

Sharon Rocha: For her it was, yes. I was a little concerned because in October of 2000, they had — well, they had moved to Modesto in June of 2000 and in October they bought their home and had a housewarming. And on the day of the housewarming her brother and his wife announced that they were going to have a baby. Well, Laci was really upset about it because she — she and Rose [her brother's wife] — had planned to have their babies at the same time, so she was really disappointed that she wasn't pregnant.

Laci's brother, Brent, in his victim's impact statement in court, also spoke of this shared timetable for conception.

> We always talked when we were growing up about how nice it would be to have kids at the same time, so we could stay close as a family.
>
> — Brent Rocha, penalty phase,
> Peterson trial

Now, the very idea that Laci wanted to time her pregnancy with the pregnancy of her brother's wife was a dangerous one. It emasculated Scott by taking the power of the timing away from him, and it created distance between Laci and Scott by bringing another party into what is the most intimate of all human activities, coming together in sexual union and conceiving. It also may have humiliated Scott by making him feel as if he was his wife's tool, much as men can sometimes humiliate their wives by treating them as baby-making machines or vessels. The idea that she was coordinating the spilling of her husband's seed with the spilling of her brother's seed could be very off-putting to her sexual partner. Finally, the plan was highly, highly desexualizing, robbing the act of its privacy.

Sharon went on to drop another bombshell, maybe not a new news item, but highly significant in light of all that has happened. Sharon spoke of what happened after the fateful housewarming.

Later that evening, after everyone had gone home, she [Laci] called me and she was crying. She was really, really upset. And I told her not to worry, you know, her time was going to come, and that's when she told me that Scott had said that he didn't think he wanted to have children. Of course that concerned me because we'd had conversations before in his presence, or they had had conversations in my presence about having children.

— Sharon Rocha, *Larry King Live*,
January 9, 2006

THIRD PARTIES

It sounds like Sharon was rooting for Laci and Scott to have children, even if Scott had changed his mind and decided he didn't want to. The very fact that she was "concerned" is concerning, not for the reasons that she mentions but because it speaks volumes about her goals for their marriage.

If my thirty years of news gathering has taught me anything about domestic distress, it's this: Whenever a third party has an agenda, any agenda, for someone else's marriage, you are in a danger zone, if not physically, then psychologically. I realize this is going to make a lot of parents of adult children angry. Many if not most of these Americans have an agenda for their children's marriage. They want to be grandparents and don't think there's a damn thing wrong with making it clear that's what they expect! Well then, they should also expect the unexpected. The world has changed since their generation.

DREAMS AND EXPECTATIONS

"There was much more pressure to have kids thirty years ago," says well-known attorney/journalist Harvey Levin, who adds that societal changes have created a higher standard for happiness and left many men longing for an alternative to a traditional family: "You only need to know a few people who didn't opt to have kids and you fixate on them. It's always wanting the freedom that somebody else has." Levin, who has tracked all of the sensational trials of our time, says he sees people aiming for much more personal gratification than their parents did and feeling deep-seated anger when something or someone gets in their way. "Today there are options not to have children, and when you get stuck in a situation where you get roped into it, you really feel tricked, because there are other possibilities now. When somebody takes that freedom away from you, it creates rage," he says.

Sharon unabashedly reiterated her agenda on the stand during her now-famous remarks during the penalty phase of the trial.

I wanted Laci to be a mother. I wanted to

hear her called Mom.
— Sharon Rocha, penalty phase,
Peterson trial

There's nothing wrong with that! But it's
naïve and dangerous for us as a society to
ignore the risks of setting goals for your
daughter's marriage, especially when you're
up against a husband like Scott Peterson,
who on the surface seemed perfect but who
was a cesspool of rage and resentment underneath.

WARNING BELLS

Sharon Rocha was furious when she learned
Scott didn't want to be a dad. In Sharon's
revealing book, *For Laci,* she lays out her reaction like an attorney: "Hearing that made
me mad. Scott knew that Laci wanted a
family. She'd made that clear in numerous
discussions, in my presence, before they
married. I had never heard him say anything
to the contrary. But then, as we've come to
understand, he was a master at telling
people what he thought they wanted to
hear. I've since heard about instances when
he told others, too, that he didn't want
children."

But it seems that Scott *was* telling Laci
what she didn't want to hear, that he no

longer wanted kids. Instead of feeling betrayed and mad over that reversal, what if Sharon had investigated and explored why? What had changed? Remember, this was a couple of years before Scott began his relationship with Amber Frey. That affair began on November 20, 2002, when Laci was already seven months pregnant, just a month before Scott murdered her.

It turns out that way back in 2000, something was up. Scott was clearly sending a signal, consciously or not, that something was going south. Perhaps he was bored with Laci and already wanted out of the marriage. Or perhaps he'd begun sensing that he was entering dangerous territory. Chances are, the secret he'd learned just a few years earlier about his mother giving away two of her children was finally percolating into his consciousness and creating new feelings in him regarding children, feelings of fear and loathing.

Psychiatrists will tell you some adults avoid having children because they themselves were molested as children and fear doing the same thing to an offspring. Some avoid interaction with children entirely. That's perhaps the simplest way not to carry a sick secret into the next generation. But the damaging facts of Scott's backstory had only been revealed to him around 1996. Undoubtedly, by October 2000, he'd finally begun getting a queasy feeling about the whole issue of children, sensing he couldn't trust himself to do the right thing, considering his own troubled family history. Hence his new declaration that he didn't want to become a father.

ROLE CONDITIONING

So why did Scott ever marry Laci, a woman whom he knew wanted children? Again, Scott's secret siblings were still very new to the Peterson family at the time of his 1997 marriage to Laci, so much so that Anne Bird didn't even go to the wedding. Scott had not dealt with that issue at all. It lay dormant. Beyond that, Scott — people-pleasing narcissist that he was — wanted to bask in the attention that, initially at least, came with the role of marriage and parenthood.

Therapists will tell you that many young couples have a fantasy image of marriage and jump in almost as if they were taking roles in a Hollywood movie, without any recognition that this is the role of a lifetime you may not want for a lifetime.

Our consumer culture feeds all this. Commercials sell the idea that you are not complete until you marry, have children, and buy all the products that come with parenthood. Many couples envision marriage as a long musical montage of wedding, baby showers, anniversaries, and other glamorous events in which they are the stars. Just like a TV show.

Given all that societal pressure, journalist Harvey Levin likens Scott's wavering on having children to the way women have always agonized over abortion. It's a struggle, back and forth: "Men are now going through the same tug of war over having children as women have always experienced over abortion."

These are questions that needed to be addressed early on. When your partner pulls a 180 on an issue that's crucial to your relationship, you need to ask why. If you can't get a satisfactory answer, chances are that you don't know the whole story. Your lover's feelings for you may have changed. Your partner's life goals may have changed. That person is hiding something from you. Scott had reportedly told others that he was hoping for infertility — a very hostile comment, given Laci's passionate desire to be a mom.

We can only speculate what might have happened if Laci had perceived Scott's new attitude for what it was, namely a loud and clear warning bell that something was dangerously amiss with their relationship. Had that comment triggered a serious reevaluation of what was happening in the marriage, through couples therapy for example, it's theoretically possible the marriage might have continued without children, or dissolved before conception could occur. Either way, Laci might still be alive.

Sharon Rocha loved her daughter passionately. This is *not* to blame her for feeling angry, but to simply try to understand the risks of some of the very *common* family dynamics at work in this case. Sharon and Laci were very typical in their dismayed response to Scott's decision that he didn't want kids after all. What Laci did next is also standard operating procedure. Let's hear Sharon tell it.

It was about a month or so later, it was around Thanksgiving time. She [Laci] and I were in the kitchen preparing dinner when she told me she's going to stop taking birth control pills in December. It had only been a month ago that Scott didn't want to have children. So we had a conversation about that, and I said, "Are you sure? Are both of you absolutely sure, because you can't put the baby back once

301

he's here?" . . . It was nothing at the time. And she said, yes, that they had talked about it and they were ready, that Scott was ready also.

— Sharon Rocha, Larry King Live,
January 9, 2006

At this point, Sharon has said the right words: "Are you absolutely sure?" But the signals she's been sending all along have been the opposite of that. She's been "concerned" that Scott didn't want children. Clearly, Sharon wanted grandchildren. While she may have been giving lip service to the cautious approach, it seems clear she was hoping for Laci to have a child or two.

BOUNDARY ISSUES

In different families, issues may manifest themselves in different ways. In some families, financial help is tied to a young couple having a child, which allows the grandmother to become even more involved in the couple's lives, making their marriage almost an extension of hers. In a psychological sense, the couple end up living in the matriarch's world. She's in bed with them. This may be fine with the wife, who may welcome her mother's practical help and attention, but for the husband it can chafe and irritate and fester as time goes on. He married a woman, not a group, and he usually wants autonomy and to be the master of his own domain.

Sometimes it's the father-in-law who's got boundary blindness. In the highly publicized breakup of superstars Jessica Simpson and Nick Lachey, *People* magazine spoke of "the Joe factor," referring to Jessica's father/ manager, whom the magazine says attended "nearly every shoot, concert, and vacation the couple went on," staying "close to Jessica. Perhaps too close." *People* quotes a family friend as saying, "No matter how nice your in-laws are, it must have been really hard to have them a constant presence." *People* quoted another source as saying Nick was irritated by Joe's incessant involvement: "He controls Jessica's life and therefore has controlled Nick's life." Whenever parents control or are overly involved in the life of their adult child, that is going to cause resentment in the adult child's sexual partner, who correctly perceives himself or herself as the one who should be the most significant other.

These are all common boundary issues. Extended-family boundary issues and their impact on marriage are very thorny subjects that desperately need to be discussed more openly in our society.

What happened next in Laci and Scott's relationship was a very pivotal moment. On the Larry King show, Sharon spoke about Scott's midlife crisis.

Larry King Live,
January 9, 2006

Larry King: Laci gets pregnant. They check it out. It's going to be a boy. They pre-named it Connor. He's building a nursery in the house. Does he [Scott] appear very happy?

Sharon Rocha: He didn't seem to be unhappy, except for on June 9 when she discovered that she was pregnant. They were at our house and that's when Scott was sitting at one end of the table and Laci and I were standing up, and Laci had mentioned that Scott was having a midlife crisis, and I asked why?

I looked at Scott and he was, you know, obviously not very happy at the moment. And Laci said, "Oh, he's having that crisis because he's turning thirty and becoming a father all in the same year." Well, I looked over at him and I said, jokingly, I said, "Oh, get over it. Thirty is not midlife and becoming a father is supposed to be a great time."

For an unstable guy such as Scott, this could have felt like the mother lode from the mother-in-law! *Get over it. Snap out of it. Get with the program, buddy.* These are the messages society sends to a newly married man who goes "off script." Becoming a father is supposed to be a great time — according to whom? While Laci insisted Scott had ultimately wanted the child and that she was justified in going off her birth control pills and getting pregnant, it can also be argued that this decision may have cost her her life. Other men in the same situation might grudgingly accept being overruled and retaliate with stale jokes about the old ball and chain when they're with their male friends on the golf course. But given Scott's family history, the issue of children was extraordinarily loaded for him, ultimately becoming the trigger for murder.

And yet Laci — from what we know of her — seemed blissfully unaware of the dangerous terrain she was in. On the witness stand during the trial, Laci's brother, Brent, spoke of never hearing his sister more excited than the day she called to say she was pregnant. He explained that Laci had been having trouble getting pregnant. Says her brother, "She had everything ready; she was so prepared, the nursery was perfect."

Perfect — except for a husband who didn't want to have a child.

After Laci went missing, Sharon spoke to investigators about the pregnancy issue, reportedly saying, "I assume if he didn't want to have a child, he wouldn't have allowed it to happen." The statement needs to be read twice to get the full yet unintended impact of Sharon's comment. *He wouldn't have allowed it to happen.*

Laci is not to blame for desperately wanting to get pregnant despite her husband's second thoughts. What I am suggesting is that we as a society need to realize that for every reluctant father who crosses the line into murder, there are hundreds of thousands of other lukewarm dads who simply become resentful and emotionally unavailable, sending their children the signal that they are a burden and creating yet another generation of psychologically damaged human beings. Can we stop the cycle? Can we make sure that any children born into this world are not just tolerated but wanted by both Dad and Mom? And for those men who decide not to have children or who change their minds, let's accept that it's their right to do so and not tell them to snap out of it.

The fact is, all of society's messages led

Laci to her decision. Scott may have even verbalized that he was ready, because of the pressures on him to lean that way. Indeed, Laci told her mother that Scott had finally said he was ready. This is what every TV commercial and authority figure is telling us to do. But clearly Scott did not want a child and deeply resented that his needs and desires were being overruled. That is a recipe for rage, especially because of the secret ingredients Scott brought to the table. And rage is the appetizer for violence. On both sides, there were far too many cooks in this kitchen.

MOMMY'S LITTLE GIRL

Other family pressures were being brought to bear on the situation, beyond the disagreement over whether or not to have kids. Every chapter in Sharon's book shows what a close relationship she had with her adult daughter — so close that Scott might have felt threatened and somewhat irrelevant because of it. This intense mother/daughter relationship could have also kept Laci somewhat childlike emotionally. It seems that Laci relied a lot on her mother's counsel, repeatedly reaching out to Sharon at key moments in her life through frequent phone calls. Example: The night before her wedding, Laci sobbed as she told her mother she was worried about losing her ethnic name when she became Laci Peterson. Her mother talked her through her jitters and calmed her down. These kinds of interactions come up frequently in Sharon's narrative.

Because of her dependence on her mother, Laci may never have developed the adult skills that might have allowed her to see through Scott and observe what was really happening with him and in her marriage. After all, shortly after they were married, Laci was in bed with Scott in the home they shared with roommates when a woman reportedly stormed in on them, a woman who was clearly Scott's lover. Laci ultimately chose to forgive this evidence of infidelity, ignoring one of the most obvious warning signs in any marriage. *Men who cheat will cheat again. People don't change unless (a) they want to, and (b) they then work very hard at changing.* For Scott to not *repeat the cheat,* he would have had to make a complete life change, hitting bottom and then seeking help through therapy or a program such as Sex Addicts Anonymous. Scott apparently did neither. And Laci lived in either denial or ignorance or both, of the real Scott.

Laci also ignored a minor alarm bell when she and Scott were first dating. Scott was, according to Sharon, fired from his job at a golf course because some money was missing. Laci totally bought Scott's story that it was all a big misunderstanding, although Sharon remembers suspecting Scott was covering up the truth or hiding something. It's clear that Laci was determined to see Scott from the very start as, "the man I'm going to marry." Or, as so many other young women before her have put it about handsome, charming guys like Scott, *He's the full package — a catch.* People are not fish. And they don't come wrapped in packages. They are complex, multidimensional, contradictory — and they always come with secrets.

TRIANGULATION AND ENMESHMENT

Enmeshed families are those that have lost a sense of where one couple and their intimate relationship ends and another couple's life begins. Living near the in-laws is an invitation to enmeshment, and that seems to be precisely what occurred here. Scott and Laci were living in San Luis Obispo, but, says Catherine Crier, "After her grandmother died in 1999, Laci wanted to move closer to her parents. The couple lived with Sharon and Ron for about two weeks before moving into temporary quarters. . . . In October 2000, with a $30,000 gift from Scott's parents, they purchased the house on Covena Avenue."

In Sharon's book, she speaks about dealing with the alarm company that handled the security system at Laci and Scott's house, saying, "My name had always been listed as the person to contact if Laci and Scott were unavailable, which had happened." Sharon also talks about coming over to feed the pets when Scott and Laci went out of town. This may have been helpful on a practical level, but at what cost to the autonomy of the marriage?

Sharon's book reveals many telltale signs of enmeshment. She says, "Laci was my daughter, my best friend." Mother/daughter/ best friends relationships can pose dilemmas, especially for the man involved with the daughter.

Says Dr. Bethany Marshall, "Men like Scott don't want to share. They want their wives all to themselves, and they feel they have to be the only one in the wife's life in order to be the most important one. So having an involved mother-in-law like Sharon could have felt intolerable."

Sharon cannot be blamed for loving her

daughter. The world sympathizes with her loss. But we can help other mothers avoid similar tragedies by learning from this case. Sharon Rocha is not the only mother to become deeply involved in her adult daughter's personal life. It's happening everywhere. Right now, phone lines are buzzing with weeping daughters pouring out their hearts to sympathetic moms who only want to help and make things better for the children they love. But at what risk?

"Sharing the love with the mother-in-law and the impending baby could have been a cataclysmic experience for such a disturbed personality," says Dr. Marshall. Or at least another factor in this case.

Another word psychologists use is *triangulation,* which is when someone in a partnership gets entangled with a third party and loses his sense of a two-person partnership, thereby feeling triangulated by the third party. In game theory, three is considered an unstable combination that can result in friction. It's unstable because there is: (1) the least powerful, (2) the second most powerful, and (3) the most powerful. What invariably happens is the least powerful aligns with the second most powerful and together they become the most powerful, effectively toppling the original most powerful, who is then knocked down to least powerful. Because this process can occur over and over again, it's considered a far more unstable combination than say, four, which would be two couples.

So Sharon, by doing favors for her devoted daughter and her secretive son-in-law and generously offering herself as the go-to person in their marriage, may have unintentionally triangulated herself with them, causing Scott to feel resentment and rage over his less powerful role as a result. The cycle is often progressive, with the codependent mother sensing there's a problem in the daughter's marriage, causing the mother to intervene more to compensate, in turn causing the son-in-law to feel even more rage and resentment, and so on.

The stress of these unstable three-way dynamics is compounded by other societal factors. The ever-increasing number of family obligations, along with the increasing work schedules of Americans, can cause a married person to feel trapped in an endless cycle of family functions: Mother's Day, Father's Day, Christmas, Hanukah, Thanksgiving, July 4, the Super Bowl, the Academy Awards, birthdays, anniversaries, and all the other events that revolve around the extended family. These are often the very times that we are given time off from work. When being with family feels like a second job, it can create a pressure cooker of stress for the person trapped in it. Also, the Petersons were living near her family, not his, so he wasn't getting the same level of involvement from his parents. This emphasis on one family over the other may have felt unfair.

It's clear Laci regularly organized many family-oriented parties and events, and in fact, these seemed to have been some of Laci's happiest moments. For a husband in this situation to tell a mother-in-law to step off and leave them alone would seem horribly rude and hurtful to the mother-in-law and the wife.

This is why I say family values kill. "Family values" is a very flawed concept that is cynical at its core because it's ego based and self-centered. It's about me and mine. What we should talk about is not family values but values, period — what's good for this world, not just what's good for the few people who share our DNA. Time and time again, we will see how a well-intentioned but misguided sense of family values plays a role in these gruesome and sensational cases.

In light of all this, Scott's suspicious behavior at the start of Laci's disappearance is very significant.

Larry King Live,
January 9, 2006

Larry King: When Laci went missing, did you fear the worst?

Sharon: I did.

King: Because?

Sharon: Hindsight, always, you know, is much easier, but as I look back at it I realize when he had called me and asked if Laci was at my house . . . I remember, when he said "missing" I remember thinking to myself "missing?" What do you mean, "missing"? You know that's not a word you use.

It's no coincidence that Scott chose to make Sharon his first call when he claimed he couldn't find Laci after returning from his now-infamous fishing trip on San Francisco Bay. Trial consultant Molly Murphy says she often sees the actions of killers as power grabs. Deep in his subconscious, Scott was taking the power back. He was saying to Sharon, Take that! I am back in control. You thought you were running this place; well, guess what, I'm in charge now.

"The dynamics often revolve around anger and control. Behind-the-scenes elements can include overly controlling third parties, like parents," Murphy says. Ironically, "anger-based triggers all come from fear." Murphy adds that a husband on the brink of murder often "feels someone's put the clamps on his freedoms and options." Why does he kill? "Because he can."

Testifying in the penalty phase of her former son-in-law's trial, Sharon Rocha turned to Scott and shouted, "Divorce is always an option, not murder!" While we can understand her rage and sense of loss and frustration, experts will tell you that in the mind of the killer husband, divorce does not seem to be a way out. When a child is on the way, divorce can feel like a life sentence, because of the specter of alimony and child support. For those men, like Scott, the murder of a pregnant woman becomes a way out of future responsibilities. "They're getting rid of two things they don't want, the wife and the child, and then hiding it," says Murphy, who sees infantile behavior in these choices. "That's what little kids do: They do something bad and then they hide the evidence."

O.J. Redux

Perhaps most perplexing is the question of why Scott Peterson thought he could get away with murder. This slaughter was clearly premeditated, as evidenced by Scott's purchase of a boat, his checking of the currents in the bay, and a myriad of other signs that point to a plotting killer. Harvey Levin is sure he has figured out that secret.

"Scott Peterson was a dreamer who wanted to be a Casanova and a pro golfer. Suddenly, he finds himself in a house in Modesto with a big pregnant wife." That's Harvey Levin's analysis of Scott's motive. As a TV journalist, Harvey Levin covered the O. J. Simpson murder from the moment it broke and sees numerous parallels between these crimes, so much so that he's convinced Scott Peterson patterned his crime after the murder of Nicole Brown Simpson. Levin says Scott assumed that if O.J. could get acquitted, so could he: "Something told Scott Peterson he could get away with murdering his wife. He did not murder thinking he would get caught. That's why he created an alibi. O. J. Simpson hit golf balls at night. Scott Peterson went fishing."

Scott Peterson was an aspiring athlete in

his school years, at one point possibly dreaming of becoming a professional golfer. Simpson was a Heisman Trophy winner who loved to golf. Scott would have been in his early twenties at the time of the highly publicized Simpson case. The trip that ended with Simpson's infamous slow-speed chase back to his L.A. home began with Simpson getting into the Ford Bronco and heading south toward Mexico with wads of cash and a fake beard. When things got dicey for Scott, he also took off, heading toward Mexico with at least ten thousand dollars in cash after dying his hair blond and growing a mustache and a beard. "Look at everything that happened, from the disguise to the money to driving to get away to the stupid alibi to the sneak attack against the wife to the fact that they were both golfers. You can say all of these are coincidences, but there are a lot of coincidences," Levin observes. Levin also notes that both hired high-profile Los Angeles defense attorneys. With O. J. Simpson free as a bird, Scott — a star in his own mind — figured he could pull off the same stunt. But says Levin, "What Scott didn't understand is reasonable doubt was never an issue. The O.J. case became laced in race." With Scott Peterson, race was not in the equation.

Scott's ridiculous mimicry of Simpson's transparent strategy shows his total lack of understanding about how the world really works. This childish thinking is the reason why Scott was able to slip so easily into the world of make-believe. After he murdered Laci, his descent into the other world of his own invention accelerated. The best example is his now-infamous phone call to lover Amber Frey about a week after the murder, on New Year's Eve. He claimed he was in Paris near the Eiffel Tower; actually, he was in California at a candlelight vigil for Laci! On another call, with his own dog barking behind him, Scott again spewed lies about being abroad. This was the sick finale to a slow downward slide into fantasy.

FEELING EQUALS TRUTH

When someone's secret life feels more authentic than his outer life, watch out. When someone feels more allegiance to his secret life than his "normal" life, that person is more easily able to cross the line and get rid of the world that feels less real to him. In the killer's mind, he is erasing the false world and liberating the real existence he so cherishes, the one he wishes he could show

318

off to the world. "Intellect is a low defense when up against feelings like sexual passion. In the end, feelings often win, because feeling equals emotional truth," says psychotherapist and cultural mythologist Dr. Martha Velez. When the secret world feels real and the real world feels false, then you're living in an upside-down world. But that's what happened to Scott as he snaked toward murder. One might wonder if Laci's life was in danger partially because she was living it on the surface and, therefore, had no idea what was going on under the surface.

With Laci's pregnancy, the marriage entered its predictable desexualized phase, going from an intimate relationship into an institution filled with goals and responsibilities, like creating a family, moving up, and keeping up with the Joneses. But sociopath Scott was jonesing for ego-boosting sex to shore up his shell of an identity.

Scott's secret affair with Amber allowed him to return to that deeply intimate sexual phase. With Amber, Scott was back in the only role he'd ever really mastered, that of the charmer and the seducer. Considering all of the women over the years he'd romanced with flowers, it's clear that Scott felt he shined in this early phase of any relationship. The reaction he got from women in the dating phase gave his self-esteem a boost, and made him feel in control, powerful, and successful, all things that he was not in the real world.

In her book, *Witness,* Amber Frey said it best herself: "After we made love and long after he had fallen asleep, I found myself clinging to him. I didn't know what I'd done to deserve this wonderful man. He was smart, charming, sexy." And this, she says, was on December 3, about a dozen days after Scott met Amber and less than a month before he would kill his wife. Three days later, on December 6, Amber's best friend angrily confronted Scott. She had learned that Scott was married and was in a position to tell Amber. Scott blurted out that he had recently lost his wife.

Trying to cover his tracks, he repeated the same lie to Amber a couple of days later. Sobbing convulsively, Scott gave Amber the impression that his wife had passed away. That's it! Now he can't turn back, not if he wants to continue his affair. Amber would later tell police tears were "pouring down out of his eyes."

What he meant to pass for grief were really tears of long-suppressed rage: rage over his mother's betrayal, rage over the possibility he might lose the illicit relationship that was giving him the only thing that passed for a real feeling in his dead inner world. And there was his rising rage as he realized he'd backed himself into a dead end.

In Scott's completely upside-down world, he figured he had to turn the lie into a truth.

Two weeks later, Laci was dead.

JUST A THEORY

So how does the perfect catch become a killer? Here's my theory, based on what I know about the case.

Give him a phony, superficial upbringing, laced with dark secrets. Suddenly dump those secrets on him as an adult. Give him an assertive wife. Add an involved mother-in-law. Tell him he's about to become a father against his wishes. Give him the ability to travel for work so he can have an affair; soon he's fantasizing about his wife dying of some mysterious ailment, or maybe an accident. Then confront him with the truth and threaten to reveal it.

For men like Scott whose authentic selves were suffocated in childhood, seduction and the first heat of early romance are the only times they can get a spark that gives them a fleeting taste of what it feels like to be human. And they will do anything to keep that spark alive. They will even kill.

In a final, stunning twist, Scott Peterson has become pen pals with one of the jurors who convicted him. The beautiful thirty-six-year-old, who was nicknamed Strawberry Shortcake by reporters because of her bright red hair, told *People* magazine in 2006 that she and Scott have exchanged about two dozen letters. She said Scott has been courteous and very complimentary. Perhaps it's not such a stunning twist after all. He's still the same old charmer he always was.

LEFT: *Former schoolteacher Debra Lafave, whose sexual liaisons with a fourteen-year-old boy made tabloid headlines, avoided prison through a plea agreement.* (AP IMAGES)

ABOVE: *Sandra "Beth" Geisel was a forty-two-year-old teacher charged with raping a sixteen-year-old student.* (POLICE MUGSHOT)

ABOVE: *Teacher Amber Jennings was accused of sending graphic images to a sixteen-year-old former student with whom she was reportedly having a sexual relationship.* (AP IMAGES)

LEFT: *Susan Polk (pictured here with her family) was accused of the murder of her husband (left), a prominent San Francisco area psychologist.* (COURTESY SUSAN POLK AND VALERIE HARRIS)

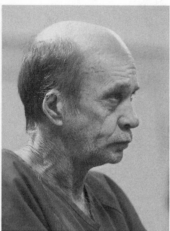

RIGHT: *Police say John Couey confessed to the abduction, sexual assault, and murder of nine-year-old Jessica Lunsford, whom he claimed to have buried alive.* (AP IMAGES)

LEFT: *Mark Lunsford holds a photo of his murdered daughter, Jessica, in an effort to get tougher prison sentences for sex offenders who target children.* (AP IMAGES)

ABOVE: *Photographer Teresa Halbach (second from right) met with Steven Avery for an automotive magazine shoot. Police say they later found her burned remains nearby.* (COURTESY TIM HALBACH)

ABOVE: *Steven Avery, right, was accused of the horrific murder of Teresa Halbach.* (AP IMAGES)

LEFT: *Graduate student Imette St. Guillen was brutally murdered.*
(COURTESY MAUREEN ST. GUILLEN)

RIGHT: *Bar bouncer Darryl Littlejohn (aka Jonathan Blaze) was charged with the murder of Imette St. Guillen.*
(POLICE MUGSHOT)

LEFT: *Lana Clarkson was found dead at music producer Phil Spector's mansion with a gunshot to the mouth.*
(COURTESY GROMMET COLLECTIBLES/FIRE-BLOOD ARMS)

RIGHT: *Music legend Phil Spector in a Los Angeles court, accused in the 2003 shooting death of actress Lana Clarkson.*
(AP IMAGES)

LEFT: *The last time Andrea Brucia saw her granddaughter Carlie was during a Christmas visit in 2003.*
(COURTESY ANDREA BRUCIA)

RIGHT: *In 2005, Joseph Smith (right) went on trial for the gruesome abduction, sexual assault, and murder of eleven-year-old Carlie Brucia in Sarasota, Florida.*
(AP IMAGES)

LEFT: *Soon after Joseph Smith was sentenced to death for Carlie Brucia's murder, the slain girl's mother, Susan Schorpen, in an unconnected case, pleaded no contest to drug- and prostitution-related charges.* (POLICE MUGSHOT)

RIGHT: *Kara Borden (left) with her sister, Katelyn (right), at the graveside service for their slaughtered parents in November 2005.*
(AP IMAGES)

LEFT: *Eighteen-year-old David Ludwig confessed to killing the parents of his fourteen-year-old girlfriend, Kara Borden, after her dad ordered him to stop seeing her.*
(AP IMAGES)

LEFT: *British national Neil Entwistle enters the courtroom in 2006. Accused in the shooting deaths of his American wife, Rachel, and their baby daughter, prosecutors suspect he borrowed his father-in-law's gun.* (AP IMAGES)

RIGHT: *Scott Dyleski was sixteen when he was arrested for the ghoulish first-degree murder of Pamela Vitale, the wife of prominent attorney Daniel Horowitz.* (AP IMAGES)

ABOVE: *Noted defense attorney Daniel Horowitz and his wife, Pamela Vitale, are seen here in January 2005, months before Vitale was bludgeoned to death by a neighborhood teenager.* (AP IMAGES)

LEFT: *Cody Posey, sixteen, is seen in court at the start of his murder trial in January 2006. Posey was charged with murdering his father, stepmother, and stepsister and burying their bodies on a New Mexico ranch owned by newsman Sam Donaldson.*
(AP IMAGES)

RIGHT: *Natalee Holloway (center) vanished in May 2005, while on a graduation trip to Aruba with more than a hundred classmates.*
(COURTESY BETH HOLLOWAY TWITTY)

LEFT: *On his honeymoon cruise through the Mediterranean in July 2005, George Smith mysteriously vanished after a night of celebrating with his bride and a group of new friends.* (COURTESY BREE SMITH)

LEFT: *According to her brother, Kathie Durst (left) was always smiling despite a very troubled marriage to real-estate heir Robert Durst (right). Kathie disappeared under mysterious circumstances more than twenty years ago.*
(COURTESY JIM MCCORMACK)

RIGHT: *Multimillionaire defendant Robert Durst demonstrated what he claimed was a dramatic encounter over a gun while testifying at his murder trial in October 2003, in Texas.*
(AP IMAGES)

ABOVE: *The Yates family in early 2001. Later that year, Andrea Yates drowned her five children. Rusty Yates's aunt, Fairy Caroland (left), says Rusty struggled to care for his troubled wife.* (COURTESY FAIRY CAROLAND)

8
RAWHIDE

If there was ever an argument for creating a culture of honesty, it's the Cody Posey case. The difference between the good Christian façade the Posey family presented to the world and the loathsome secret life this clan actually lived just might be the difference between heaven and hell.

With his cowboy hat and his winning smile, thirty-four-year-old Paul Posey seemed like the ideal family man. A church-going ranch manager in southern New Mexico, on the surface he was the American dream personified. His brother, Verlin, described Paul this way on television during a Court TV interview: "He was hardworking. He believed in God and country." ABC News personality Sam Donaldson, who owned the sprawling New Mexico ranch Paul Posey managed, described the Poseys as "the all-American ranch family."

But who was Paul Posey behind closed

doors? Was he the man who surfed the Internet for incest porn, using such keywords as "father daughter incest"? Was he the man who beat his toddler son, Cody, so badly the child's diapers overflowed with urine and feces? Was he the man who later forced young Cody to kill his own dog? If you believe some three dozen defense witnesses who testified, Paul Posey was not a man who protected and loved his family. He was a cruel, sadistic brute.

July 5, 2004, was just another day on the ranch. Except that Cody, who was by then fourteen years old, just couldn't take it anymore. Cody admitted that, unable to endure any more of his family's sick secrets, unable to withstand any more abuse, he picked up a gun and, at close range, put a bullet through his father's head. Cody also picked off his stepmother, Tryone, and her thirteen-year-old daughter, Marilea. He then used a backhoe to drag all three bodies to a manure pile, where he buried them. Consider the symbolism of the manure pile in light of testimony that Cody was called a "shithead" by his parents, one of many insults they directed at him, according to witnesses.

Cody confessed to investigators. He admitted that he shot his stepmom first, firing twice at Tryone's head as she sat reading a book on the couch. Hearing the shots, his father raced in from outside. Cody, standing near the refrigerator, fired again, this time at his dad. Paul Posey dropped to the floor, leaving Cody's stepsister exposed as she came in. Cody shot her too. Marilea's body twitched and convulsed. Cody shot her again. She stopped moving.

Cody Posey's Confession

Q: All right, Cody. You need to tell me what happened.

A: I got tired of him hitting me. Yelling and screaming at me all the time. He hit me. I couldn't take it anymore.

Q: So what did you do, Cody?

A: I tried getting rid of him.

Q: How?

A: Get him off this planet 'cuz I'd be better here without him.

Q: So what did you do, Cody?

A: I shot him.

Q: With what?

A: .38 special.

Q: Where's the gun, where did you shoot him?

A: In the head.

Q: Where was he standing?

A: He was walking through the door . . . kitchen door.

Q: Where did you get the gun, Cody?

A: Marilea had it in her saddle bag for shooting snakes. . . . Shot her too so she wouldn't go tell or nothing.

Not exactly a Norman Rockwell portrait.

Soon a jury was being asked to decide a perplexing question: Was it cold-blooded, premeditated murder by an unruly teen who disliked his dad's strict discipline? That's what the prosecutor argued. Or did Cody snap after years of physical and psychological abuse? And how did sex play into it?

See No Evil

This was a case in which the secrets really spilled out in court. Sordid themes. Nasty details. The prosecutor claimed these secrets were actually the fantasies of a budding psychopath. But the defense argued they were all too real. With TV cameras in the courtroom, the case was covered extensively on Court TV. The testimony stunned and outraged the nation. Witness after witness testified to seeing Cody physically, mentally, emotionally, and verbally tormented by his father and stepmother. The accounts were so consistently shocking that Court TV polls showed overwhelming support for the teenage killer. Ranch hands testified to seeing Cody's dad whip, punch, stone, and in other ways torture and humiliate the boy, who was said to carry the workload of a grown man despite his young age. Teachers testified to their discomfort as the boy's parents insisted on outlandishly harsh punishments for Cody when he committed minor infractions. Others said they saw Cody cower and look down when his parents were around.

Of course, it makes you wonder why nobody took drastic action to get the boy out of harm's way. A thick social-history report by the defense team's mitigation specialist documents Cody's extraordinarily dysfunctional upbringing. When Cody was about seven, before Tryone was even in the picture, he was taken to the emergency room. The boy said the injuries on his backside came from a severe beating by his father, first with a wooden paddle and then, when that broke, with a two-by-four.

The defense report says the sheriff's department was notified, but criminal charges were never filed and the complaint was dismissed by a child protection agency as an isolated incident. This would seem to be a clear-cut failure of the government's responsibility to protect a helpless and innocent little boy. The defense says a couple of other complaints to the child protection agency by Cody's biological mother's side of the family went nowhere. The abuse just escalated after that.

Those who say they saw signs of Cody's mistreatment over the years had all sorts of excuses for why they didn't stop it. Some worked for Cody's dad and feared for their jobs; others said Cody offered innocent explanations for why he sometimes had bruises and even a black eye. Paul Posey allegedly told those few who dared to confront him to shut up and mind their own business, pointing out that Cody was *his* son, as if the boy was his property. This is how a community keeps it secrets: deferring to intimidating dads, ignoring unpleasant truths, accepting unbelievable explanations, going into denial. See no evil, hear no evil — until you're subpoenaed to testify at trial. But by then, it's too late.

By the time of his trial, Cody was sixteen and looking more like a man than a boy. He took the stand in his own defense and told story after story of abuse. The boy alleged his father punched him, choked him, almost drowned him, slapped him, dragged him with a rope, insulted him, and cruelly punished him through isolation, sometimes even depriving him of food and water. He claimed his father forced him to shoot his beloved dog after it injured its leg, even though Cody offered to use allowance money he'd saved to get the animal to a vet. He said his dad and stepmom called him degrading names, like "stupid" and "dumb-ass," verbal abuse that was confirmed by other witnesses. One ranch hand said Paul consistently talked down to Cody, telling him he was "bad, worthless, dumb, and stupid." According to the defense, Paul and Tryone also called Cody a "faggot" and a "pussy."

CARNAL KNOWLEDGE

But Cody had an even more shocking accusation to make against the father and stepmother he killed. He said something really awful happened the night before the carnage. He testified he was called into his parents' bedroom. His father then ordered him to have sex with his stepmother, who was already in bed.

The State of New Mexico vs. Cody Posey, Defendant's Testimony
Cody Posey: As I stood in front of the bed, Tryone pulled down the covers and was lying there completely naked. . . .

When Cody first dropped this bombshell during his confession, investigators did a double take.

Cody Posey's Confession
Q: They wanted you to have sex with your stepmom?

A: Yeah. She was like, well, we're not related, we're not blood, come do it. And I didn't want to. I thought it was wrong.

Q: Okay.

In the confession, Cody went on to say that when he refused to have sex with Tryone, they tortured him. Cody says as Tryone pulled him down to her breast, his father branded him on his arm.

A: He had like a welding rod and a torch there. That's how I got these burns.

Q: That's where you got those burns?

A: He was like do it, do it. . . .

Q: Where'd he get the torch from?

A: He had this little bitty torch that he used to carry in, carries around to melt pipe and stuff.

Cody was finally spilling his guts, making up for all the times he kept quiet.

Prosecutor Sandra Grisham insisted this was all a big fabrication on Cody's part to justify his killing spree. But Dr. Susan Cave, a clinical and forensic psychologist who interviewed Cody, told me on the phone that the boy has the marks to prove it. "He says he bit her" and they seared his skin in return. "When he got arrested for the homicides, they saw the burns. Those are verified," says Cave.

The morning after this bizarre bedroom scene, Cody says his father slapped him in the face with the back of his hand during an argument over chores.

Defendant's Testimony
Cody Posey: I was getting overwhelmed by what happened to me. . . . I remember going into the barn, putting away the tools, and just thinking to myself about my emotions and why I had to be the one who was hit and why I had to be the one who had the situation the night before.

I more or less lost my mind. . . . I didn't know what I was thinking. I didn't know what I was doing. I was overwhelmed and I lost control of my emotions.

The long and twisting road to triple murder goes way, way, way back. It started long before Cody was born and slowly morphed into a dysfunctionality so profound that the local sheriff in New Mexico said, "In my thirty-six years of law enforcement, it's the saddest case I've ever worked."

A CHIP OFF THE OLD BLOCK

Almost a decade before Cody killed his family, he lost his grandparents on his father's side. It was reportedly a murder/suicide. Cody's grandmother Linda shot and killed her husband, Jay, and then turned the gun on herself. They left behind two sons, Paul

332

and Cody's uncle, Verlin. Even though money troubles were mentioned as the motivating factor in a suicide note, Cody's defense attorney, Gary Mitchell, believes the murder/suicide was primarily in retaliation for abuse: "Jay Posey had major confrontations of a physical nature with his wife, Linda. She couldn't stand the abuse anymore," Mitchell told me. According to the defense theory, Jay's abuse and Linda's murderous retaliation bear a striking resemblance to what happened between Paul and Cody. Abuse, followed by retaliation and murder. Abuse, retaliation, murder. This is how violence is handed down, generation to generation.

The jury would never hear any of this. The judge said no. He only allowed a dry social-studies report that mentioned intergenerational abuse at sentencing. Still, Pandora's box had swung open. The media picked up on it. As so often happens in trials, the secrets swirled through the air outside court, along with an emotional debate over the Posey family's history and whether it was really as violent as some insisted.

Jim Forrester, a silver-haired retiree, claimed he saw evidence of abuse in three generations of Poseys. During the sentencing phase, Forrester offered gut-wrenching testimony about the last generation. He told the court he visited the home of Cody's birth mother, Carla, to repair a heater. Cody was just a toddler at the time and his parents were already parting ways. Paul was there and warned his young son to stop running around near the heater. When the boy kept playing, Forrester says, Paul began beating the child.

The State of New Mexico vs. Cody Posey, Defense Witness

Jim Forrester: He pulled off his belt and then hit him fifty or seventy-five times. He was hitting him on his face, head, back . . . he had giant welts all over him. . . . Urine and feces was running out of his diaper down to the floor.

Forrester said he tried to stop the beating but it took him and two others to finally hold Paul back. Over the phone, Forrester recounted the incident again, painting an equally disturbing picture, saying Paul "just grabbed the buckle and went to work on this kid." And by the time it was over, Cody "couldn't even scream anymore. All he could do was gasp."

Forrester told me he also knew Cody's grandparents, Jay and Linda, and says he is convinced Linda killed Jay and then took her own life because she was "afraid of another ass-whipping." Forrester says a few weeks before the murder/suicide, he spotted Linda sitting in a vehicle waiting for Jay and approached her, only to be shocked by the condition of her face.

"Oh, man, I have never seen anything like this. It was like a horse had kicked her with both feet in the side of the head. It was just blue and black, and her eye was like hanging, almost ready to pop out. I mean this was bad. And I said, 'Linda, what happened to you?' And she said, 'Oh, God, don't let Jay see you talking to me, get gone, please,' so I took off."

Forrester told me he ran into Linda again a couple of days later, when she was again waiting in the car. At that point, he says, she told him that Jay had become enraged when he walked into the kitchen and saw her laughing with a man who'd been waiting to see him. "And as he walked by her, he blind-sided her, and she said she doesn't know what he hit her with, she knew it wasn't his fist. . . . She woke up in the middle of the night still on the kitchen floor and he was watching TV." Then, Forrester said, Linda added a warning, "and I can't tell you the exact words. But it was something like 'I will never take another one like this. He will never beat me again.' "

Forrester also claimed he saw Jay beat Cody's father when Paul was in his early teens. "I saw him beat the kid the first time with a rope, and he hit him so hard down across the top of the head. Doubled up rope, like a roping rope . . . He whipped him down across the head, I don't know seven, eight times. . . . It was just whack, whack, whack, whack, whack, whack, whack. And he ripped his ear loose at the top and we thought he was going to have stitches, but ended up, they just kind of put stuff back together and gauzed him up. They were cowboys, you know, they're tough."

A few short years later, it was Cody's turn. Paul continued the cycle of what Verlin has described as stern parenting and others have called child abuse. Cody is the spitting image of Paul. When he looked at his son, Paul saw his own mirror image, and he was going to teach him a lesson, the same lesson he had learned.

Perhaps the most significant thing Forrester told me was that he could trace the abuse back yet another generation, to Jay's parents. "I have sat at the table and listened to Jay talking about his dad beating him with buggy whips, and tying him up and leaving him tied for days." Forrester concluded, "Who knows how far back it goes? If each generation thinks that's normal, how long has it been going on?"

Forrester knows his accounts of intergenerational abuse have been fiercely contradicted by Paul's brother, Verlin Posey, who has gone on television and the Internet to challenge Forrester's accounts and defend his family, particularly Paul's behavior toward Cody.

From the time Cody was a little bitty baby, any time he got a spanking, his mother's family kept telling him it was abuse. My brother was the disciplinarian. With Cody's mother and her family, it was anything goes. So automatically you have a good parent/bad parent problem there, and he was trying to avoid that.
— Verlin Posey, Court TV Online,
February 8, 2006

Verlin says Cody has exaggerated the abuse he says he suffered at the hands of Paul.

Well, Cody originally testified to eleven instances of abuse in his life in his confession, and when we got to trial, it had grown to fifty-some-odd. My brother was trying to raise a man out of a boy that was admittedly skipping school and smoking dope and being a juvenile delinquent at times. How far would you go to prevent your child, your teenage son, from going down that path? I'm sure at times he probably crossed the line.

— Verlin Posey, Court TV Online,
February 8, 2006

But others suspect Verlin is in denial.

THE POSEY PATTERN

"I think the statistics are real clear, that abused children tend to abuse their own children," says Cody's attorney, Gary Mitchell. "And the odds of that happening are about one in three. And I think that is a very conservative number. It's probably far greater than that, particularly if somebody has endured long-term abuse and more than one or two instances of abuse."

In short, Paul would have had to have done some extraordinary work on himself to avoid becoming an abusive father. But the concept of a cowboy like Paul going into therapy, or getting some other kind of psychological help, is hard to imagine.

"Men are not socialized to seek help," says Dr. Stacy Kaiser, a Los Angeles therapist, who adds, "Men are supposed to be independent. They're supposed to be able to fix their own problems. . . . You know how men won't ask for directions to a location?" Well, they rarely ask for directions in life either. It would be especially humiliating for a man like Paul, who was raised in a cowboy culture.

BOUNCED AROUND

When Cody was still a toddler, his mom and dad split up. It's believed Carla had a drug and alcohol problem during the first years of Cody's life, according to both the prosecution and the defense. She reportedly joined the military to clean up her life. Carla returned several years later to get custody of Cody, who had been living with Paul during much of this time. Paul had remarried twice, ultimately settling down with Tryone, whom he married in 1999.

CINDERFELLA SYNDROME

Among the witnesses who testified for the defense, a number said that Tryone Posey had been very open about her disdain for her stepson way back when he was in elementary school. "She was very ugly and very verbal about him," Jan Callaway, a local parent, testified. "She said that she hated him and that she was not going to let him get in-between her and Paul." Another mother testified that "she said he was worthless and that he was a horrible child," adding, "She couldn't wait until his mother came, maybe she could get rid of him that way, but under no circumstances would he come between Paul and her."

Cody's attorney called it "jealousy. Insecurity causes jealousy and jealousy causes insecurity. She had found security in Paul. She was jealous of Paul's time and the attention he was going to have to show to Cody. I think she was jealous of the time Cody was going to take away from her and Marilea. . . . Every time you want some time alone, there is always this child around."

"The other dynamic in this family is that Marilea was the golden, perfect child and Cody was the dark child," says Dr. Cave, who reviewed a thousand pages of discovery on the case. "She was Tryone's daughter, so she was perfect, and Cody was this castoff son that Paul didn't really want. Cody was a slave at home. All he did was labor intensively." You could call him Cinderfella. As shrinks will tell you, fairy tales do come true, because they're based in human truth.

The underlying psychological cause of the

mean-stepmother syndrome is unconscious anger. The stepmother feels rage at the stepchild because that child is a flesh-and-blood reminder of the husband's old lover, with whom the current wife feels a sense of competition — especially when the old lover did a stint as a stripper, an insinuation the prosecutor made about Cody's mom. And Tryone's hatred of Cody was only going to get more intense, because it's impossible to compete with a dead woman who remains young forever in the memory of those who survive her.

ANOTHER DEATH IN THE FAMILY

By April 2000, legal papers were drawn up to terminate Paul Posey's parental rights over Cody. The modification agreement states, "The Petitioner shall not be liable for any child support, as he is giving up all parental rights." Giving up parental rights is a very big deal. It speaks volumes about one's attitude toward the child in question. There are conflicting reports as to whether Paul signed all the paperwork. Either way, fate intervened, bringing Cody back into Paul's grasp.

Just a few months later, as ten-year-old Cody, his mother, and her new husband, were setting off on a new life together, they got into a terrible car accident that left Cody's mother dead. Suddenly, at the funeral, Paul sauntered back into Cody's life, with a police officer in tow. A cousin of Cody's mother who was at the funeral testified that Cody was terrified of going back: "He just kept saying over and over, 'Don't let him take me, don't let him take me, he beats me.'"

Cody's fiercely protective aunt Corliss claims Paul was after the social security money that came with Cody, which the defense estimates was about $600 a month. Cody's lawyers claimed Paul and his wife were having money problems and needed cold, hard cash.

> The dollar amount didn't matter. He never loved Cody, Cody was property, and he told me this much. He also told me that he didn't care if Cody ended up hating him, so I'm sure social security was the motivation. He picked him up July 31, 2000, and the social security began September 1, 2000. So you tell me.
> — Corliss Clees, Court TV Online, February 7, 2006

What happened once Cody was back on the ranch with dear old Dad became a matter of furious debate between prosecutors and Cody's defense team. In essence, prosecutors accused the defense of putting Cody's dead dad and stepmother on trial, through a long parade of defense witnesses who painted a very ugly portrait of life in Posey country.

MAYBERRY? MAYBE NOT

The cast of small-town characters who took the stand to testify on Cody's behalf seemed right out of an episode of *Mayberry R.F.D.* There was Emily Nutt, the soft-hearted Sunday-school teacher. She testified that when she first saw the Posey family, all starched up in their church clothes, she thought they looked darn near perfect. She was thrilled to have such a promising family enter her church community. But Ms. Nutt soon became disenchanted, testifying that Paul and Tryone both favored Cody's step-sister. "I really tried to focus on Cody, because Marilea had all the encouragement in the world from her parents. . . . They were always hugging and touching on her, always telling her what a good student she was and how beautiful she was."

Ms. Nutt said Cody was such a whiz at Bible drills, memorizing and reciting scripture, that she wanted him to take part in a statewide Bible study contest. The Sunday-school teacher said Paul and Tryone championed Marilea's participation but wouldn't let Cody take part. His infraction? His defense team says there's evidence the boy was being punished for taking off his long-sleeved dress shirt and wearing his T-shirt at school.

Ms. Nutt said she begged Cody's dad to let him take part. "I said, 'Oh, please, Paul, he's worked too hard, he's too good at it and it's very important to him.' " She testified that the father reacted by saying, "How does allowing a bad boy to compete in a state competition glorify God?"

Cody's attorney, Gary Mitchell, says religion was used by Paul as a cover. "Religion becomes a real crutch to people in these types of situations and an excuse for them."

Psychiatrists also have a term that might apply to Paul's self-righteous religiosity: *reaction formation.* Says noted Los Angeles psychoanalyst Bethany Marshall, "Reaction formation is when you react against a feeling of badness by being super good, like the sex addict minister who preaches hellfire and brimstone from the pulpit, or the rageaholic who becomes sickly sweet."

Back at the ranch, Dad was surfing . . . the Internet, that is, for porn, according to Cody's defense team. With prosecutors calling the attempted rape of Cody a "fairy tale," the defense was determined to show a pattern of sexually deviant behavior by his father. Their biggest weapon in that war was the hard drives of the computer in Paul's office.

Over prosecution objections of character assassination, computer analyst Joe Burchett said he found evidence of thousands of Web pages containing porn, plus lots of searches for incest porn between 2002 and 2004. He testified that one search used the key words "free incest stories," which brought up hundreds of incest-related photos and articles. Many, claimed Burchett, were extraordinarily graphic. Some, he said, dealt with father/daughter rape. Other searches included "sunbathing daughters," "father-daughter incest," and "my sexy wife photo album," all key phrases that allegedly popped up during the search of Paul Posey's computer.

Dr. Cave suspects Paul turned to Internet porn in the wake of the murder/suicide of his own parents, as a form of escape: "For men, sexuality is a big distraction from death, from their own fear of death." But how does this incest-porn surfing dovetail with what Cody says happened the night before the killings? Says Dr. Cave, "It becomes this power thing, sex and domination. It becomes blended." In other words, the defense claims Paul tried to force Cody to have sex with his wife to show that his power over the boy had no bounds and to further humiliate him.

Prosecutors argued that Cody could have been the porn surfer, either out of his own curiosity or to set up his father as the bad guy. But defense experts countered that some of the date and time stamps listed the very times Cody was in school. Prosecutors insisted Cody could have altered the time and date stamps, but that suggestion left Ted Coombs, a forensic computer scientist who has testified at many trials, rolling his eyes.

"It's like trying to find every cockroach in the kitchen. You think you've gotten them all, but turn on the light at midnight and it's a scary sight," says Coombs, explaining how there can be several notations on your computer for every keyword you enter and every website you visit.

"Most people think that by erasing their Internet history or by dumping their cache files that, somehow, they're wiping out evidence of their surfing history. They think it's gone because it's no longer visible to them," says Coombs, adding, "Those people are wrong!"

SECRET FILES

Coombs says most people who surf the Web use Internet Explorer as their browser, and "little known to the average user, Internet Explorer keeps a secret file or files called Index.dat . . . which keep a record of every single Web page you've visited and the time and date you visited it." Coombs suggests we visualize it as a spread sheet listing the time, date, and name of every website you visit, along with all the search parameters. And it's all buried in your computer.

So, for example, you Google the word "incest" and it takes you to a certain website. Both the entry and the result will end up on your Index.dat file. Coombs says, "There's more than one date associated with each file. There's the file creation date, there's a last access date, and a last updated date." Coombs adds, "There can be multiple Index.dat files on your computer."

His conclusion? It would be virtually impossible for a youngster of Cody's age and computer experience to surf the Web and then change these hidden markers to make it look like the porn sites were visited while he was at school. And even if he had, Coombs believes such changes would be obvious to the experts who studied the hard drives.

By the way, Cody would have had to finalize his murderous plotting while he was on Zoloft. Did we mention Cody was put on the antidepressant just a few months before he murdered his family? Psychologist Susan Cave says Cody's parents put him on Zoloft because Cody was "getting angry" and sassing his dad: "I see the Zoloft as just another control measure by them."

Experts suggest Zoloft be administered to a child in conjunction with psychological therapy, but Cody's parents did not send the boy to a shrink for regular counseling. "They didn't want anybody outside the family to know the family secrets. Of course they're not going to put him into therapy," says Dr. Cave.

THE OMERTA VOW

The structure of this family revolved around keeping secrets. It was as if each immediate member of the Posey family had taken the same oath that Mafia members are said to take: the Omerta vow, also known as the

348

"law of silence." Basically, it means, once you are in the family, you do not rat to law enforcement or the outside world about the secrets of the family. Consequences for betraying this code are severe and can include torture and death. In much the same way, Cody Posey knew that he had to remain silent about the abuse to survive in *his* family. One of Cody's friends, Gilbert Salcido, said he often saw Cody bruised: "One time he had a big ol' black eye and said, 'I got hit in softball.' We're all, 'A softball couldn't do that.' He finally told us his dad had punched him." The defense mitigation report confirms that the few complaints that did come into the family protection agency boomeranged against the boy. "Indeed, the complaints served not to protect against but to escalate the commission of violence against Cody: He was beaten in punishment for 'telling' on his parents," reads the defense document.

So, in order to survive, it would appear that Cody had to protect his abusers with his own silence. He had to cover for them. He had to lie for them. When he failed, he paid for it dearly. Even when he succeeded in keeping the secret, he suffered.

John Bradshaw addresses this very issue in his book *Family Secrets* when he writes,

"The very act of keeping a secret generates anxiety in the person, who must be constantly on guard against disclosure, avoiding particular subjects and distorting information."

With Cody, keeping his secret went so far as refusing to shower in front of others for fear of revealing bruises on his body, wearing long-sleeved shirts in the heat, and making up stories about why he had a black eye and other injuries. Beyond the pain of the abuse itself, just imagine living with that level of anxiety. What boggles the mind is the monstrous arrogance and hypocrisy it would take to severely punish a child on the pretext of teaching him right from wrong while simultaneously forcing him to lie to his teachers and others to hide one's own shameful behavior.

Those who make their family live by the code of silence undoubtedly tell themselves they are simply exercising their right to privacy. And many, many families do live by this code. The head of the household demands that, whatever private hell exists behind closed doors, the family projects an idealized self to the world that seems darn near perfect to everyone else. Even members of the extended family are not privy to the secrets. Cody's mitigation report laid out this syndrome perfectly, describing what happened when Cody's uncle and aunt stopped by the ranch *the day before the killings.* The defense document describes how Cody and his dad had been arguing over how to break a horse and that Verlin and Shanda Posey reportedly "noticed nothing amiss between Cody and his father. Cody seemed 'normal' and joked and laughed with his aunt." According to Cody, in an interview after his arrest, he and his father remained at odds with each other for the rest of the day after their argument but when people were around, "we were the All-American Family."

If any of this rings a bell, it's because this is perhaps *the most common secret* law-abiding citizens share with those who end up involved in a crime. In some ways, we all automatically put up false fronts whenever an *outsider* approaches the ring of family secrecy. In fact, we could think of every family as two families: the *real* one and the *phony* one everybody else sees.

This is why so many families argue over what their dead relatives were really like. A grown nephew loves the dearly departed uncle Jack and bristles when Jack's own son is finally free to reveal the dead man as an alcoholic and a wife beater. The nephew never saw what Jack's son secretly lived through and assumes the son is just bitter. This happens constantly within families.

All of this raises the question, Where do we draw the line between legitimate privacy and secrecy? The right to privacy is a basic human right that helps guarantee our freedom to make individual choices and avoid unreasonable intrusions into our lives. Secrecy implies you have something to hide because you, or someone else, has done something wrong or shameful. Theoretically, privacy is not shame-based. Secrecy is.

If someone wants to keep his or her own dark secrets, that's one thing. Forcing somebody else, a child no less, to become a co-conspirator in secrecy is quite another. It's manipulative, coercive, and shame-producing, and it amounts to yet another form of abuse.

CONTROL FREAK

Dr. Cave sees the relationship between Paul Posey and his son as one long exercise in control and power-flexing by a man who in his depths felt very powerless and worthless and sought to compensate for it: "They just want control and power over somebody."

When it comes to playing God, there's no more captive audience than your own kid. When it comes to playing dictator, there's no region easier to dominate than your own family. Dr. Cave observes, "If you're talking about a dictator of a country, like Saddam Hussein, you would call him a malignant narcissist. So it's moving in that direction. But for these people, their power kingdom is usually just their little family unit, or anyone who falls within that sphere."

While newsman Sam Donaldson, the ranch owner, says he never saw any abuse, Dr. Cave says that's because Paul wouldn't abuse Cody in front of anyone he considered more important or more powerful. Instead, it was the ranch hands who say they saw their boss abuse an overworked kid.

Slim Britton is a cowboy right out of a Marlboro commercial, lanky and weathered. His testimony was the high-noon moment of the trial. Wearing blue jeans, cowboy boots, and a western vest, Britton got up out of the witness chair to demonstrate the abuse he says he saw. Holding a metal hay hook, Britton said that Paul hit Cody with the sharp implement, angry that the boy couldn't lift the heavy bales. Britton also testified that Paul hit Cody with a lariat for not moving an injured calf fast enough. "It nearly knocked him off his horse," said the fifty-five-year-old Britton. "I've seen people who've been taken apart with it. It's like being hit with a piece of steel cable."

Hurting the Helpless

Speaking to Court TV, Britton also revealed something about Paul that wasn't allowed into the trial: animal abuse. He claimed Paul once smashed a rock into a heifer's eye, maiming the animal. Such acts of cruelty, he said, were not unusual for the ranch manager.

Jim Forrester agreed, claiming Paul abused many animals, once even shooting a helpless kitten that was meowing on his porch. "Paul just went and got his .357 or something and . . . blew it all to hell, and then told Cody to get it in the trash." And now, when he sees someone abusing animals, "I just figure they're abusing their wife and kids," Forrester said, which is generally what psychiatrists say. In a poignant aside, Marilea's biological father, Jake Schmid, described Cody's expression like this: "The only way I can describe it is if you've ever seen a dog that's been whipped."

If there is any indicator of how upside-down the Posey world was, it's that Jake Schmid, whose daughter was shot dead by Cody Posey, took the stand in Cody's defense and said he harbored no animus toward the boy.

One of the many bizarre facts of this case is that after Tryone and Jake divorced, Tryone married Paul and Jake married Paul's second wife, Sandy. You might have to read that over a couple of times to get your brain around it. In clinical terms, this is what is known as PDWS, postdivorce wife swapping.

Sandy Schmid testified that during her marriage to Paul, she protected Cody from his dad. She described a surreal incident in which Cody, only about six years old at the time, had been ordered by his father to fill up a horse trough with water using a Dixie cup as a punishment for something he did. Said Sandy, "When Paul left, I told Cody to just put the hose in the trough and finish filling it up." Sandy also testified that her ex-husband had a taste for porn, both on the Internet and on television.

Of all the shockers to come out of this trial, Marilea's dad, Jake Schmid, delivered the coup de grâce when he took the stand out of the jury's presence during the sentencing phase of the trial. Jake told the judge he would have murdered Paul himself if he had figured out then what he ultimately came to believe, namely that Paul was having sex with thirteen-year-old Marilea. "If I had known it, I would have killed Paul, and I would have killed Tryone for allowing it," Schmid said in court.

When I asked Cody's attorney about the molestation claim, Gary Mitchell was very careful to use caution, emphasizing, "I have no proof of that. I do know that Jake Schmid, Marilea's father, thought that to be the case because he testified to that — he made a statement to it in front of the court. . . . But I have no evidence one way or another. I know that all Cody ever said about it was that his father would go into Marilea's room, and spend about thirty minutes there at night after she had gone to bed. He didn't know what was going on."

Obviously, Paul is not around to defend himself against any of these accusations.

The morning of the killings was shaping up to be a classic summer day in New Mexico, bright and hot. School was out and Cody, say witnesses, saw himself more isolated than ever on the ranch. Forensic psychologist Christine Johnson testified that in the months leading up to the killings,

Cody suffered the added anxiety of being moved by his parents from one school to another, cutting him off from friends and a Hispanic girlfriend his parents didn't want him to see. Said Johnson, "Stressors were increasing, helplessness and hopelessness increasing, reaching a point of despair."

Cody's maternal aunt says that her side of the family had already been long shut out of Cody's life. Dr. Susan Cave sees the isolation of a child by cutting off family and friends and switching schools as a common method abusive parents use to keep the abuse secret and maintain control over the child: "As soon as it looks like somebody's figuring it out, they move." It's all about keeping the secrets secret. But in a matter of seconds, the equation changed. Cody opened fire and killed the only people who could stop him from talking.

So now everyone knows all the nasty big and little secrets of daily life in the Posey household. While prosecutors insisted some details were exaggerated and others made up out of whole cloth, that doesn't nullify the impression the public took home. If even a tenth of the accusations against Paul Posey are true, he was a violent man and an abusive father with some very dark tendencies.

Imagine for a moment that Paul had been able to see the future, to know that all of his dirty laundry would be exposed to the world after his death. How might that have affected his behavior? Would he have thought twice about hitting his son or calling him bad names if he'd known that, one day, his actions would be memorialized in a nationally televised court proceeding, forever joining his family name to the issue of family violence?

This raises yet another fascinating question. How would *any* of us act if we were certain that our secrets would ultimately be exposed? So many deep, dark secrets do end up being revealed one way or another, because of a crime, a divorce, a last will and testament, a lien, a lawsuit, an unauthorized biography, or just gossip.

It's worth thinking about. How would you feel if your darkest secrets involving family and sex were exposed? How would you fare if every word you've Googled in the last few years was published for the world to see? How would you come off if friends, relatives, and business associates took the stand and told anecdotes about your worst behavior? What kind of portrait would a prosecutor or defense lawyer paint of you? Few of us would emerge completely unscathed.

358

Most of us will never find ourselves in that situation. But, as this case shows, secrets can sometimes turn to murder in an instant.

THE VERDICT

And in the end? "We lost the battle and won the war," said defense attorney Gary Mitchell of the verdict. The jury's decision? They found Cody guilty of first-degree murder for killing Marilea, guilty of second-degree murder for killing his stepmother, and guilty of manslaughter for killing his dad.

But, in a stunning twist, the judge decided not to sentence Cody as an adult, which could have gotten him life in prison, ensuring his confinement for at least fifty years before he would have been eligible for parole. Instead, Cody will go to a juvenile facility until he's twenty-one, and could get out much sooner.

In handing down his sentence, the judge said he didn't buy the prosecutor's argument that Cody showed psychopathic traits and could not be rehabilitated. In the end, the judge ruled in favor of hope, that Cody can become a new kind of Posey and break the cycle of violence. Said family observer Jim Forrester, "I think if anybody breaks it, it will be Cody." But when you think about it, it's too late for him to break the cycle.

He's already killed three people.

CAN YOU RELATE?

"I understand what Cody went through; I was humiliated and hurt by my stepmother. I was hit every day, but I can't give Cody Posey a thumbs-up for killing his family." So said a woman who agreed to speak to me on the condition of anonymity. She told me she and Cody had experienced a remarkably similar pattern of abuse.

After her mother died when she was a preschooler, she went to live with her father and stepmother. She, too, was isolated from her mother's family and treated differently than her step-siblings. She was also beaten and humiliated by her stepmother and was convinced her stepmother only tolerated her because of the social security check she brought in thanks to her deceased mother.

This woman said, "I know from experience my first ideas were: kill myself, run away, starve myself . . . so that I can tell the world that there is something desperately wrong here." She says she became anorexic "to get back at my parents, to make them look bad. I just wanted to get back at them any way I could. But I never thought of taking a gun and putting it to their heads. And I don't think I should give Cody the okay

360

for that. I can't believe he is going to go to jail for only five years for that. I think he's a killer."

But one thing this woman didn't experience was sexual abuse. Dr. Cave says that was the final trigger: "I think that whole sexual abuse thing is what set him off. He had pretty much decided he could live with this until he turned eighteen. But that pushed him over the edge."

But did that nightmarish incident really happen, or did Cody make it up?

If Tryone hated her stepson, then why on earth would she want to have sex with the fourteen-year-old virgin? We may never know the answer to that question, but there are clues. Dr. Cave says that according to Cody, Tryone and Marilea had just returned from a rare weekend trip and were unpacking when Tryone and Paul began arguing. "She never went anywhere without Paul, so, who knows, he may have had some little jealous snit. But they were arguing and I think it's because they [Tryone and Marilea] were gone."

It was some time after this argument occurred, Cody says, that he was summoned in to have sex with Tryone. This would be Sunday evening, July 4, 2004. Funny that this would all happen on Independence

Day, for that night Cody would finally declare his independence.

It Could Happen

Let's try and put ourselves in Paul's shoes at this juncture. We know he was a man obsessed with controlling and dominating his family. We have reason to believe he was a man obsessed with porn that veered toward incest and swinging. We have evidence that he was angry at Tryone for showing some independence with her weekend trip away from him. That in itself would be good reason in Paul's mind to bring her down a notch, to show her who's really the boss.

And what would be the best way to pull in the reins? What would be the ideal way to dominate his wife and control his son simultaneously? The very best way to blend all his sick urges into one demented act would be to emerge after dark as the sexual master of his two slaves. While Cody says the naked Tryone was beckoning him to her, Paul was right there, with a torch in his hand.

S&M, D&S

It's quite possible that Paul and Tryone had a sexual relationship characterized by dominance and submission, whereby the submissive pleases her master by acquiescing to his demands, no matter how inappropriate. In fact, in the D&S world, the more inappropriate the better. And what possibly could be more inappropriate than this ménage à trois?

In Paul's twisted world, Tryone's offering of her body to his flesh and blood might be what he would demand from his submissive as a show of love, respect, and subservience. It would be the perfect way to humiliate Cody and Tryone all at once. Let the games begin. But Cody refused to play along, and things turned really ugly. The slave was punished with a branding. And the next morning, there was a slave revolt.

People are not property. You don't own your kids. And if you treat them like property, when they grow up, they might want to get even. On July 5, 2004, Cody became a man in the Posey family tradition.

Now he must learn how to become a real man.

9
DIRTY TRICKS

See if this rings a bell. You know someone — a friend, business acquaintance, or lover — who is *trouble.* You sense danger, but you just can't seem to walk away. There's something about this person that intrigues you and sucks you in like a magnet. No matter how much they stir things up and destabilize your world, somehow you can't bring yourself to shake them off. You've let them into your life, against your better judgment.

Most of us have known someone like this at one time or another. Some of us have gotten stung.

It's the profile of a *borderline personality.* Shrinks say borderlines can be incredibly charming. The theory is, they don't know who they are. Something went wrong very early in life and they failed to develop a sense of self. So they mimic whomever they're with. Whatever you like, whatever your values, tastes, and beliefs are, they mirror all of it right back at you. That can be a very pleasant experience. They totally re-affirm you. That's why you enjoy being around them. They make you feel validated and important.

Unfortunately, there's a very dark and dangerous side to the borderline personality. Because they don't know who they are, they don't know where they end and you begin. They have no sense of borders or boundaries. When they want something, they don't care that it doesn't belong to them. They become determined to get it, with a singleness of purpose that is unnerving in its intensity. And when they want *you,* watch out.

This is precisely the position that aging actor Robert Blake found himself in after getting to know one Bonny Lee Bakley. A woman of mysterious means, the stocky fortysomething blonde was hell-bent on marrying a celebrity. When Bonny set her sights on Blake, she proved impossible to shake. The short, tough-talking former star of the TV show *Baretta* was in his mid-sixties. Once considered one of the wild men of Hollywood, he had finally calmed down. He was reportedly sober and lived according to a predictable routine. He was also a tad too confident that he had mastered life and could handle whatever surprises came his way.

Then he met his match — Bonny. And Bonny met hers, too. As we shall see, each suffered enormously as a consequence of their association. But even as the malignancy of their relationship became impossible to ignore, seeping like a toxic tide over their respective lives, neither seemed capable of pulling away, severing the ties, or even altering their behavior to make the situation less volatile. It was as if they fell into a trance that overwhelmed their sense of self-preservation and rationality. The question is: What was Bonny getting out of the relationship that caused her to stay in it even after she told others she feared she might be killed? And what did Robert get out of his interactions with Bonny so that he kept having them, even as he flew into rages and fits of frustration over her cunning ways?

The increasingly popular study of *victimology* centers around analysis of the victim and the relationship between the victim and the victimizer. It also explores how the victim sometimes plays a role in his or her own victimization. In this case, you could argue that Robert Blake played a role in being victimized by Bonny. Bonny would also play a role in becoming a victim herself when she was ultimately murdered after dining out with Robert.

While Robert Blake was found not guilty of Bonny's murder in the criminal trial and insisted that persons still unknown are responsible, it's clear these two were a lethal mix. No one disputes that they fought explosively over her pregnancy, her desperation to marry, his determination to get their baby for himself, and countless other issues.

As we study the ever-more-twisted entanglements of these two damaged characters, we may find that the dynamics are not quite so foreign as we'd like to believe. While Bonny Lee Bakley was a manipulative seducer and con artist, she is certainly not the first woman to plot marrying a man solely for his social status, or to silently plan getting pregnant in order to snare him. And Blake is certainly not the first man to have sex with an unknown woman after only a cursory chat, or to want a sexual relationship with no strings attached. Each thought they were using the other. Both were into cynical, dangerous games, the very games that are secretly played every day all across America. See if you recognize any of the moves.

Blake and Bakley met, sort of by chance, at an old showbiz hangout, a bar that's since been shuttered and forgotten. Chadney's was right across the street from the *Tonight Show* studios in what Johnny Carson used to sarcastically call "beautiful downtown Burbank." Bonny had gone there one night, knowing it was a hangout for older B-list celebrities. When she saw Blake's familiar mug, she was like a predator drone locking onto a target. At least that's how renowned Hollywood private eye Scott Ross sees it.

"I'm sure she spent the first ten minutes telling him how wonderful he was and what a great actor he was and yanking his ego before she started yanking his other parts," says Ross. He told me Blake and Bakley proceeded to walk out of Chadney's, get into his car, drive to a nearby parking lot, and have sex in his vehicle. Some first date.

"She wanted to go back to his house and have sex. And Robert, being Robert, would never let anybody in his home." Hence, the parking lot sex. But I asked Scott, Why would Blake go anywhere with a groupie he'd just met? "She's fueling his ego. She's cheap, she's free, she's available, she's willing. There's no energy. There's no effort.

There is, theoretically, no obligation. . . . Robert's mindset was that Redd Foxx adage: Women over forty, they don't tell, they don't swell, and they're grateful as hell."

Blake paid a terrible price for that misogynistic mindset. Not only would Bonny tell, she would swell. And she would put Blake through hell. The story of how Bonny Lee Bakley ultimately became pregnant with Robert Blake's child, despite all his efforts to the contrary, is a study in mutual manipulation and polyamorous perversity. Scott Ross says he knows every last sordid twist and turn. He should.

Three years after that hot and heavy first date, Scott Ross joined up with Robert Blake to be his private investigator. Ross got the call just hours after Bonny Lee Bakley was murdered on the evening of May 4, 2001. By the time of her death, she had achieved her goal. She had become Mrs. Robert Blake.

She and her famous husband had just eaten dinner at an Italian restaurant in Studio City called Vitello's. After the meal, they returned to Robert's car, a black Dodge Stealth. She got in. Blake told police he'd forgotten his registered gun back at the restaurant and claimed to have walked back a block and a half to get it, leaving

Bonny to wait inside the Dodge. He says when he got back to the car, Bonny was dying, the victim of a mysterious assassin who had shot her in the head and the shoulder as she sat in the passenger seat. One witness said her window had been rolled down. Blake didn't use a cell phone to call 911 but instead ran for help. It wouldn't be long before he became the prime suspect in her murder, although it would take cops almost a year to arrest him.

MOTH TO FLAME

This was the biggest Hollywood murder story since the O. J. Simpson case, and when the news broke that Mrs. Robert Blake had been gunned down, the media went into frenzy mode. News choppers whirred over Blake's rambling Studio City compound. Emotions ran so high that, unbeknownst to anybody, Blake went to live with investigator Ross and his pretty, gregarious wife, Lisa, in their San Fernando Valley house and remained in hiding there for months. Lisa says after Blake arrived at their home, "He broke down, just completely broke down into wracking sobs, and said, 'I wish I would have stayed in the car. Then my family wouldn't be going through this and I'd be dead too.' He looked and sounded com-

370

pletely hysterical." When I suggested to Lisa that Blake was an actor well known for his ability to produce tears on cue, she replied, "Who am I? I'm a Valley housewife, for crying out loud. Who the heck am I? I didn't know he was acting for me. I had no idea. I honestly thought he was truly, truly upset by what had just happened."

Bonny's family pointed the accusatory finger at Blake. They insisted that the actor, whose most acclaimed role was that of a murderer in the 1967 movie *In Cold Blood,* was a cold-blooded killer himself. Blake's supporters countered that Bonny was a con artist who'd made scores of enemies, and that any one of them had a motive to kill her.

Whether you believe Blake pulled the trigger or not, it seemed he and Bonny were locked into what one forensic criminologist called "a dance." On one level, the conscious one, Blake had wanted nothing to do with her beyond the occasional sex she'd offer when she was visiting L.A. from her Memphis home. But on an unconscious level, Blake was drawn to Bonny like a moth to flame for a number of reasons. First of all, they matched. Like attracts like. Their childhoods had uncanny similarities. Both Blake and Bonny were born into what have been

371

described as highly dysfunctional working-class families in New Jersey. According to Court TV's Crime Library book on the case, both claim to have been physically and psychologically abused.

Author Gary King writes that Bonny claimed to have been sexually abused by her own father when she was seven and "would later say that he died before she became old enough to kill him." According to Bakley family attorney Eric Dubin, Bonny was a "neglected child . . . picked on for having dirty clothes." It's interesting to note that Bonny's maternal aunt disputes these characterizations, telling me she never saw any signs that Bonny was abused or neglected as a child, although she described Bonny's dad as a troubled man with a drinking problem and notes Bonny eventually went to live with her grandmother. In any event, both Bonny and Robert gravitated toward show business, seeking the positive feedback they felt they could never find at home.

Bonny fantasized about stardom as a way to blot out the perceived pain. By the time Bonny bombed as a singer, Blake was already a star. His real name was Mickey Gubitosi and he'd gotten his big break at an astonishingly early age. By the time

Mickey was five, his family had moved to L.A. Soon he was cast in the now classic *Our Gang* series as one of those adorable little rascals. From the very start, he was considered a natural talent, one who could reliably shed tears. In later life, he would describe how he felt love coming from the audience, love that he apparently couldn't find at home.

Even Blake's ardent supporters don't seem to dispute the assessment of well-known clinical psychologist Dr. Judy Kuriansky: "He's a drama addict." I asked Dr. Kuriansky if she was theorizing that, because Blake came from an abusive environment, he would be attracted to an abusive, drama-filled situation. "Absolutely," she replied, "and invites it. There's no question in my mind. He participates in it and needs it, desperately needs it."

Bonny was also highly addicted to drama. Putting two drama addicts together just multiplies the turmoil. It's exactly what happens when you put two raging alcoholics together. There's nobody around to slam their foot on the brakes. Essentially, it would appear that Bonny and Robert, unbeknownst even to themselves, went on a long drama binge together, with deadly results. But why?

To understand the tango between these two similarly traumatized individuals, we must go way back to their formative years. Unconsciously, they were drawn to each other because of their shared scars. They were kindred spirits, whether they would admit it or not. That's how the subconscious works, always coming back to the early childhood traumas.

We are drawn to what we know, what feels familiar, even if it hurts again, perhaps *in order to be* hurt again, to reexperience the hurt in an attempt to purge it. That's when we get in touch with our real selves. When the original pain is reexperienced, the person whom we squashed in order to survive the trauma comes alive again within the psyche. I'm back! it says, gasping for air. The "original me" has been freed. The excitement, the adrenaline rush of the drama, makes us feel doubly alive. It's a high, and we can become addicted to the intoxication. *Drama addict* is one way to describe a person trapped in this cycle. Another way to describe the experience is *negative excitement.*

Blake and Bonny met during the most serene years of his life. While Blake has an astounding 161 acting credits to his name, his very last credit is *Lost Highway* in 1997, well before his first meeting with Bonny. He had essentially retired and was existing on a routine that reportedly stressed exercise, Alcoholics Anonymous meetings, and superficial socializing. He had seemingly conquered his addictions one day at a time, but he may very well have been bored. After the wild life he had led, reading the paper, lifting weights, and going for target practice with one of his many guns wasn't going to cut it for long. Cue Bonny Lee, enter stage left. Boy, did she add drama to Blake's story line, supplying plenty of negative excitement for the actor, just as she'd brought drama to other celebrities she'd encountered long before him.

Christina Scheier told *CBS News* she and Bonny had been best friends since they were kids growing up in New Jersey, and said Bonny was always obsessed with stardom, determined either to be a celebrity herself or to be with one. Bonny was only in her twenties when she embarked on her quest in earnest. "She went to see Tom Jones, Frankie Valli, and she really stalked Frankie," Scheier told the reporter.

THE STRIPPER SCAM

I'd heard this crazy story that Bonny had once shown up half naked at country music legend Jerry Lee Lewis's home. I called the house and the singer's sister, Frankie, picked up the phone. With a thick Southern accent and a sly sense of humor, the spirited woman told me I didn't know the half of it.

"She just knocked on the door," Frankie told me from her "big ol' house" in Ferriday, Louisiana. Frankie said her famous older brother grew up in the home that she later turned into the Lewis Family Living Museum, complete with "real laundry and real dirty dishes."

Frankie said that sometime in the early eighties, Bonny Lee Bakley simply showed up at the Lewis family home. She told me Bonny walked in holding a portable boom box. "She just played some music and she just stripped down to a pair of bikinis. Looked like a pair of thongs almost, and no bra." Frankie says she watched in amazement. "She danced all over the little living room and she was quite colorful and very pretty. She had tassels on those breasts. She sure did. It was a little bitty string around the nipples. I remember that. She was something."

Frankie told me the young stripper was so impressive that she called her famous brother: "I said, We've got a real live wire, you've got to see this one. If she's broke, she's crazy. If she's rich, she's eccentric. He said, Well, send her up. I've got a room full of nuts I'm looking at now." While others have also claimed to have introduced the two, this is how Frankie says Bonny Lee Bakley entered the life of one of her idols, the music legend known as "the Killer." In short order, the Lewis clan got to know the sexy spitfire who insinuated herself into their lives, bringing her business along with her. Frankie noticed she was entrepreneurial in a cunning way, mailing sacks of letters and getting a bundle of mail back. Bonny "used many, many names," she recalled. It would turn out she had dozens of aliases.

A couple of years before she met Blake, Bonny was arrested in Arkansas. Authorities reportedly found more than half a dozen driver's licenses and a handful of social security cards in her possession, along with a batch of stolen credit cards. It would turn out this was just the tip of the iceberg in Bonny's world of complicated con games. According to private investigator Scott Ross, Bonny used those many IDs to rent post office boxes around the nation for her lonely-hearts scam, so she could write letters posing as a variety of beautiful women in search of Mr. Right.

Because social security numbers were

seized, her case ended up in federal court, entitled *U.S.A. v. Bakley.* Originally facing several counts that could have landed her serious jail time, Bonny managed to get all but one of the charges dismissed. She ultimately pleaded guilty to one count involving misuse of a social security number and was sentenced to three years' probation and a $1,000 fine. She was not supposed to leave the state of Arkansas without permission, according to the terms of her probation. By this time it was February 1998. Just a few months later, she would meet Blake in Burbank, California.

Rounding out her rap sheet was a misdemeanor drug fine and a run-in with the law over a couple of bad checks years earlier. Considering the many con games she played, Bonny had maintained a relatively clean criminal record. Scott Ross says his probing of the case quickly revealed why. He believes Bonny's victims were so embarrassed they'd been duped as part of a lonely-hearts scam that most didn't want to go public with it. For most of them, the amount of money they'd lost wasn't worth the effort or humiliation that would have resulted from pressing charges. Who wants to admit they're so desperate for companionship they've answered sleazy ads?

"The con was: Send me money and I'll come see you," said Ross, who told me his in-depth investigation into Bonny's past turned up about eight examples of con. "The first one was: I'm running an ad and you responded. The eighth level was: Put me in your will."

Ross says he has evidence that, over the years, Bonny had conned tens of thousands of men into sending her money, sums that could range from twenty dollars to thousands. "We went to some of her box drops, and we got other boxes that she had because Robert had the keys to get into them. And we had about three months' worth of letters. Those letters probably totaled over two thousand." Robert Blake also kept some of the letters Bonny sent to him, evidently sensing he might one day need evidence of her character. Still other letters, sent by Bonny to strangers, were obtained from various sources, including acquaintances and relatives, according to Scott.

Investigator Ross said that after he collected all these letters, his defense team turned them over to the prosecutors trying Blake for murder. The letters were later returned to the defense team by the prosecution through the discovery process and stamped "legal discovery." Ross says this mountain of letters was booked as possible evidence, but adds most of this material never actually made it to trial. Ross allowed me to view copies of some of these letters, which were handwritten or typed single-spaced. Purportedly written by Bonny or at Bonny's direction, they offer a fascinating glimpse into the secret world of lonely-hearts scams.

The standard Level 1 letter read like this. "Hi Single Guy, I'm this young pretty still single gal who wants to get to know you. I'm 24 and a half years of age and I measure around 38-27-38. I'm only 5'2" so I have to watch my weight carefully, I do go up from 120 to 130 quite easily. But don't worry I'm not fat and I promise I never will be. . . . I don't know what else I can say actually my first letter and all. I am into sex with the right man whom I want to have a relationship with. . . . It is my dream to have a man of my own again to live with. I'm not sure what it would cost, what do you think? I would need a lot of gas and a motel room for one night and food and a small amount for who knows what emergency. I think I would need either $150.00, $175.00, or perhaps even $200.00. Do you possibly have this much extra that you could spare right now so that I could come immediately? If you could please send it along with your phone number so I can call you and you can tell me the way to your place. If you wish to get to know me first and make sure I'm pretty enough then just send me a twenty and I'll part with a bunch of my sexiest pictures. Hurry I need you now! I will give you my telephone number in my next letter or my phone call to you. Do you have a cassette player? I will send you a tape my Uncle produced of me if you send me $20 for pics. Love you Lots, Lee."

Scott Ross said Bonny sometimes included nude photos of herself and sometimes sent naked photos of other women, saying they were of her. Ditto for X-rated home videos. Ross claims Bonny sometimes asked men to send her X-rated tapes demonstrating their favorite sexual positions, so she could learn what they liked. "People would send her videotapes. In fact, we turned over 110 videos . . . to police." Ross contends Bonny would then turn around and sell those graphic tapes to other strangers.

Another typical letter, purportedly from Bonny to a man, reads like this: "Darling, I know I should have been there by now. But I've had some bad luck along the way — Please let me explain what has happened I

381

got about 130 miles from home and the drive shaft fell down I pulled to the side this couple stopped & drove me to a garage that does towing I waited there while they went and towed it back. . . . I was gonna call you and see if you could Western Union the money somehow so I could come on the rest of the way but I got scared and chickened out I figured you might get mad at me. . . . So 'if' you're not real mad and disappointed with me for having a heap and you still want me please send me the two hundred forty soon as you can get it by two day priority mail and I will get my mom or sister to drive me there."

Sometimes the letters would come from a so-called third party urging the man to send her friend, Bonny Lewis, some money. Scott says a worthless stock certificate would be thrown in "as security." Sometimes, excuses would be made for having taken the money but not shown up: "I have been very sick for three months, very sick." The money, said that letter, had been used for emergency medical expenses. Some postmarks indicate that one man sent out five letters to what he believed were five different women at five different post office boxes around the country. The defense contended that all those P.O. boxes led back to Bonny's business, in which she corresponded with men using an assortment of names and addresses. In effect, she was posing as many different women.

THE LONELY-HEARTS CLUB

But Bakley family attorney Eric Dubin said the extent of Bonny's cons had been exaggerated by Robert Blake's camp in an effort to poison public opinion. "My experience is that guys don't send women money unless they feel they are getting something out of it. And what they got was Bonny Lee Bakley stroking their egos in letters. The con was the fact that she would never show up, or never date. She wasn't a prostitute," Dubin said. He likened it to a 900 phone-sex number, where the woman tells the caller she looks like a Dallas Cowboys cheerleader. "But the reality is different. Everybody knows that."

Another one of Bonny's former lawyers, prominent Los Angeles attorney Cary Goldstein, echoed that sentiment. "It's almost like these guys deserved to be taken. In a sick way, one might morally justify what she did. It was almost like 'fair game.' If you're stupid enough to do this, then you deserve what you got."

Indeed, in the legal discovery are some

letters purportedly from men responding to her. One starts with freeway directions to his home and then cautions, "Don't come if you are on your period I don't want you to get sick on road. Don't give anybody a ride. Be sure you are not pregnant or have VD or Aids. I guess you protected yourself. Love, Bob."

To me, that letter, though it made me laugh, is very sad. It speaks of ignorance and longing mixed up with coarseness and some affection. Most of all, it screams loneliness. There are so many lonely men out there who will do just about anything for the soft touch of a woman. I feel for all those pathetic, desperate men, although I know most had other options. There are better ways to escape loneliness than lonely-hearts clubs.

That hardly any of these conned men had the stomach to pursue her legally is proof they were ashamed of their secret efforts to find companionship in this manner. Says Scott Ross, "This was something that people were embarrassed about, the fact that, number one, they're looking at lonely-hearts clubs, or the backs of these low-end soft-core porno magazines, the fact that they're corresponding with women from these low-end throwaway newspapers. . . . The kind of thing you see in newspaper dispensers with pictures of half-naked women on the front, these were the types of magazines that she advertised in. . . . It's an admission that you're picking these things up. It's also an admission that you're stupid enough to send this woman twenty dollars from this idiotic ad, and I think it was embarrassing." Bonny was well served by the secretiveness of these men. Their shame and desire to hide their foolish actions protected her operation and allowed it to continue.

But if you feel sorry for these lonely guys, Eric Dubin says Bonny also deserves our compassion and understanding. Dubin points to Bonny's struggle to overcome what he insists was a brutal upbringing that left her with very low self-esteem: "All this stems from a horrific childhood and wanting to show everybody that she was special and become a celebrity." Frankie Lewis described Bonny as cheerful on the surface but melancholy underneath. Her observation was that Bonny was, in her heart, very lonely too. That's one of the reasons she was probably so adept at hitting the right notes with these forlorn men.

And, says Cary Goldstein, there was a Robin Hood aspect to Bonny's mischief: "She would give jobs to friends in need and family. I mean, she was getting in stacks of mail and they would have to sort the mail. She had prewritten letters of different types. An A, B, C, D, or E letter. They would make the calls and say, Okay, this one gets a B letter and this one gets a C letter, depending on what stage of the scam they were in. Do I ask for bus money or airfare, that kind of thing."

SMART COOKIE?

What seems clear from studying her complex scams is how clever, organized, and determined Bonny was, along with being a hard worker. Defense investigator Ross says he found evidence that Bonny worked diligently on her letters, writing practice missives, with cross-outs and misspellings, then refining and improving them until they were ready to go out. This is work! If Bonny had only put all that concentration and effort into a legitimate business, imagine how successful she would have become. According to *Blood Cold,* the well-researched book on the Blake case by Dennis McDougal and Mary Murphy, those who knew Bonny thought she could have succeeded on the up-and-up. They quote her ex-husband and the father of three of her children, Paul Gawron, as saying, " 'In one word, I'd describe her as a thief. . . . If she had put her mind on something else, she could have been a whiz. It's just a shame that everything she did was crooked.' "

This was a choice that Bonny made based on what she was comfortable with, which — in turn — was based on her rough childhood. While we tend to envision grifters as hard-boiled realists, they are often sentimental dreamers seeking what they view as well-deserved payback for hard times. Often psychologically damaged by childhood trauma, they are not so much looking to succeed as they are battling to win their perceived war with the world. In their minds, they are heroes cast into a heartless life, forced to play dirty to survive. This story line begins as a way of surviving a difficult childhood by romanticizing it and continues into adulthood.

Bonny was the star of the movie playing in her head. Grandiosity and magical thinking is par for the course. So is complication and drama. Being a normal, successful businesswoman would have been far too dull for Bonny's inner story line. The complications, adventures, and hijinks that come with scamming strangers are much better material for a drama addict, who needs to romanticize and glorify her daily life. It would certainly be interesting to examine our own lives and try to pinpoint when, how, and why we create unnecessary drama and rationalize our worst behavior by romanticizing it, either in our work lives or our love lives, or both.

Frankie Lewis recounted a prophetic conversation she had with Bonny. "She wanted to be a star and she couldn't even sing. So I don't know what kind of star she wanted to be. I kept asking her: What do you want to star in? 'Well, I'm going to get married again.' I said, Okay, but that's not going to make you a star. 'Oh, yes it is.'"

BLACK WIDOW

How many times Bonny was married continues to be a subject of hot debate. Scott Ross claims Bonny Lee was married well over a dozen times. The Bakley family attorney scoffs at that, saying the number is more than a couple, but he really doesn't know for sure. One Internet site lists ten husbands. Other published reports say eleven. Some claim she got quickie Mexican divorces that weren't binding for some of the marriages. At the end of the day, it seems to be anybody's guess.

But Frankie Lewis says what's not guesswork is Bonny's relationship with men. "She was a black widow spider. She had a very bad mean streak." Could it have had anything to do with her being sexually assaulted by her own father, as Bonny claimed? Such a horrific experience at the impressionable age of seven could make a woman very angry. If she was never in analysis, the rage might turn into hate for men in general, and a desire to seek revenge against all of them. "She hated men worse than God hated the Devil. That's the way she put it," says Frankie.

"Trapped in a victim/victimizer mode" is how Dr. Kuriansky put it: "She was out to take advantage of men and did. She was out to humiliate them and to use them, and she was highly successful at it." Dr. Kuriansky says what happens with someone who has been victimized on a sexual level is that they can snap and decide to "identify with the aggressor." The psychologist says the sexually abused child might say to herself, " 'Screw that, I am going to end up reversing the roles. I am never going to be abused again, because I am going to take advantage of people and do them one better, so that it never happens to me again.' So she's continuing to reenact the early drama. Only this time, she is the abuser."

One elderly man who claimed to have suffered at Bonny's hand was DeMart Besly, a self-described handwriting analyst who says he married her in the late 1980s. He became so furious at Bonny, he later wrote a manuscript about her called *Ubiquitous Bonny, Mistress of Sham! Of Lust, Greed, and Deceit!* He was peddling this work to various publications, and his angry letters were stamped "legal discovery" in the murder case.

One letter, dated January 1994, warns, "Bonny is still operating from her Memphis home. I called her number last week . . . and received the following message, 'I'm not home right now, but if you are the guy I've been writing to, give me explicit details in coming to you, and send me one hundred dollars.' "

In another letter, the retired military man, then in his eighties, explains how he met Bonny though a lonely-hearts outlet and began corresponding with her. He called her "a greedy, grasping gold-digger without a single positive trait," and claimed Bonny got another octogenarian to pay for tens of thousands of dollars in cosmetic surgery. "She's made a fortune in this racket since her late teens and is now approaching her thirty-eighth year. Her targets are the elderly, hopefully with one foot in the grave and the other on a banana peel. . . . It remains to be seen how much longer her phenominal [*sic*] luck will last."

Some of his anger should have been directed at himself. Though elderly, he clearly still had a relatively sharp mind, sharp enough to know he was inviting danger by marrying someone he met through lonely-hearts correspondence. De-Mart Besly admits in his letters that he "married the gal to really check her out." That's the wrong reason to get married, and he suffered the consequences. In one sense, he victimized himself.

Another husband, William Weber, was in his eighties when he reportedly married Bonny. The Florida senior had responded to a personal ad Bonny had placed and she reportedly just appeared at his home. CBS News said that days after the marriage, Bonny disappeared. "Bonny was into my grandfather's life for one week and basically walked off with eight thousand dollars," Weber's granddaughter told the network. But experts say Bonny protected herself legally by getting married, as she could argue she was permitted to use his money. Where did she get the idea of using marriage as a strategic tool?

Way back in 1976, when she was turning twenty, Bonny briefly married a Greek immigrant *she* had met through a lonely-hearts magazine. In her divorce petition, she claimed she realized only later he wanted to marry her to become an American citizen. She accused him of extreme cruelty. Soon after, she married her cousin Paul Gawron and they had a daughter, Holly, and a son, Glenn.

Bonny gave birth to her third child in 1993. She had named her daughter Jeri Lee Lewis, but the singer didn't take the bait, according to his sister Frankie: "He just laughed. He said, Well, the kid's got to have a name." It was only after Bonny's murder, almost a decade later, that Lewis issued a statement saying, "As saddened as we are to hear of anyone dying, we want it made clear that I have never fathered a child by Mrs. Robert Blake, Bonny Lee Bakley, to whom my name has been attached since her murder."

The statement goes on to say that years earlier, Bonny had been an "avid fan" who crossed the line, "harassing my family. . . . She moved to Memphis in the hope that I would leave my devoted wife, Kerrie, and our son, Jerry "LEE" Lewis III, and marry her: merely a figment of her own imagination. . . . Her stalking of my family, as well as her threats to kill our son, landed her in a Memphis court room. As a last ditch attempt to form a relationship with me, in 1993 she charged she was carrying my child and stories to this effect appeared in the tabloids." The press release says Lewis was out of the country at the time and couldn't have conceived the child. In the end, Bonny's husband Paul reportedly claimed the child and took the baby in, raising her as his own.

This is much more frightening stuff than any mail-order scam. Bonny Lee Bakley, long before she ever met Robert Blake, had tried to worm her way deep into another celebrity's life, honing tactics she would later use to greater effect with Blake. When her efforts failed, the Lewis family claims she resorted to threats.

This is classic borderline-personality behavior, according to Dr. Judith M. Sgarzi, a forensic criminologist and co-author of the book *Victimology: A Study of Crime Victims and Their Roles.* "Once a sociopathic or borderline personality gets you, then they sort of operate on this love/hate mentality. If you are with them, then they love you to pieces. If you are against them, then all hell breaks loose. That is where I see her personality is. They don't have a middle. They don't have a medium that they can do." And that is why they are so scary and dangerous.

Robert Blake was soon to get a taste of this. But it turns out Blake could be scary too. In the end, one is left to wonder who was zooming who.

Isn't It Romantic

"Hi, I hate to tell you this but the pill did not work for me." According to the Smoking Gun website, this undated letter from Bonny Lee Bakley informed Robert Blake that she was pregnant. This would become one of the prosecution's court documents. Blake was reportedly furious.

The baby girl was born on June 2, 2000. So Bonny would have been impregnated by Blake approximately nine months earlier, in the fall of 1999. The Smoking Gun says it also obtained the transcript of a "late-1999 telephone conversation" Bonny allegedly had with Blake. In it, he urges her to get an abortion, but she says she won't.

Bonny Bakley: "The thing is, is . . . I just . . . I can't be that awful to kill it, but obviously you can."

Robert Blake: "You swore to me, you promised me, you promised. You said, 'Don't worry, Robert, no matter what, I will have an abortion. You never have to worry about me getting pregnant. I'll take the pills,

I'll have an abortion, okay, relax, enjoy yourself, I care about you.' And that was all a lie. And not a little lie. That's a big lie. That's the kind of lie that God looks down and says, 'Hey, wait a minute.' . . . That's a big, awful, mean, vicious lie."

In fact, according to Bonny's daughter Holly, Bonny was *trying* to get pregnant. In the criminal trial, the twenty-four-year-old Holly was cross-examined by Blake's attorney and acknowledged her mom had asked her for help with a fertilization monitor. "She was trying to find out her most fertile day," said Holly. "Your mother was *trying* to get pregnant?" the defense attorney demanded. *"Obviously,"* said Holly.

Holly also testified to Blake's rage, saying that after learning of the pregnancy, he would call her mother and she would pick up the phone to hear Blake "yelling, cursing obscenities" when he thought Bonny was on the line. In the civil trial Holly testified that "sometimes I would answer the phone, and he wouldn't know it was me . . . he'd say, 'Don't fuck with me, you bitch. You don't know who you're fucking with. I'll kill you.' I would say, This isn't Bonny, it's Holly, and he'd say, 'Put your fucking mother on the phone.' "

The drama was in full swing by this time,

and the drama addict was on a dry drunk. Here's a man who has it made, and yet he allowed this dangerous woman into his life and relied on her assurances that she would not get pregnant. You have to ask yourself, Why? Why would he do something so terribly self-destructive? Could it be that his need for excitement overwhelmed his better judgment?

How many of us do the same thing, on a smaller scale? We're bored. Nothing seems to be happening in our lives, so we pick a fight with someone or become obsessed with an insignificant issue that suddenly seems monumental. Often the best course of action in life is no action at all. But sometimes doing nothing is the hardest thing to do. And if you don't have drugs or alcohol to keep you distracted, you can go stir crazy. Sober Blake may not have been aware that his addiction had jumped from substances to situations.

Sadly, this pattern had been going on a long time. Robert Blake had a history of histrionic behavior in relationships. In a deposition taken for Blake's civil wrongful-death trial, his former wife, actress Sondra Kerr, made some shocking claims. The mother of Blake's two adult children, Delinah and Noah, Sondra was married to Blake for more than two decades.

According to Court TV's reports on the deposition, Kerr described her husband as an angry, controlling liar. "He said that I was a lesbian," Kerr is quoted as saying. "He told the children that I abused them sexually, told them that I was a drug addict." Kerr said Blake could get quite violent. She claimed that once "he grabbed me, got on top of me," and started "slugging me" with his fists. But her most startling quote concerned an alleged plot to have her killed after they separated and she began dating. "He had put a contract out on me and the other man I was seeing at the time. . . . He said to kill me," she testified. She added a telling comment: "He always used to say, 'If you ever leave me, I'll have to kill you.' . . . I'm embarrassed to say that I thought it was passionate."

I think a lot of people confuse emotional volatility with passion. Intimate passion, ideally, is about loving feelings you have toward your intimate sex partner. When that magic is gone, people often try to drum up passion in unhealthy ways. Arguments, threats, accusations, and generally dramatic behavior may feel, for a second, like passion. But they're fool's gold.

A lot of couples do the same thing with

intimacy. They've lost that special connection of intimacy in sex. So they try to get a spark going in other ways, through bickering or other sick interactions. It's a poor man's intimacy.

I mention this because, while Blake is an extreme example of a drama/passion addict, we all do this to a certain degree, and we all put up with it. We need to remember that we always have other options. No matter what your partner is doing, you don't have to play. Sondra Kerr said she confused Blake's threats with passion. But it would appear she didn't get that clarity until a long time after they had parted ways. What would her life have been like had she refused to participate at the time? It actually took me a long time to understand this very simple life concept: I do not have to interact with anybody who puts me down, makes me feel bad about myself, or makes me feel uncomfortable. Ever.

But back to Bonny.

BACKUP PLAN

The pregnant Bonny was trying to quell Blake's anger, but she was also working another angle. Enter Christian Brando, the handsome but troubled son of actor Marlon Brando. Bonny's daughter testified that her mom was carrying on an affair with Christian Brando at the same time she was seeing Blake. One would play the role of her leading man, the other would be the understudy in case the first actor walked out.

There is a famous phone conversation in which Bonny is trying to decide who to go with. She asks a friend, "Who would you go for? Blake or Christian? I'd probably feel more safe with Blake." The friend responds, "Blake ain't gonna let you hustle him. . . . Blake's too slick."

Bonny probably considered Blake the safer choice, because Christian Brando had already killed a man. An inebriated Christian had gunned down his half-sister's boyfriend after she'd complained to Christian about him. Christian pleaded guilty to voluntary manslaughter and did several years in prison. A probation officer had recommended a lenient sentence, saying Christian suffered from "chemical-induced brain damage and a lack of self-esteem," according to a report in *The New York Times.*

But even Christian seemed fed up with Bonny's scamming ways and told her so in a phone conversation, warning her she was lucky someone didn't put a bullet through her head. With Blake ignoring her, Bonny named her baby Christian Shannon Brando.

While Christian reportedly seemed open to the idea of being a father, Bonny didn't give up on Blake.

One fascinating letter, purportedly from Bonny to Blake, goes like this: "Hi! Why did you disconnect your phone numbers? . . . You were wrong when you said I did this for publicity. . . . I thought it was safe to let myself fall for you, I wish now I would have paid more attention to your career throughout the years. Maybe I would have seen some warning signals. The only two things that stick in my mind are the movie where you played an Indian. I recall saying to my Grandmother, 'this Indian actor is much better looking than Redford.' She told me that's Robert Blake he's not an Indian he's Italian. I said, 'why then doesn't he have an Italian name?' 'He must have changed it,' she said. I asked her why didn't he change it to something Italian then? Years later we were watching you on Carson and she said, you ought to go after him, he's more down to earth than that conceded [sic] snub [sic] Frankie Valli you're chasing after. . . . I remembered this the night I met you and finally took her advice for your sake I wish I could have gone for the abortion. However, I was so in love I couldn't imagine not having it. You are everything I had always

400

wanted to be. When I realized how difficult it was, I decided it was more gratifying to only allow myself to fall for those who had already accomplished what I was too lazy to continue to seek for myself. When I am with someone of your caliber it feels a thousand times better than with a commoner. But the down side of course is when it does not work out it is also a thousand times worse. Well I guess I'm due any day now. Its suppose [*sic*] to be a girl so I guess I screwed that up too. . . . What I don't understand is why didn't you simply say you had met someone else and never wanted to see me again? That would have made me want to get rid of it a lot faster than the cancer story I'm pretty sure you made up. But then I guess you didn't know that about me. Another thing I guess you didn't know is that I'm really foolish when I'm in love and I would have been content to have just gone on seeing you once in a while, that's all. You never would have had any contact with the baby and I would have been glad to support it, because I would have been in a much happier state of mind knowing I could look forward to being with you again. . . . Even if you hate me it's not the baby's fault I wanted you too much, it still needs you. Why don't you talk to me? Love, Me and the baby."

And that's the condensed version! Forensic criminologist Judith Sgarzi says, "The borderline personality can be seen in some ways like the stalker, who turns and decides when you reject them you really do love them, and if they just keep trying and gnawing away and following you and sending you letters that you'll see the error of your ways." Bonny also came after Blake with lawyers.

BABY-NAPPING?

Attorney Cary Goldstein, who has handled many celebrity cases, says Bonny came to him to represent her in her dealings with Robert Blake. "She wanted to marry him and was using the baby to do it," Goldstein told me.

Why didn't Blake pull a Jerry Lee Lewis and just ignore her? The answer is the baby, who suddenly went from being called Christian to Rosie. Said Blake's private eye, Scott Ross, "Robert was old school . . . Italian. You protect your children. Robert looked at Rosie and instantly fell in love. That was his daughter and nobody was going to get near her." Ross sums it up this way: "Robert agreed to marry her for the sole purpose of having her move into, not his house, but the compound. He wanted Rosie. Rosie is the absolute focus."

All this time, Bonny was on probation for her Arkansas conviction, which meant she wasn't supposed to travel to Los Angeles. Still, Bonny showed up, new baby in tow. This is where accounts differ. Bakley family attorney Eric Dubin claims what happened next was actually a child kidnapping. "Blake convinced Bonny to bring the baby out and hired a lady to act like a nanny . . . so Bonny would leave the baby and they could have lunch." He maintains Blake set Bonny up by then having someone approach her under the guise of authority and warn her she was violating her probation by being in Los Angeles. "Blake said, Go, go, go, don't get in any trouble, Rosie's fine . . . and Bonny was in such a panic because she was in violation being out here." So, fearful of going to jail, she fled back home without the baby, who was now in Blake's control. It would seem the schemer had been out-schemed. Later, said Dubin, Bonny filed a kidnapping report with police, which was "dropped in exchange for them to marry, and that's why they married. It's like the true American love story," he said with a chuckle.

Scott Ross calls the kidnapping theory

idiotic. "The reality is, you cannot kidnap a child if there is no custody issue. . . . He is the father, which is why there were no charges filed in this alleged child stealing or child kidnapping."

Ross insists Blake married Bonny because, even though he knew he could win full custody, he feared that she would get visitation rights and he could lose the child during holidays.

Cary Goldstein says Blake's team rammed a prenup down Bonny's throat that was so lopsided he urged her not to sign it. "It was a setup. If she didn't dance to his tune very specifically, it was like she could lose the baby, she'd have to move out. Forget money. She'd never see a dime. . . . It was definitely part of a plan to capture the child." But, says Goldstein, Bonny ignored his advice and signed it anyway, thrilled to be on the verge of becoming Mrs. Robert Blake, Hollywood celebrity wife.

Some Marriage

But Blake had other surprises in store. He insisted on what's called a "confidential marriage." This is a special certificate that basically keeps the marriage out of the public records. And then there was his name. "I specifically remember that she was upset that he was marrying her under the name Michael Gubitosi. She wanted to be married to Robert Blake. She wanted to be married to a celebrity, and that was troubling her greatly," said Goldstein.

Her attorney also claimed that Bonny had begun fearing for her life after she, Blake, and his Hulk-sized handyman took a trip to the desert and she sensed danger over her shoulder. "She told me, If anything happens to me, if I'm killed, Blake did it. I think he's trying to kill me."

Bonny taped many of her phone conversations. Prosecutors obtained one conversation, which may or may not have been recorded by her, in which Bonny referred to her fears:

Bonny: You're not planning on having somebody shoot out my tires or something, are you?
Robert: Shoot out your fuckin' — oh, Jesus Christ . . . What the fuck is it gonna take? You know, I signed a marriage contract, I fuckin' married you. You're movin' out here and you still think I'm gonna shoot out your tires.
Bonny: Ha, ha.
Robert: You may have a lot of enemies in the world. You know, you've been at —

what — what you've been doing, you've been doing a long time. And I'm sure there's some little old man in Peoria, Illinois, that's saying, you know, "One day I'm gonna find that bitch that didn't send me" whatever the fuck you were supposed to send him —

Bonny: Ha, ha.

Robert: — or whatever, and you're going to walk out your door and some old guy with a cane is gonna hit you.

Bonny: Ha, ha.

Robert: But it ain't me.

What's really bizarre about this conversation is that both parties seem to be aware that it's being taped. Blake appears to be putting on the record that Bonny had lots of enemies, but he's not one of them. Bonny got on record that she was suspicious of Blake, but was careful not to admit anything about her mail-order scam. The dance is in full swing. This kind of espionage in relationships is not as unusual as it might seem. These days, taping someone on the phone is a breeze and a lot of people do it, even though laws vary from state to state on the legality of taping someone without their knowledge and permission.

People also have e-mail conversations with

an eye toward how they might be quoted. We live in a world where, between security cameras, phones, Internet time stamps, and computerized receipts, we are creating a record of our every move, just in case we might need it. It's made many people hyperconscious of their own behavior and alert to ways they can use this technology to their advantage, to paint themselves in a good light and someone else in a bad light.

BLAKE'S TOUGHEST ROLE

It was a Friday night in May 2001 when Blake and Bonny went out for a leisurely dinner at Vitello's, one of his favorite restaurants. They had been married for about six months, but she had been living in the house in the back of his compound for only a very short time. According to the book *Blood Cold* by McDougal and Murphy, the newlyweds were already arguing over money and Bonny's access to her daughter Rosie, who was being raised by Blake's grown daughter, Delinah. Bonny was sure her line was being tapped, and just days before the murder she discussed with a friend a "step-by-step scheme to retrieve Rosie and return her to Memphis," according to the book. Bonny never got a chance to put that scheme into action. Before long, she was dead.

It was almost a year later that Blake was arrested and charged with Bonny's murder. At a news conference, police stated bluntly, "We believe the motive is Robert Blake had contempt for Bonny Bakley. He felt he was trapped in a marriage he wanted no part of." Blake was also charged with solicitation of murder. Blake was accused of asking others to kill Bonny. Prosecutors said Blake suggested to prospective hit men that the murder could take place outside Vitello's Restaurant.

In the criminal case, two stuntmen were to be the prosecution's star witnesses. Both said Blake had tried to get them to kill Bonny. But in the trial, the credibility of each man fell apart. Both, it seemed, had a history of drug problems and bizarre behavior. Blake's defense team tore them apart. There was testimony that one of them, on a drug binge, thought satellite dishes were tracking his movements and people were tunneling under his house. Said one reporter who sat in the courtroom, "The prosecution made the argument that you're not going to solicit Rhodes scholars to kill your wife. These are going to be shady characters to begin with. However, if there is a history of mental problems associated with drug activity and their memories are a bit foggy, then that calls into question their whole story." Given the paucity of physical evidence, the lack of witnesses, and the inability to connect Blake to the gun that was found in a nearby trash bin, that was enough to create reasonable doubt.

Even as the trial geared up, bizarre behavior was going on outside court, courtesy of Robert Blake himself. Blake borrowed a guitar and performed for the assembled TV news cameras next to a hot dog stand. He sang "Somewhere Over the Rainbow." It was almost as entertaining as the time he sat down with Barbara Walters for a highly promoted TV special. That was back when he was still locked up in what he called a concrete box, awaiting trial. Dressed in jail clothes, he gave a riveting, wide-eyed, command performance, speaking in a voice choking with emotion of his love for his little daughter Rosie and denying killing his wife.

Even though he didn't take the stand in his trial, the tape of his impassioned interview was played in court, affording him the best of both worlds. He told his side without being subjected to cross-examination. In his first live interview after he was found not guilty, he told Barbara Walters, "You saved my life."

Bonny's daughter Holly was said to be devastated by the verdict. Another source of hurt for Bonny's family? Rosie was later adopted by Blake's daughter Delinah.

STARS IN THEIR EYES

Bonny's lawyer, Eric Dubin, told me it's time society realized celebrity trials are not normal cases: "Forget the guise of trying to treat them like every other case and recognize that the burden of proof is going to be higher," because "to the everyday person," Robert Blake feels like "an old friend." I agree with Dubin that when it comes to the big crimes like murder or child molestation, jurors have a hard time convicting a celebrity. For lying to investigators in a stock scandal, Martha Stewart got jail. For probation violations stemming from drug abuse, Robert Downey, Jr., did time. But they both did relatively brief stints in the clinker, and still got star treatment along the way. Examples of Hollywood stars doing anything approaching life in prison are virtually impossible to come by.

I saw it myself in the Michael Jackson case. The jurors got stars in their eyes. But can I really blame them? I was surprised at my own reaction when Michael once complimented my smile. When Michael walked by, even hardened reporters would perk up if they made eye contact with him. Inside the court, the bailiff seemed tickled when Michael would ask her for candy before the jurors walked in. Stars have a charisma that can be hypnotic. That's why they're stars.

Jurors, like all human beings, are driven by their unconscious, which seeks power and glory. In their unconscious, if they side with the celebrity, it's kind of like being their friend. So in a way, they become part of the celebrity world by association. In their unconscious, it makes them feel like a star, too. Encouraging all this is the fact that jurors in a high-profile case are treated like celebrities themselves, shielded from the media and whisked in and out of court. The enchanting VIP sensation wears off after the trial ends and the celebrity waltzes out of their lives. I believe that is why — in the Jackson case — several jurors woke from their trance after the trial ended and told the media they actually thought he was guilty, although they voted otherwise.

The final factor, which cannot be underestimated, is the quality of legal representation that stars attract. It's not just the money. The defense lawyer who lands one of these big-celebrity cases becomes an instant media star. That attorney, often part of a "dream team" of high-profile lawyers, criminologists, and private investigators, is going to do everything to win. A high-profile case can be a career maker or a career ender. So they leave no stone unturned. It becomes a war. Often, the government-salaried prosecutors simply can't compete with the sheer zeal displayed by the defense team.

This brings up the issue of reasonable doubt. This is where I see these brilliant lawyers working their magic most. In the end, you can have reasonable doubt about anything. Will the sun come up tomorrow? It depends. I might not be here, so how can I say for sure? It's that kind of thinking that these defense attorneys cultivate during the course of the trial, brainwashing jurors into viewing every outlandish alternative theory as equaling reasonable doubt about the prosecution's version of events. They turn the concept into something it was never meant to be, essentially insisting jurors throw their common sense out the window. As someone once joked about the O. J. Simpson case, if he did it, where's the videotape of the murders? This dovetails naturally with what's called the *CSI* effect, the desire for clear-cut evidence that is 100 percent infallible. It's just not going to happen in most cases.

But celebrities can get nailed in the civil case that often follows a criminal trial. Exhibit A: O. J. Simpson, acquitted of killing his ex-wife, Nicole, and her friend Ron Goldman in the criminal trial, but found liable in the civil wrongful-death case. In civil trials, there is a lower burden of proof, namely *preponderance of the evidence* as opposed to *beyond a reasonable doubt.* Also, in a civil case, you can force the defendant to take the stand, which you cannot do in a criminal case.

And Bakley family attorney Eric Dubin, avoiding the potholes of the criminal trial, snatched a significant victory in the civil case. He forced Blake to take the stand for seven extraordinary days of testimony. He said he decided to do it after Blake lunged at him in the courthouse. Dubin said, "We had some words and he kind of charged to fight me. It was broken up before he could get to me. . . . At that point I realized I had him at an easier point to push buttons. When I say push buttons, I mean I needed to show the real Blake. . . . He has a horrific temper," and Dubin was determined the jury would get to see it. They did.

Dubin says Robert Blake was so mad

about being forced onto the witness stand, the actor threatened him. "It was something like, You better watch out, Junior. . . . I stood up and told him he better bring his gun again. In fact, the judge called it a bad B movie at one point."

In the end, with a lower burden of proof, the civil jury found Robert Blake liable for Bonny Lee Bakley's wrongful death, awarding her four children $30 million in damages. Dubin called it "a monumental victory." He said it was all worth it to see the reaction of Bonny's daughter Holly: "Honestly, I don't ever think I've seen somebody's psyche or self-worth or inner happiness inflate like Holly's did. It was unbelievable. It had nothing to do with the money, because the kids never expected to win and to this day have never asked me once anything about, When are we getting the money?"

And it's a good thing too. Robert Blake filed for bankruptcy protection. He says he's broke and has begun working as a ranch hand in Malibu.

WATER FINDS ITS OWN LEVEL

Dr. Judy Kuriansky makes an obvious but important point about the celebrities Bonny was able to get close to. "The three celebrities she hooked up with were three highly disturbed men: Robert Blake, with his own tortured mind; Jerry Lee Lewis, who married a thirteen-year-old; . . . and Christian Brando. I mean, these are not milquetoast!" Indeed, it could be argued that Bonny wouldn't get a word with most stars before being escorted away and warned to stay away. That she was able to get close to these three celebs says more about them than anything else. But once they exhibited the bad judgment of stepping into Bonny's world, they found it very hard to get out.

BLAME THE VICTIM?

Some would call Bonny's murder a *victim-precipitated homicide,* arguing that her behavior gave not just Blake but many other men motives for killing her. People are very wary of this concept because nobody wants to be accused of "blaming the victim." For one thing, it upsets the victim's relatives. Eric Dubin, the lawyer who fought in court for Bonny's children, told me, "The concept that she deserved to die or put herself at a high risk to be killed . . . is a bit off." He says the moral of this story is simply, "Thou shall not kill." Period. "Because you really hate someone, or because they are really inconvenient, or because they've really done you wrong, you can divorce, you can sue, you can hate, you can bad-mouth, but you can't blow somebody's head off. You just can't."

But *Victimology* co-author Dr. Sgarzi told me, "When it's a borderline it doesn't matter if you move or divorce or change your address, it's a never-ending story for most of them." While she agrees that the moral solution is never murder, she is simply saying that sometimes a victim's behavior can be a factor in provoking violent reactions against them. To pretend otherwise is to simply be in denial.

I asked Dr. Sgarzi, If borderlines are unstoppable, how do you protect yourself from one? "The only way you can protect yourself from a borderline is to keep your borders and set limits. And if you want to know if you're dealing with a true borderline, set limits. . . . Say, You can't do this and you can't do that. If they freak and they go berserk, that's when you know you have a borderline." And she warns never to give in on the limits you've set, because if the borderline thinks they can push you, "they'll take 175 percent."

In the end, it would seem that borderlines are untreatable by medication and can only, in the best-case scenario, learn to control their manipulative impulses. Sadly, they often have unfulfilled lives packed with disappointment, and even tragedy. Says the doctor, "What I see is that the only border-lines that people put up with are family members, because they have to." In fact, says the doctor, when a borderline is brought in for treatment, "I want to get under my desk." If you ever see one coming, crawl under yours.

10
TEENACIDE

In a deeply religious community in the heart of Pennsylvania Dutch country, some folks had been preparing for the end of the world. Instead, they got a different kind of apocalypse — a double murder.

Even as the victims were buried, secrets were unearthed that shed light on some of the dark forces that spawned this crime. Inside one extremely pious home, a teenager named David Ludwig cultivated a love affair with guns and an obsession with sex. David was allegedly having a secret sexual relationship with a fourteen-year-old girl. When her mother and father found out, they forbade him to date her. So, using one of the pistols from his family's arsenal, David gunned the parents down.

David Ludwig's decision to kill his young girlfriend's mother and father will haunt him forever. Having pleaded guilty, he will now spend the rest of his life in prison. He has *no* chance of parole, except for the highly unlikely possibility of a commutation by the governor. Imagine a nineteen-year-old coming to terms with that stark reality. David destroyed his own future and devastated his family. He will also forever live with the fact that he violently robbed five children of their parents.

David was well known for his work ethic, his natural leadership abilities, and his entrepreneurial spirit. In prison, he has reportedly been tutoring his fellow inmates. You have to wonder what led this handsome, promising young man to deliberately choose a murderous course of action on November 13, 2005? How did he arrive at this monumental miscalculation? Was he in some way unwittingly groomed to make extreme choices by growing up in a household overflowing with weapons? Or did David simply have a biologically based mental problem? Or was it both?

David's attorney, Merrill Spahn, describes his client as a "very troubled young man." The lawyer told me the teen has serious psychological problems, although they didn't rise to the level of insanity as any kind of legal defense against murder. Out of respect for David's privacy, the attorney wouldn't reveal his psychiatric diagnosis.

Spahn added that, while he refuses to judge or criticize David's family, the teen's "environment" was one of a multitude of factors leading to the crime.

David's deeply religious father not only collected dozens of weapons, he reportedly made meticulous plans to help his family survive in the event of a world upheaval, an apocalypse as prophesized in the Book of Revelations in the Bible. Revelations speaks of death, famine, and plagues, but also of the rewarding of the faithful. According to their church pastor at the time, David's father worried that world chaos might erupt as a result of Y2K problems at the turn of the millennium. In his own way, David's father was obviously trying hard to protect his family. But did any of this doomsday thinking unconsciously inspire David's plan on that fateful Sunday when he brought guns to his girlfriend's home for a cataclysmic confrontation?

In a statement released just days after the killings, David's distraught parents expressed their profound sorrow and shock. While asking for privacy and insisting they had "no interest in discussion" with the media, they acknowledged that the murders have "challenged everything about us." It's a challenge that must be faced in order to avoid similar horrors in our own lives.

Decide for yourself if this disaster was based on a family recipe whose main ingredients were religious obsession and gunplay, to which David then added his own teenage angst. No one can dispute that it was a very messy dish.

On November 14, 2005, David Ludwig, then eighteen, slammed his parents' red Volkswagen Jetta into a tree. It was the climactic end to a police chase that wound through Indiana, speeds topping one hundred miles an hour. When the car's airbags finally deployed, David and his fourteen-year-old girlfriend, Kara Borden, had made it nearly six hundred miles from the scene of the crime. They had managed to elude authorities for just over twenty-four hours. Both David and Kara walked away from the crash, Kara crying hysterically. She had every reason to cry.

When cops searched the car, they found a cache of several guns and ammo. They also found an ominous-looking outfit, complete with gloves, a hood, a stocking cap, and a stocking mask, all in black. Back east, in their hometown of Lititz, Pennsylvania, the girl's parents lay dead, each with a single gunshot to the head.

A friend told authorities David and Kara

were "involved in an ongoing secret intimate relationship of a sexual nature." Their secret got out. Her parents ordered the relationship terminated. Blood spilled.

BLOODY SUNDAY

Saturday night, November 12, 2005, Kara Borden reportedly stayed out all night. Police say she had told her parents she was at a sleepover. But when she returned early that morning, her mom and dad weren't buying their daughter's story. Convinced that their underage daughter had spent the night with David Ludwig, they demanded that David report to their house for a come-to-Jesus talk. It would certainly be that.

According to the prosecutors, before David came over, he asked Kara if her father had a gun and she said no. Prosecutors add that Kara's dad knew David had a history with guns and was concerned. But apparently not concerned enough to call the cops.

When David arrived at the Bordens' ranch-style home, he was prepared for battle. Dressed all in black, he reportedly carried a duffel bag that contained several weapons. Kara's dad is said to have told David to leave the bag outside, apparently unaware that David had also tucked a gun into his pants. Inside the home, they had a heated conversation that lasted about forty-five minutes. According to Kara's fifteen-year-old sister, Katelyn, her parents didn't want David and Kara dating anymore. Kara's dad ordered David to stop seeing his underaged daughter. This apparently was unacceptable to David, who, by all accounts, was quite smitten with Kara. For this young man, the idea of not ever being able to be with Kara again must have felt like the world was ending.

There is a theory that one can sometimes attract what one fears. Imagine growing up in a home literally planning and preparing for world chaos. This would naturally create in a child an *expectation* that calamity was bound to enter his life. In David's impressionable young mind, epic violence may well have seemed predestined and inevitable. The only question was when.

Katelyn told the cops she saw her father leading David to the front door to leave when all hell broke loose. After his capture, David allegedly confessed to detectives about what happened next: "Ludwig explained to Detective Geesey that he 'drew the pistol and shot her dad in the back as he was going down the hallway to the front door.' " The prosecution documents quote David as saying he then returned to the living room: " 'I shot Kara's mom as she was sitting in the chair. . . . It was an intentional murder, I intended to shoot them, and I did.' " Both victims were shot at close range. They were both fifty years old.

Katelyn says she raced to the bathroom, locked the door, and hid, while she heard Ludwig calling out for Kara. Then silence. Cops were called and surrounded the house. After a couple of hours, they realized David and Kara were long gone.

ALONG FOR THE RIDE

At first, police assumed Kara was a kidnapping victim and issued an AMBER Alert for her. After their arrest came the stunning news that Kara had left voluntarily with the young man who had just slaughtered her mom and dad. Police say that revelation came as David confessed to the murders. Although David initially pleaded not guilty, police say he told them everything, even confirming that the murder weapon was the handgun found under the driver's seat of his parents' mangled car. Also in that car were a .45-caliber pistol and a mini rifle.

Detectives say Ludwig told them that after killing the Bordens, he couldn't find Kara. So he got into his car to look for her. "After traveling approximately fifteen feet, the defendant saw Kara running down the road toward him. Ludwig then opened the door, and Kara got into the car. Kara told the defendant she wanted to stay with him, and they drove west with the intent to 'get as far away as possible, get married, and start a new life.' " Police say Kara also "acknowledged going with him 'of her own free will.' "

Kara has not been charged with any crime. Still, the girl got a lawyer. Attorney Robert Beyer told me his client is yet another victim. He said her behavior immediately after the shootings has to be put in context: "She was in absolute shock for days, if not weeks. This was *not* something she knew was going to happen or had any idea would happen, and she kind of reacted, as opposed to acted, at the time." Some experts in adolescent behavior theorize Kara was under David's sway at this point. Waving down the alleged killer to get into his car might have been some expression of loyalty. As we shall see, there are some indications that David may have thought of himself as a budding religious leader. Some bloggers claim he had plans to start his own quasi church in a barn, reportedly with the encouragement of his dad.

"A lot of times older males, eighteen or

nineteen, will find a girlfriend who is younger than them because they know they will do whatever they ask them to. It's easy to take advantage of them," says William Lassiter, manager of the Center for the Prevention of School Violence, a think tank on youth violence based in North Carolina. It can also be a sign of insecurity on the young man's part. "They will go find somebody who is younger than them" because they know the girl is inexperienced and will be more likely to buy their act.

Teenage Bloggers

As David's conservative dad was reportedly using his military skills to fortify his home in the event of a world meltdown, his son was entering dangerous territory in a virtual world. This child of traditionalists was digging a high-tech tunnel to freedom of expression. But it was a cyber rebellion that couldn't be seen from the sidewalks of the old-fashioned little town.

Lititz is a leafy, picturesque village in the heart of Amish country, about an hour and a half's drive west of Philadelphia. A deeply religious community, Lititz has forty-five churches for a population hovering at about ten thousand. The area is a bastion of political conservatism. Because of the Amish presence, with their horse-drawn carriages and antiquated dress, the whole region seems deeply rooted in yesteryear. Except for the teenagers.

Kara Borden and David Ludwig were two popular teens in the community. Both were being homeschooled and reportedly met through a Christian homeschooling network back in May 2005.

With blond highlights in her brown hair, a petite body, pretty features, and a bubbly nature, Kara Borden was a particularly cute fourteen-year-old. She babysat for neighborhood children and played soccer. David Ludwig, too, on the surface, seemed a perfectly ordinary teenager. His homeschooling didn't seem to keep him from being a part of the larger community, although he often had his dad in tow. He played trumpet in the Lititz Community Band with his father, who played tenor saxophone. David was also a lifeguard at the local recreation center and reportedly held a job at a nearby electronics store.

Both David and Kara were raised in an extremely religious environment, but they didn't seem to be rebelling against that. David often signed off, "God Bless." Kara's profile on the popular teen blogsite Xanga read: "i love the lord . . . i go to church . . . i love all my friends! YOU GUYS ARE SOO AWESOME!" Under INTERESTS, she wrote: "JESUS!! Church, my youth group."

Still, when it comes to determining the essential ingredients for this recipe for disaster, we need to look at what Kara added to the mix. She seemed to have a little something going on in the flirtation department. There's one photo of her wearing sunglasses on the end of her nose and a cap turned sideways, making a *V* sign with her fingers. She's pouty and sexy. I would call the photo "very Britney," as in Spears. This is not to attack her. At five foot one and hovering at around a hundred pounds, she is what the boys would call "hot." It was just her. I doubt she could have turned off the special sparkle that turns boys on.

Still, according to MSNBC.com, Kara lied about her age on one of her Web pages, listing herself as seventeen and naming "partying" as one of her interests. One neighbor said Kara's mother had expressed concern about her interest in boys in general and David in particular. "At one point, they had cut off her Internet service because of her connection with David," the neighbor told the Associated Press. But the effort was futile.

Teenagers just have too many ways to

communicate with one another. They can send text messages on cell phones. They can have private e-mail accounts that can be accessed through anyone's computer via the Internet. Ditto for instant messaging and websites like Xanga and MySpace. "Most parents I know have learned how to use e-mail and the Internet and Google, but how many of them know anything about text messaging? How many know about Xanga and blogs or anything like that?" asks Mike Shelley, the pastor at the Lititz Christian Church, which the Ludwig family had attended. "I think the children are much more savvy than the parents . . . and so I think it's a great challenge to parenting."

But many parents appear too rigid to even attempt to explore the latest networking sites to see what's really going on out there. The popular crime-blogging grandma who goes by the username OptyMyst calls that intellectual laziness. She's learned how to navigate deep into the maze of Internet networking and concludes that if she can master it, so can any other parent or grandparent. What this cyber-sleuth says she learned about David Ludwig is fascinating.

David's MySpace photo is of a good-looking young man, but one who seems somewhat confrontational. He is leaning into the camera, unsmiling, with messy hair. Typical teen-boy cool. Among his Xanga interests were "pulling stupid pranks, having soft air gun wars, and various other things." Prosecutors contend that high among David's "various other" interests was having sex with Kara.

A lot of nonevangelicals have a skewed view of Christian kids as nerdy Goody Two-shoes who never feel the need for fun and who just read the Bible and pray all day. Nothing could be further from the truth. Sex is an overriding issue for *all* adolescents, including Christian teens. This fascination comes from universal biological urges that overwhelm any and all ideological or religious boundaries. Intellectual concepts, even religious ones, are hardly a match for raging hormones. Simply telling these teens to rely on faith and exert the willpower to remain abstinent is an ineffective strategy that can lead to tragedy.

There is evidence that David was struggling in his own way to integrate his sexual feelings into his faith-based life. He was reportedly trying to create something half-way between a church and a nightclub. This is a perfect example of how teenagers, whose thoughts often lean toward fantasy, can come up with inappropriate solutions.

On David's MySpace website, his friends, including Kara, posted typically goofy teen photos. At first glance, there didn't seem to be anything ominous about them. But Opty-Myst says she mirrored, or copied, David's Xanga site before it was pulled off the Internet. She then hosted some of his pages on her own site for everyone to read. They reveal David purportedly had big plans to create something called the Barn. In the summer of 2005, a few months before the murders, David and a friend reportedly felt inspired to clean up the upstairs of the family's barn. In his blog, David promised a place "we could come to after our Monday night and Friday night youth meetings . . . to worship and diligently seek God's face." One posting jokingly asked if the Barn was "The Ludwig Loft?" In another posting, someone suggested they build a bar. Opty-Myst says some of David's friends claimed the Barn was also a place to make out, adding, "I think David used God as a way to get young girls."

If such a barn in fact existed, the idea that teens would be partying there wouldn't be shocking in the slightest. Like anyone their age, evangelical teens have a desire to be "cool." For example, both Kara and David were said to be into Christian hard-core music, which can be very similar to regular hard rock. We've all had the experience, while driving, of tuning into what sounds like a typical rock station, only to eventually figure out that it's Christian programming. You're rocking to the beat and suddenly the word "Christ" pops up. It can cause the nonfaithful to temporarily lose control of their vehicle as they desperately lunge for the tuning knob.

On the day of the killings, Kara was reportedly wearing a sweatshirt with the name PILLAR on it. That popular Christian rock band has an "underground army" devoted to spreading the group's message. To join that army, you must fill out an "enlistment form." The group once embarked on "the Warriors Tour." Their site described a recent album's theme as dealing with "being pulled at from different directions and the people who always tell you who to be and what to do." The militaristic imagery combined with religious overtones could be a combustible combination for defiant Christian teenagers grappling with all the coming-of-age issues that adolescence brings. For David, it might not have been such a leap to show up like a mighty warrior at his girlfriend's house. After all, they were already living dangerously.

Friends told police that David and Kara often traded flirtatious messages and inappropriate images of each other electronically. Police say they found pictures on Ludwig's computer of fourteen-year-old Kara in various stages of undress. Kara allegedly took seminude photos of herself and then messaged them to David, via cell phone or e-mail. Again, while this may seem totally out of character for homeschooled Christian kids from ultraconservative households, the fact is that teenagers are teenagers and will always be attracted to the forbidden.

But would inexperienced young Kara have come up with the idea of stripping for the camera on her own? Doubtful. This was surely a sign that she was under the spell of her older boyfriend, who must have seemed quite worldly. Also, in this evangelical culture, the females are conditioned to do what the men in their lives dictate, and this is an example of how that chauvinism can backfire.

It appears David grew up in a home where challenging males was verboten. Brett Lovelace, a crime reporter for the *Lancaster Intelligencer,* says the Ludwigs belonged to a very male-dominated religious community: "Women have the diminished role of the passive. The males are in control and set the tone and agenda for the females." Naturally, if David were trying to follow that example and set the tone for the female he was dating, it would be easier to do so with a younger girl, who would be less likely to challenge him. These choices are not random or by chance. They have everything to do with the culture inside the home. But why did Kara, described by neighbors as a well-behaved and likeable teen, bite?

KILLER BOREDOM

This tragedy also puts the spotlight on another signature of Christian fundamentalism: homeschooling. "How is school and crap?" Kara blogged to a friend, adding "Mine is really boring . . . sigh . . . oh well ttyl [talk to you later]."

It's significant that Kara expressed boredom with her homeschooling, undoubtedly a common problem for older homeschooled kids. Homeschooling is controversial to begin with, inspiring a lot of impassioned debate. A 2003 CBS report called "A Dark

Side of Homeschooling" profiled the horror stories of some homeschooled children who were neglected and abused. The report sparked an uproar, with homeschooling advocates calling it a smear job. Proponents of homeschooling can be extremely passionate, insisting that homeschooled kids often do better on standardized tests and excel in their adult careers.

Dr. Phil has even weighed in. He concluded that properly run homeschooling that includes a lot of extracurricular activities can be wonderful for younger kids. But, Dr. Phil added, it can hinder social development in teen years: "Once kids get to high school, social development is important. They become more independent. They want to interact on their own. . . . And so they don't do well in a homeschool environment" once they reach those high school years.

Dr. Phil's comments raised the ire of homeschooling advocates, but I think he's right. I can very easily see how homeschooling could become suffocating for a teenager. Teenagers' whole reason for living, at this stage of their development, is to separate from their parents and form their own identity and belief system. In a lot of ways, they learn who they are by learning how they differ from their parents. That's why teens are so notoriously argumentative with their parents. That crucial separation is hard to accomplish when you're living and breathing in your parents' shadow and under their thumb 24/7/365.

"A lot of focus on education today is on testing, and the reality of it is, going to school is an education in itself, just by socializing kids. And that's one of the greatest lessons kids can get out if it: How do I interact with other people?" says William Lassiter, the youth violence expert.

Kara's lawyer says this tragedy has underscored the futility of trying to shield your kids from the dangers of the world at large, an impulse he says runs particularly deep in the fundamentalist Christian homeschool crowd.

"They think that by homeschooling and by tightening the rope around these kids and making the world small, they've got the control," says attorney Robert Beyer, when in reality there are many ways to slip the parental noose.

Pure Insanity

Even the most well-meaning parents can live in ignorance and denial of who their children really are and how they *really* behave. This is a morality tale about the dangers of trying to control your kids too much and how that parental urge to control can boomerang. Many parents idealize their kids' behavior and sanitize their sexual development. They often have a very difficult time watching their children grow up and develop into sexual beings. The parents can develop a blind spot, unable to see the evidence of their kid's budding sexuality, even when it's right before their eyes. You could call it the "my dog doesn't have fleas" syndrome. A parent convinces himself that his little girl is not having *those* thoughts. But of course when she hits puberty, she does!!

To give you an idea of how upset Mike Borden must have been over the idea of his fourteen-year-old daughter having sex, *People* magazine quotes a minister as saying Mike gave his older daughter, Katelyn, a "diamond ring to symbolize that 'he would do everything within his ability to help her stay pure until she was married.'" *Pure!* Quite a word. So to have sex outside of marriage is to be impure. To have sex when you're fourteen is to be very impure.

I'm not condoning underage sex. Fourteen is too young, in my opinion. Besides, it's against the law. But framing virginity in the context of purity is medieval. We don't become impure — dirty — when we have sex, either in or outside of marriage. This is very shame-based thinking. Giving your daughter a diamond ring is also unhealthy from a psychological standpoint. Men give diamonds to women when they're going to marry them and engage in a long-term intimate relationship. That's why diamonds have a proprietary sexual overtone. Remember, diamonds "are forever." It's inappropriate for a father to give a daughter a diamond ring in exchange for chastity. The unconscious message is, You belong to me, not any other man. It's overcontrolling and betrays a role confusion. Dad is not a suitor. This is not to suggest there was anything untoward going on sexually between Kara and her father. No one has suggested that!

To me, it's just another symptom of the patriarchal evangelical Christian ideology, in which the father's role as head of the household is magnified so out of proportion that he has all the latitude in the world to be inappropriate. During the funeral service, the reverend who delivered the eulogy alluded to Mike Borden being a "spiritual leader" in his home and "a bit of a perfectionist," although he added that both Mike and his wife were "mighty warriors of prayer." While this all may be said with the best of intentions, it's very dangerous to send a message that Dad is perfect and all-knowing. As these events so tragically proved, he is not all-knowing. Sometimes, Dad doesn't know best and doesn't even have a clue. So, while Dad giving his daughter a diamond ring should be seen in the context of the culture he was living in, it's still weird.

Weirder still was the lifestyle of David's father. When authorities raided the home of the devoutly Christian Ludwigs, they found a cache of fifty-four guns, including three assault rifles and lots of ammo.

Nancy Grace, CNN Headline News, *November 17, 2005*

Nancy Grace: Where were these guns? I want to know! Where is the collapsible mount for the machine gun? Where was that? On the dining room table?

Brett Lovelace, Reporter, *LANCASTER IN-TELLIGENCER:* As they are searching the house, they are coming across all these weapons, just out in plain view. Not in locked cases, not secured in a safe. They are just out there for David or anyone else in the house to come across, take, and leave with.

Later the *Lancaster New Era* reported the weapons were found "in a locked room in the house," meaning they were not all over the place for anyone to grab. Yet authorities have noted search teams saw "in plain view gun cases . . ." In any event, David was able to get his hands on enough firepower to make murderous mayhem. The inventory list collected by the police is mind-boggling: several Ruger minis with scopes, several Remington 870s, a buckhorn rifle with scope. The famous names are all there: Colt, Winchester, Glock, Smith & Wesson, Walther, German Luger, Beretta . . . the list goes on and on, not to mention the considerable ammo. Wasn't this the very home where David Ludwig was being home-schooled? In retrospect, we have a right to ask, What did David learn inside that home? What values was he being taught about violence? Should he have been home-schooled in a weapon-filled environment?

BUNKER MENTALITY

But other, even more astounding secrets would pour out. Soon came the reports of a secret bunker in the basement of the Ludwig home, a bunker David's family had reportedly built for when the apocalypse comes. Brett Lovelace also reported on this stunning development for the *Lancaster Intelligencer* and spoke to me about what he learned: "The Ludwigs were very much fundamentalists . . . they believed that the Y2K, when the millennium changed, that there was going to be this apocalypse, that there would be some sort of world chaos. And they had prepared for that. . . . They had created a bunker under their house . . . where they could all stay for an indefinite amount of time." Lovelace told me that even after the millennium passed without catastrophe, the Ludwigs kept food, including big bags of rice and grain, and bottled water in their bunker.

This could explain the large number of guns. Said Lovelace, "Some of those guns that they were collecting and had kept there may have been to protect them from an attack or from other people who were trying to get at their supplies or their food in the event of a world meltdown." Imagine having a man who was worried about *that* as the spiritual leader of your household. What kind of a teenager might this family produce? David Ludwig?

What's astounding about all this is that David's father doesn't have the typical résumé of an extreme survivalist fundamentalist. He's a pilot for a commercial airline.

The pastor of the church the Ludwigs once attended told me he talked to David's dad about his fears: "Mr. Ludwig did have a lot of concerns in Y2K time. He did discuss it. So I do know that he made several moves at that time in preparation for what he was expecting to be the worst scenario. . . . As for his bunker, well, he has been trained on how to build those things. I believe that's his military training."

Trying to understand the religious survivalist mentality, I asked Pastor Shelley what the views of his church are on the apocalypse. He told me it was an area of great debate: "The only thing they tend to agree on is that there will be a return of Christ to the earth at some point in time. . . . A lot of people believe there will be a great war, that there will be great destruction." Upon the return of Christ? "Most people believe it will happen before that, and that the return of Christ will be necessary to avoid total annihilation. I believe that Jesus did say he would return and I believe he gave us many signs. . . . I don't think he said anything specific enough to make us know exactly the right moment in time. And I think the church has proven over history that we don't know."

Over the centuries many have discussed

and debated the meaning of the Book of Revelation. It seems that every generation wonders if the disasters and crises of its time are indications that the end of the world is near. Many have prepared themselves to be ready when the time comes. The Ludwigs' preparation involved accumulating enough firepower to wipe out an entire village.

The issue up for scrutiny is not really religion, it's violence. How these churches deal with violence is the question. I asked the pastor about that. He told me he didn't make a big point about being nonviolent or antiwar: "We talk a lot about forgiveness. We talk an awful lot about reconciliation. We talk an awful lot about walking in peace with one another." But it would seem that David Ludwig was walking the other way, away from peace, toward his own private war.

NIGHT PATROL

Examining Ludwig's computer equipment, police say they found a sinister eighteen-minute video featuring David and a friend. On the tape the two young men are dressed in dark clothing and handling various firearms and ammunition inside a "secured room within the Ludwig home." They allegedly leave the house with the weapons and drive to another house, where they plan "an armed forcible entry . . . by climbing onto a roof and entering through a dormer window." The affidavit filed in the case goes on to say that Ludwig and his friend "talked about using their weapons to shoot and kill family members inside of the residence."

Although the nighttime home invasion was never carried out because too many cars were passing by, cops say the video then proceeds to capture some disturbing conversation between the two young men. They allegedly talk about continuing their "night patrol" by going to the Borden home. Police say they discuss having sex with Kara and her sister, Katelyn, and note "the sex would constitute statutory rape." They talk about having to "shoot a guy named Jonathan if he found out about it." Who Jonathan is remains a mystery, but the emerging portrait of David Ludwig as a sex-and-violence-obsessed teen shocked a community that had prided itself on raising good Christians. There is no evidence that Kara's sister was in any way involved with these boys, but rather that she was the unwitting subject of their charged fantasies. Detectives believe this was one of several "night patrols" the two boys carried out with home invasion on their minds.

Given the number of guns in David Ludwig's home, no one should be shocked by any of this, says the soft-spoken youth-violence expert William Lassiter: "Kids are going to be curious. They're going to seek out that weapon and feel the power that they get from it." Lassiter says he knows this from studying the boys who've brought guns to school in response to bullying: "The biggest thing about bullying is that there is a power imbalance in place. The bully has more power than you as the victim, and that weapon is a great equalizer."

Bullying doesn't just happen in the schoolyard. In the culture David grew up in, where fathers have all the power, teens can feel bullied by their parents and the fathers of the girls they want to date. When David was summoned to Kara's home to get dressed down by her dad, he brought along "the great equalizer." Had the father not had so much power, perhaps David would not have felt the need for such a monstrous overreaction. When society doesn't allow you to talk back, you might be inclined to shoot back. When communication is warped by inflexible religious dogma, kids are emotionally and intellectually abandoned. Their messy feelings are simply deemed *impure*.

Kara's attorney, Robert Beyer, makes the

point sarcastically: "When you've got a problem and you go to your parents and ask how do I solve this logistical problem, and their answer is to go pray, well, Jesus, thanks for the help." Pastor Shelley counters that prayer and practical advice are not mutually exclusive.

Other critics say the overcontrolling patriarchal structure of the homeschooled Christian fundamentalist world also discourages the intervention of real-world institutions like psychiatry and law enforcement. Says OptyMyst, "The first thing I would do if somebody told me someone is coming over with guns is call the police. But they don't, apparently . . . which is mind-boggling to me." Keeping it in the family of the faithful is part of the insularity that can keep much-needed intervention and objective advice out of the equation. Under these circumstances, there is no opportunity for outside professionals to spot the very warning signs to which family members have become blind.

REPEAT BEHAVIOR

David had at least one other disturbing incident that should have served as a bright red flag. In the spring of 2005, David reportedly took off with another underage girl without getting her parents' permission. Journalist Brett Lovelace told me he broke the story of their trek to the Ludwig family's hunting cabin in a remote area of north-central Pennsylvania. David was armed with guns and lots of cash that he'd allegedly gotten from his family's bank account and was planning some sort of extended stay. But did anyone call the police? Apparently not. "The girl's parents were worried and were coming to the Ludwigs asking for help. They were able to make contact with him and he did come back," said Lovelace. Again, no charges were ever brought. The families worked it out among themselves. "They aren't going to rat out each other, in other words," says OptyMyst, adding "that speaks to the communal aspect" of their religion.

Internet postings in response to the news of an earlier incident didn't mince words. Said one, "Hasn't anyone ever heard of the term 'nipped in the bud'? This guy was sending out all kinds of signals that he was TROUBLE and everyone seems to have chosen to look the other way." Had police and prosecutors gotten involved the first time, David might have gotten the reality check he so obviously needed. Kara's lawyer says the religion's insularity fosters "a real misunderstanding of what the world is like."

Soul Searching?

So has the tragedy sparked any soul searching in this ultraconservative community? Not really, says Kara's attorney. "A lot of these people don't think they ever make any mistakes. They are doing God's work." The pastor of the Lititz Christian Church begs to differ: "We've certainly asked over and over and over and over and over again: How did things get here and why did they come to this place?"

One obvious answer: too many guns! But folks in the area don't seem inclined to rethink their position on guns. Reporter Lovelace says his informal survey of local gun shops showed many families in that county have dozens of guns in their homes and think nothing of it. One gun-shop owner told him that "half the people in this shop right now have more than fifty guns in their possession in their homes." That means what was happening in the Ludwig home was *not* an aberration. People say they're "collectors" or "hunters." This is true across the red states and some blue ones too. Even in famously liberal Massachusetts, Neil Entwistle was accused of borrowing a gun from his stepfather-in-law's "collection" to murder his wife.

Says school violence expert William Lassiter, "I can tell you right here, right now, in the state of North Carolina, no politician is going to win running on gun control. I don't care if they're Republican or Democrat. You are just never going to win on that issue. . . . If anything, we're going the other direction, looking for more ways for people to possess weapons."

One area resident even told me, "I am anti-guns, and when I look back, if I took inventory of the guns I own, I probably have about ten or twelve. I've had a gun since I was twelve." Huh? How can you be antigun and own guns? I'm confused. But that's America for you. We all say we're against senseless violence and yet we're all fascinated with the instruments of violence and tune in nightly to watch people use them to hurt one another. It's like saying we want lower gas prices while we drive around in gas-guzzling SUVs.

There's a lesson here for all parents, religious or not. Kids do not listen to much of what parents say. They are more likely to copy what their parents do. If you don't want your child to resort to violent solutions, then don't embrace violence yourself. Having a home filled with guns is inviting violence into your life. In that sense, David Ludwig is also a victim — of his upbringing.

That Dog Won't Hunt

David Ludwig knew how to use a gun. He often went hunting with his dad. There were photos of him on the Web proudly gutting deer. Along with self-defense, hunting is perhaps the most common justification for gun ownership. Certainly David's hunting experiences helped him become very good at aiming and firing a gun. But by immersing David in this hunting culture, was his family also training him to become comfortable with killing? Hunted animals often die slow, agonizing deaths. Other times they may drop to the ground, instantly killed by a perfectly aimed shot. Either way, a youngster who repeatedly views that process becomes accustomed to the notion of death and dying. It's not that big a leap from a four-legged creature to a two-legged one. Both have eyes and ears. Both bleed. Both feel pain.

In the wake of the boy's arrest, David's lawyer described him as scared, anxious, and confused. Now that he knows his fate is to be a life spent in prison, he may also be depressed and angry. His lawyer tells me that he is struggling to adjust to life behind bars. The attorney added he wouldn't be surprised if David one day decided to tell his whole story in the hope of helping others. The lawyer said there are still secrets in this case that have not come out, but he wouldn't elaborate.

Kara, her sister, Katelyn, and their younger brother, David, are now orphans, being cared for by relatives. The Bordens are also survived by two adult sons, including one who recently returned from serving in Iraq. Kara is said to be haunted by guilt. Imagine how this will impact the rest of her life. Unlike David, she is walking free, having committed no crime herself. But the tragedy of her parents' death at the hands of her boyfriend will undoubtedly be the defining moment of her life and the theme of her life story. If she stays put in her community, she will always be *that* girl. If she leaves to find a new life, she will have to decide if she wants to share this horrific story with her new friends or create yet another secret.

11
ANGELS OF JUSTICE

Sometimes an eleven-year-old girl has to be kidnapped, raped, and asphyxiated for politicians to get it together.

Sometimes a nine-year-old girl has to be abducted, tortured, and buried alive for bureaucrats to take action.

I'm talking about the ghastly sex killings of Carlie Brucia and Jessica Lunsford.

These two Florida girls gave their innocence and their lives, and in the outrage that followed, laws were enacted. Nobody asked them if they wanted to be the sacrificial lambs for legislative change. Their screams went unheard, their tears unnoticed, until finally their small corpses turned up. Only then was there enough clamor to toughen the laws against child predators. Why does horror have to be the opening act in the carnival known as social progress?

It was Super Bowl Sunday of 2004. Eleven-year-old Carlie Brucia was walking home from a friend's house in Sarasota, Florida. It was just after six in the evening. Her life was about to take a hideous turn, through no fault of her own. The sixth grader who loved pizza and her cat, Charlie, had innocently sauntered into a deadly vortex. Powerful forces beyond her control were swirling around her. Little Carlie, all blue eyes and blond hair, was about to become the victim of an unhinged, drug-crazed sexual predator. Joe Smith was a husband and a father of three young girls. But the dark side of this average Joe was about to extinguish a child full of light. He found her at the intersection of self-pity and rage.

At this very moment, the whole world was about to become completely obsessed with Janet Jackson's right breast. This was the very day Miss Jackson "accidentally" exposed her breast, which was adorned with a sizable sun-shaped nipple shield, during her Super Bowl halftime performance with Justin Timberlake. It would go down in history as the "wardrobe malfunction."

I was at home in Los Angeles, getting ready to head out to a satellite TV studio for a live interview on a national cable news show. I seem to remember my subject was Michael Jackson's legal woes, because I recall thinking how omnipresent the Jacksons were, between Michael and his famous sister Janet.

I was actually only half watching the Super Bowl halftime show, ducking in and out of the bathroom where I was putting on my makeup, catching only occasional glimpses of Janet and Justin's performance. They seemed to be doing fine. I missed the breast exposure, which was only on for seconds. By the time I'd wrapped up at the studio, Janet's boob was getting the kind of coverage normally reserved for a terrorist attack. I could hear the story being heavily promoted as I pulled out my earpiece. Everybody was breathless. *Oh my God, did you see it?*

The "good people" of America were having a Super Bowl–sized orgy of self-righteousness. Across the land, the phone lines had lit up. Mothers and fathers were railing against the media powers that allowed such "indecency" to be broadcast across the globe.

But during all this, a real crime was being committed against a helpless child named Carlie. As parents dragged their "traumatized" kids away from their TV sets, Carlie was being dragged into the depths of hell. I was later to wonder why the outrage over Carlie's brutal rape and murder was nowhere near as frenzied as the national apoplexy over Janet's flash of flesh.

Personally, I was disgusted . . . not by Janet's breast, but by the reaction to it. I marveled at the hypocrisy of America's puritanical culture. Since the statistics show porn is pervasive in middle America, wouldn't those porn surfers be from the very same households that went into an uproar over Janet's exposed titty? *Oh, but not in front of the children!*

What's so awful about a woman's breast? I remember the first time I saw a woman sunbathing topless in Europe and I realized nobody was aghast. Kids were playing. Dads were tanning. It was natural. It was beautiful. Why is America so conflicted over sex? If we could just learn to see a woman's body as a beautiful gift of nature, as opposed to an object of shameful lust, then we could view nudity as divine instead of dirty. A revolution in our attitudes toward sexuality might reduce our crime rates, particularly when it comes to sex offenses.

Janet Jackson reportedly became the most frequent query in many search engines in 2004. How many men across America were privately fantasizing about Janet's breast while publicly denouncing it?

Can we find meaning in the coincidental timing of these two incidents and the ripple effect each had on society?

TELL IT TO THE JUDGE

Thirty-seven-year-old Joe Smith was flying on drugs, lots of them, combinations of them. He says he was so wasted he really doesn't remember much of what happened after 4 p.m that day. Smith claims he was trying to kill himself because his wife had just told him that their marriage was ending because of his severe drug problems.

Here's exactly what Joe Smith told the judge: "I found out she didn't want me. I lost my business, my family, and my self-control. . . . I just wanted to die that day. I copped a bunch of heroin, cocaine, and began injecting, hoping I would overdose. It was different than any other time. I think it was mixed with something."

Joe Smith was about to hit bottom with a thud so hard it would be a lead story on cable shows for months. Tragically, he grabbed an innocent little girl on his downward tumble, as if his pathetic life were her fault.

Smith claims he was in a blackout during

his binge. But prosecutors argued that a man in a drug-induced blackout wouldn't take actions that show premeditation and wouldn't take elaborate steps to cover up his tracks.

Probable Cause Affidavit

SARASOTA COUNTY
DEFENDANT Smith, Joseph P.

. . . the Defendant observed Carlie Brucia walking home through the parking lot of Evie's Car Wash on February 1, 2004. The Defendant then maneuvered the vehicle he was operating to a location, in a premeditated manner to conceal his actions, where he was able to approach Carlie. The Defendant then forcibly abducted Carlie from the parking lot of the car wash and drove her from this location. Through the means of homicidal violence, the Defendant then murdered Carlie Brucia.

Joe, is that You?

Smith certainly wasn't counting on a surveillance camera at the car wash catching him in the act. One just happened to be aimed in his direction. So it captured the crime on tape, recording the very moment he grabbed little Carlie's arm while she walked along the rear of the car wash and led her away. A movie director couldn't have framed it better.

Carlie went missing on Sunday evening, but it wasn't until Monday morning, when the owner of the car wash came to work, that the case got its big break. Owner Mike Evanoff told me he noticed police with bloodhounds going back and forth near his business. Evanoff says he approached a detective, and "I told him that I had a camera in the back of the car wash and would you like me to check it, and he said, basically, don't worry about it because they were too busy and they were running around."

Thank God Evanoff ignored the cop's advice and checked out his surveillance tape anyway. Evanoff had nine cameras around his establishment as part of a digital video recording system that cost about $10,000 and would prove to be priceless. Camera number nine was the one in the back. "I went to camera nine and he'd [the detective] given me a roundabout time of about six o'clock when the girl went missing. I programmed the DVR at six o'clock and it jumped right to Joe Smith abducting Carlie

Brucia." Evanoff explained that his digital video system is motion activated. It will only record when there's significant movement. Since the car wash was closed at the time of the abduction, Joe and Carlie's motions were just about the only movements that triggered the record function. That's why the stunning kidnapping scene immediately popped up.

"I sat there and I was in shock. I got chills." He was especially taken by the image of golfers in the far distance, at the driving range he also owns. While they were practicing their tee shots, 150 feet away a little girl was being kidnapped. Evanoff called the cops back and soon he was surrounded by law enforcement.

Within minutes of that video being viewed by police, an AMBER Alert (America's Missing: Broadcast Emergency Response) was issued for Carlie, effectively putting the general public to work. Bob Hoever, director of special operations for the National Center for Missing and Exploited Children, explains the basic concept behind AMBER Alerts: "Typically, when a child is abducted, it's like looking for a needle in a haystack. The more eyes and ears you have, the smaller that haystack becomes." TV and radio shows were interrupted by the familiar

459

high-pitched emergency tone. The scroll went across the bottom of the TV. But this wasn't a test or a tornado. It was about a missing sixth grader and a mystery man. The media saw the tape and went wild.

"I was getting calls. They wanted to know why law enforcement didn't put out the AMBER Alert earlier," says Linda Spagnoli, a child advocate who was working as a spokesperson for Code AMBER, a company that distributes AMBER Alerts to hundreds of thousands of websites. "In retrospect, she was dead before anybody knew she was missing," Spagnoli said. In fact, experts say most kidnapped children who are murdered are killed within three hours of the abduction.

Spagnoli explains that authorities did the right thing, given the circumstances. It turns out there are very specific criteria for when an AMBER Alert can be issued. According to the Department of Justice, rule number one is "law enforcement must confirm that an abduction has taken place" and that "the child is at risk of injury or death." There should also be "sufficient descriptive information of child, captor or captor's vehicle to issue an Alert." Without that information, the general public wouldn't know what to look for. While we might like to see

AMBER Alerts go out immediately for all children reported missing, that would be wildly unrealistic and would overwhelm the public with reports that aren't specific enough for them to act upon.

More than two thousand children are reported missing every day in the United States. But only a minuscule percentage are really in danger. A good number are runaways who had a fight with Mom or Dad. Some get lost. Or there has been an innocent mixup about who was supposed to be where when. Or they're parental abductions in which the child is easily located. How are cops supposed to separate the life-threatening abductions from the pack until there's concrete evidence of a crime?

To give you another perspective on the complex and hard-to-define issue of missing children, let's examine the most recent information available. According to data supplied by the Department of Justice, in one year, 1999, more than *a million* children went missing in some way, shape, or form from their caretakers! Sounds shocking — until you read the fine print. About 800,000 kids were reported missing to law enforcement or missing children's agencies, but the vast majority of those cases were quickly resolved. In what are often the more serious cases, 58,000 children were abducted by non–family members. But for the entire year, only 115 children were the victims of the most dangerous "stereotypical kidnappings" by a stranger or slight acquaintance.

In 40 percent of those stereotypical kidnappings the child was killed, and in 4 percent the child was never recovered. Put another way, more than half of those 115 children survived. That would seem to leave *fewer than 60 children per year* as victims of the kind of deadly kidnappings that make headlines. Again, these are *estimates* from a study that cautions there is a margin of error.

Still, when you consider that one deadly abduction is too many, these statistics are unnerving. Especially when you read that "nearly half of all child victims of stereotypical kidnappings and nonfamily abductions were sexually assaulted by the perpetrator."

Despite media focus on the abductions of *younger* children, the study showed "teenagers were by far the most frequent victims of both stereotypical kidnappings and nonfamily abductions." In most cases, the victims were girls, with sexual assault being a common motive.

In Carlie's case, Spagnoli says the AMBER Alert was properly triggered, as soon as cops saw that tape with Carlie being led away by Joe Smith. That video was just what the cops needed to separate this case from all the others that are not the classic kidnapping we've all come to fear.

It's crucial to save the AMBER Alerts for use *only* in the most life-threatening cases, because it's such a powerful tool. All fifty states now have AMBER Alert programs. Additionally, AMBER Alerts are now being issued over the Internet and cell phones. AMBER Alerts started out as a partnership between law enforcement and broadcasters. They've evolved into a rapid notification system that uses any and all technology, including large flashing highway signs that will list a suspect's license plate and vehicle model. Even many truckers get AMBER Alert notifications on their text messaging panels.

And the system is working. The Department of Justice says, "More than 265 children have been recovered since the AMBER Alert system began in 1996," most of those since it became a coordinated national effort in 2002. Bob Hoever says the number is actually a lot higher: "We'll never be able to measure the deterrent value of people thinking twice now about abducting a child because they know everybody around them is going to be looking for them." He adds there's evidence that quite a few kidnappers have let their young victims go upon hearing that an AMBER Alert had been issued for that child.

Paradoxically, the widespread use of the AMBER Alert program may be causing many Americans to hear more often about child abductions, causing them to assume that the problem of child abduction is getting worse in America. The experts I spoke with caution that while it's impossible to say for sure, the problem does not seem to be worsening and may be improving. However, because of the increased attention the issue is getting through AMBER Alerts and true crime shows, it feels to many Americans like a growing crisis.

For all these reasons, it's crucial that AMBER Alerts not be overused but rather triggered only in cases like Carlie's, where it's clear a dangerous stranger abduction has taken place and there's enough information to deem the public's involvement useful.

But was this really a stranger abduction?

As the video of Carlie being led away was played repeatedly on news outlets, phone calls began coming in identifying the burly white man on the tape, who had tattoos and was wearing a mechanic's shirt, as Joe Smith.

FAMILY MAN/DRUG FIEND

Smith's one-time associate in the auto-repair business, Ed Dinyes, told reporters he was one of those who called the sheriff's office within minutes of seeing the tape to say it looked like Joe, all right. Ed knew Joe as a guy who could fix a car in record time. He never thought he could be a kidnapper.

Dinyes said he knew Joe as an attentive dad who spent much of his free time taking his three girls, then aged three, four, and six, to the beach. "That's how I know him, as a family man," Dinyes told *Newsday.* "I don't know him as a killer."

Deputies soon caught up with Smith. And when they did, the pathetic secrets of this "family man" came spewing out. Authorities were able to put him behind bars immediately because he was violating his probation on a cocaine charge. Soon there was a raging controversy over why the judge hadn't already put him in the clinker for failing several drug tests during the previous year while he was out on probation. After all, Carlie would still be alive if Smith had been behind bars. But the judge defended himself, reportedly saying that

465

probation officials assumed that Smith was getting drug treatment at a local nonprofit center.

Turns out "Dad" had a long rap sheep, having been arrested about a dozen times, mostly on drug offenses. But it wasn't just drugs. A look back at Smith's criminal record clearly foreshadows what was to come.

In 1993, Smith was sentenced to sixty days in jail after a woman said he hit her in the face with a motorcycle helmet.

In 1997, Smith was accused of grabbing a young woman and threatening to cut her if she screamed. But he was acquitted. Like many criminals, it seems he has a dual personality with a very charming side. "He actually went up and took the stand and apparently was just so believable. He said he was trying to save the woman," said Mike Saewitz, a reporter for the *Sarasota Herald-Tribune* who researched Joe Smith's troubled history, "and I think that was part of his persona. . . . He was very persuasive and very good with words and very smooth."

Earlier that same year, a female copy editor from Mike's newspaper was shopping when she was approached by Smith. It was the middle of the night, Mike said, "and he was waiting outside of the cash-and-carry with a knife tucked into his pants. . . . He lured our copy editor . . . over to a car. He said his car was broken down, and the cops came in at that point and arrested him and only got him for possession of a weapon."

Four years later, Smith went to prison for more than a year for prescription fraud. He got out in early 2003, about a year before he murdered Carlie. But he was rearrested within days, on drug charges. At that point, he could have done hard time. Instead, he was sent to drug treatment.

WHO LET THE DOGS OUT?

In the wake of Carlie Brucia's rape and murder, there was a lot of screaming over why Joe Smith was out on the streets in the first place. Fingers were pointed at judges, at probation officials, at politicians, and at each other. This accusation/ass-covering pattern happens in many high-profile murder cases, because the defendant so often has an extensive criminal history.

"This man should have been in jail," says Linda Spagnoli, repeating the mantra of every anticrime activist. "He had an exhaustive record . . . and he just kept getting out on probation and parole."

One big underlying problem? Jail overcrowding. It's almost impossible to keep every man who exhibits violence toward women locked up because so many men do it.

THE ADDICT'S SPIRAL

The underlying question is: Why do we have so many broken, violent men? As the shrinks will tell you, the answer is multidetermined, meaning there are lots of reasons.

Drugs are certainly one factor. Violent sexual urges can be unleashed by drugs. Drug addiction also fosters the spiritual bankruptcy that can allow a human being to cross that line into the unimaginable. Any recovering addict will tell you this. When you do drugs, your sensations are temporarily heightened by the narcotic, but the price you pay is the dulling of your senses overall. The high of drugs is so pleasurable that nothing else can compete. So when you're not doing drugs, you crash into an abyss. All you crave is the experience of being high again.

Because the addict builds up a tolerance, it usually takes more and more of the drug to achieve the euphoria of that first life-changing high. That's the progressive, destructive cycle of addiction. You don't see drug addicts doing a lot of gardening or needlepoint or crossword puzzles. Ordinary activities do not rate on the drug addict's excitement/pleasure scale. Everything seems dull compared to the delirium of being high. Ditto for ordinary sex. Dull.

When ordinary sex goes out the window, the sex drive remains and still has to be fulfilled. As the addict's downward spiral progresses, his sexual urges become perverted. What's going to get him off when he's flying on crack or heroin? Something kinky, something different, something that rises to the level of excitement set by drugs. Dangerous or "rough" sex might fit the bill.

Another component is the drug user's plummeting self-esteem. He can't easily approach age-appropriate women for consensual sex because (a) they wouldn't be interested, and (b) the addict is so filled with shame and self-loathing he wouldn't dare try — without a knife. This leads to isolation and a growing resentment toward the very women he's attracted to. He becomes furious at that which he covets. As the paranoia grows, he thinks they're rejecting him. He feels vengeful. *I'll show them.*

Addicts live in denial. They know they have made a mess of their own lives, but they don't want to admit it, especially not to themselves. That would mean having to face themselves honestly, admit their mistakes, and make humiliating amends to those they've hurt. It would mean having to change, to get clean and stay clean. It is so much easier for the addict to blame everyone else, anyone else. The rage they are feeling is actually toward themselves, but they don't have the courage to self-confront. It's easier to lash out.

Malice is a key ingredient in the poisonous brew simmering in the addict's psyche. He feels like the victim and wants revenge. He is developing the desire to hurt someone, to see them suffer, for spite. *Everybody hates me. Nobody gives a shit. Fuck them! I hate them all. Fuck everyone. I'll get even. I'll make them suffer.*

Suddenly, in the addict's drug haze, he has crossed a line. He has reverted into a primitive savage. He will attack the easiest prey, a small child. For him, civilization no longer exists.

This hypothetical scenario dovetails neatly with the real-life facts of addict Joe Smith. His addiction was in full bloom. He'd had two incidents involving adult women. He had been rejected by his wife. She had kicked him out of the house and he was living with a friend. Then she'd told him she wanted a divorce. He became crazed and vengeful and savagely lashed out. It could have been at anybody. It was at young Carlie.

Joe Smith said as much to the judge after he was found guilty, trying to explain his unspeakable crime. "I was very angry at myself and very high. I knew . . . it was wrong but I could not stop." This was Joe's plea for mercy. He was trying to avoid the death penalty.

He explained that as a teenager growing up in Brooklyn, he abused drugs daily. He said he moved to Florida to get a new start, but chronic back pain and surgeries left him with an even more severe addiction to painkillers. "I knew I had a big problem, and I tried a number of times to get help."

The judge ruled in favor of the death penalty.

To blame all these types of incidents on drug addiction alone would be simplistic. Another component is the societal dynamic between men and women. Why do so many men view females as prey? I actually had an expert in family violence, who shall remain nameless, become upset with me when I suggested there is an epidemic of male-on-female violence in this country, and it has something to do with the state of being male in America today. "Oh no," I was told, just before he cut the interview short, "it's just

471

that America is a violent society. Women can be violent, too."

No Contest

Yes, women can be violent, but when you look at the litany of monstrous rape/torture/murders committed in this country, you'd be hard-pressed to find one committed by a woman.

A U.S. Department of Justice study on sexual assaults found that "females were more than six times as likely as males to be the victims of sexual assaults known to law enforcement agencies. More specifically, 86 percent of all victims of sexual assault were female." One fascinating statistic says that "the year in a male's life when he is most likely to be the victim of a sexual assault is age four." That's right. Once a male gets past his childhood, his risk of being sexually assaulted plummets. The study says "a female's year of greatest risk is age fourteen." But still, she faces a greater threat of sexual assault throughout her life than does a man. Of sexual assault victims who are thirteen years old, 90 percent are female. Looking at sexual assault victims who are nineteen years of age, 95 percent are women. This is obvious. Everybody knows this. Just look at the news.

If you turned the tables for just one day and showed women raping and killing men at the rate that men are currently raping and killing women, you'd have the government declaring a national crisis. But we regard this business of men killing women as business as usual. *Why?* It's time for us to call it what it is — a crisis! We as a society need to start acknowledging our sexist view of murder.

Women are certainly not perfect. Right now, there is an epidemic of female teachers having sex with their young male students. But they're not binding the boys' wrists and strangling them.

That is what Joe Smith did to Carlie. According to prosecutor Debra Riva, "The child was taken quick and quiet. . . . Bindings were put on the wrists so that she would be unable to resist. He took her to a place where she wouldn't be seen and [he was] unlikely to be caught."

Smith eventually confessed to having "rough sex" with Carlie, telling his brother he got "carried away." Detectives found a semen stain on the back of Carlie's shirt. It matches the genetic profile of Smith to "1 in 92 quintillion," which is a one followed by eighteen zeroes, according to the FBI DNA expert who testified at Smith's trial.

Prosecutors say Smith raped and strangled the little girl, then dumped her body on the grounds of a church. The Buick Century station wagon Smith borrowed from a friend and was using that day showed signs of a violent struggle.

But did Carlie struggle when Smith first approached her?

In the Eye of the Beholder

"I've watched that video of Joseph Smith taking Carlie frame by frame. . . . Not once does Carlie pull away from Joseph Smith. Not once does she back off. Not once do you see any fear in her eyes." So says Steve Eckmann, who recently started a group called the National Voice for Children. His website contains blogs and chats filled with furious debate over the ten seconds of video showing the abduction and what it really means.

Eckmann says the video left many wondering, "Why didn't she just fight? Why didn't she just kick? Why didn't she just scream?" Eckmann has reached his own conclusion, a controversial one at that: "I see a young girl who recognized Joseph Smith. . . . She didn't see him as a danger."

This is significant because of the other big question that has long floated around this gruesome case: Did Carlie's mother know Joe Smith? Almost a year after the crime, the *Sarasota Herald-Tribune* reported that "rumors repeatedly have circulated that she knew Joseph P. Smith . . . although there has been no evidence to support them." Susan Schorpen has reportedly said no, she did not know her daughter's killer.

Those rumors began after published reports that Joe and Susan both frequented the same bar. When I reached the bar owner on the phone, he was not happy to hear from yet another reporter. I managed only to blurt out one question — Did he know Joe Smith? — when I got an earful: "Listen, I'm going to make it clear, one more fucking time. I'm tired of telling people this. The guy never fucking came in here. If you did your homework, honey, you would know about it, instead of trying to make a fucking dollar. The guy never walked in this bar, once, in his fucking life." How about Susan Schorpen? I asked, but the phone had already gone dead.

Carlie's grandmother Andrea Brucia, said she would love to know once and for all whether that long-running rumor of a Smith-Schorpen connection is true or not. After all, Joe Smith and Carlie's mom did have one thing in common: drugs.

But according to Lieutenant Chuck Le-saltato from the Sarasota County Sheriff's office, "the mother had been known to be involved in drugs, but the relationship between her and Joe Smith, there was no correlation. It was never proven that they knew each other."

Finally, someone claiming to be Susan Schorpen herself weighed in on this issue with a blog entry on the National Voice for Children's website. Steve Eckmann, who runs the blog and has presided over a heated blog debate regarding Susan's behavior, is convinced the writer is indeed Susan herself. This writer says,

> As for the idiots who can not comprehend what they read and hear from the news and the trial . . . I did not know Joe Smith. You're cruel and incredibly sick. Get a life.
> — Comment by sue (yeah, it's me),
> May 19, 2006 @ 3:33pm

What the kidnapping video may actually reveal is not that Carlie knew her abductor, but rather that children don't always behave the way we *assume* they would in this kind of situation. We take our cues from movies and TV about how a child should react when she's grabbed and pulled away by a stranger. We think she will scream and kick and claw, because that's what we see in fictional accounts. The fact is, kids are conditioned to listen to and obey adults. When a grown man comes up to lead her away, the child may simply become compliant, given that she is undoubtedly confused, scared, and in shock over what's unfolding.

THE COLISEUM OF CRIME

From Internet blogs to television talking heads, crime in America today is a national pastime and even a national obsession. Dozens of cable TV shows devote themselves to the latest and greatest gruesome murders. An entire network has sprung up around the premise of cameras in the courtroom.

Don't get me wrong. I'm not knocking it. I'm part of it. I'm one of the people who keep showing up on those cable shows to pontificate on this trial or that arrest. And I'm addicted to the Court TV show *Forensic Files*.

There are many ways society benefits from our love affair with violent crime. The average American knows far more today about DNA, Luminol, facial reconstruction, blood spatter, hair and fiber evidence, and handwriting analysis than they did a couple of decades ago. Now we have full-scale analysis of every major trial, from gavel to gavel, from jury selection to sentencing.

In this day and age, when the government believes it can wiretap and search through garbage cans with abandon, it's vital for Americans to have access to what's going on in America's courts. What started as a polite call to open up local courtrooms to cameras has now become a chorus screaming for universal video access in all courtrooms, even the U.S. Supreme Court.

This is an age of voyeurism. When the cameras are rolling, inside and outside court, secrets are the plot points that keep us riveted. But it's not just the secrets of the defendants. Often the victims' families find their dirty underwear tossed out onto the courtroom steps for everyone to see. Not only do these crime victims have to suffer through the hell of hearing in nauseating detail about how some sicko raped, tortured, and murdered their beloved children, they also have to endure the personal humiliation of having their private problems revealed to the world.

Today's courtroom is an arena. Anyone who steps, or is pushed, into the pit of justice can be ripped apart. It's even happened to the judges and lawyers. Cops who've testified have had their reputations torn to shreds. Mark Fuhrman, the detective from the O. J. Simpson trial, is the ultimate example. Amazingly, he managed to reinvent himself as an investigator, author, and media pundit. The arena concept harkens back to the days of the Roman Colosseum, except today, instead of good acoustics, we've got TV satellite trucks beaming a constant stream of humiliations and misfortunes around the world.

The Carlie Brucia case is perhaps the most glaring example of this kind of courtroom spectacle that I've ever seen, and it's not to blame the reporters. We all have to do our jobs.

THE MOTHER LODE

Officials told me Carlie's mom was no stranger to law enforcement before this tragedy, and she was no stranger to law enforcement after this tragedy. Deputies report making dozens of trips to the mother's home over the years.

In January 2006, Susan Schorpen was arrested in St. Petersburg, Florida, on charges of possessing crack cocaine and facilitating prostitution. She was picked up by an undercover cop who suspected prostitution, although she had not committed it. She pleaded no contest to both charges and did jail time. According to the Associated Press, Susan Schorpen "has said the pain of losing her daughter led her to . . . take drugs to numb the pain."

In another heart-wrenching twist, as Susan grappled with her own legal problems, her older brother, Kurt, was killed when his speeding truck swerved off the road and hit a tree. It was almost two years to the day after his niece had been raped and murdered. He was said to be close to her. The local papers said Kurt also had a drunk-driving conviction and a drug record.

When the trial ends, the spotlight fades — until you do something wrong. Then the high-intensity lamps flick back on and expose you again.

Please don't ever think reporters relish the chance to zero in on the misfortunes, addictions, or character defects of somebody who has lost a little girl to rape and murder. *Sarasota Herald-Tribune* reporter Mike Saewitz put it this way: "Just a few months before the trial [of Joe Smith], another man had been stabbed at the mother's home. It's hard, from our standpoint. You know, do you ignore it, do you cover it? In the end, the media often does cover some of these things. And it's tricky. You don't want to be insensitive *and* you want to tell the truth, and you've got to go with that."

BUSYBODY NATION

The truth is that most Americans are over-confident of our ability to keep secrets in today's intrusive world. Every day, there's another news story that shatters the false assumption that what we do in our private lives can easily remain private. The times they are a-changin'. Just read the *Times*.

Two modest examples. On Monday, August 14, 2006, *The New York Times* reported on a proposal to require security cameras at the entrances and exits of New York City's 250 or so nightclubs. It was put forth as a way of fighting crime in the wake of the horrific murder of Imette St. Guillen, who was last seen alive leaving a lower Manhattan bar. But gay activists expressed alarm, noting that cameras could discourage people who are not "out" about their sexual orientation from going to gay bars. "It smacks of Big Brother," complained one gay man. The next day, in the same paper, there was an article about a completely different subject — or was it? This story detailed Yahoo!'s introduction of a computer system to analyze "what each of its 500 million users do on its site: what they search for, what pages they read, what ads they click on." Indoors or out, on the computer or at a club, someone is going to be taking notes. If not now, soon. It's just a matter of time and technology.

Once somebody is arrested, society gets the green light to accelerate into super-scrutiny. Your every orifice is probed, if not literally then figuratively. Psychotherapist Lew Richfield notes, "If you're going to break the law, then you take your chances about having your life exposed. That's fine. Let criminals think about that, that every-thing you do after you break the law be-comes public. . . . It's part of being caught."

However, this intense scrutiny also applies to people who have simply been accused but have not yet gone to trial. The sudden spotlight can come as a shock to the man or woman who has been arrested. Some are paraded in front of the media's cameras in what's known as the "perp walk." While defense attorneys are known to bask in the hot media glare, their clients often break out in a cold sweat.

After Mary Winkler, a mother of three, pleaded not guilty to the murder of her preacher husband in Tennessee, her very capable attorneys got her out on bail, despite what authorities called a confession. They warned the media to "please respect her privacy" as she went off to live with a friend and work at a dry cleaners while waiting for her trial to start. But the warning may not have had much impact on working journalists whose first responsibility is to get the story and learn the truth. Some reporters may have decided that Mary's behavior while she was out on bail was a relevant angle that could help solve the riddle of why her husband had been shot in the back and left to die, while she was arrested at a beach resort in another state with her three kids and a shotgun in the minivan. Later *Good Morning America* snagged an exclusive interview with Mary's father, who said she lashed out after years of physical, mental, and verbal abuse, adding, "I saw bad bruises."

Secrets don't reveal themselves by themselves. The very definition of *secrecy* is "something hidden or concealed." It's usually going to take some probing and prodding to flush it out into the open.

A California psychotherapist who specializes in marriage and family issues, Dr. Richfield notes that even the shrink's office is not a completely secret safe environment: "I have to work under what's known as the

Tarasoff Law. If I have information that someone is going to be hurt, I have a duty to disclose that, to the police, to the intended victim, to the social workers." Dr. Richfield says that covers serious threats or indications of impending suicide, murder, child abuse, elder abuse, or spouse abuse.

Yes, in the end, the truth will come out. The secrets will bleed through and reality will triumph over appearances. Especially if you're anywhere near a courthouse. And there's a good reason for it. Information is power to force change.

If We had Only Known

"Carlie called me Grandma," Andrea Brucia told me. Now a homemaker, Mrs. Brucia has also been a substitute teacher and has a business background. Speaking to me over the phone from her Long Island home, she presented an image of calm and common sense. She explained that Carlie's dad, Joey, is her stepson, and has been so for thirty-three years. So, in essence, he is her son, which made Carlie her granddaughter. Andrea says she's the last person you'd ever think would become an activist. But her unimaginable loss has made her precisely that.

Andrea's mission now is to get laws passed

in New York and other states that will boost the rights of parents who are not living with their children. That was the case of her stepson, who lived in New York while his daughter lived with her mom, Susan, in Florida.

"They were married just a very short time," Andrea explained. Carlie was born in New York but moved with her mom to Florida when she was just a toddler. Andrea told me it was only after Carlie's death that she and her son found out about Susan's secret life: "We were shocked. We knew she was not Donna Reed by any stretch of the imagination. We never knew that Carlie was living in an environment where her mother was using drugs. And there were apparently numerous police calls to their house. And you know, you find this out after the fact and it was, like, so, so disturbing to us. If we would have had any knowledge of this . . . Joey would have definitely gotten custody of her."

Andrea Brucia went on to spearhead legislation in New York that would require noncustodial parents to be notified when a parent who has custody of a child is arrested for a felony. She'd like to see this notification law in every state in the land, explaining, "With the amount of divorces in this country and so many long-distance relationships — maybe the mother is in California and the father is in New York — you don't know the other parent's lifestyle. You don't know what's going on unless the child says something. And very often, like in our case, no matter what the mother does, a child protects their mother. That's just the way it is. That's almost a law of nature."

The question is, Why doesn't this notification system for the "other" parent already exist?

Privacy is one reason. Noted Santa Monica criminal defense lawyer Steve Cron warns that it's very dangerous to base any notification law on something as flimsy as an arrest: "The presumption of innocence is supposed to mean something. People get arrested all the time and charges are never filed," due to lack of evidence. Attorney Cron also worries about any law that would, in essence, tattle on one parent to another parent: "Custody battles are often vicious. So if they find out their ex has been arrested, gee, that's like hitting the lottery." Cron envisions scenarios where the notified spouse would use the arrest information as a weapon, not just to regain custody but to get the arrested parent fired from work and humiliated in the community. New York state assemblyman David G. McDonough, who is pushing the legislation, told me he had heard similar complaints and may change the proposed legislation to require notification of the noncustodial parent in the event of the custodial parent's *conviction* on a felony.

Either way, says McDonough, the law would have to go into effect on a national basis to be truly effective. He is hoping that New York will be able to set the precedent for congressional action, which is how these campaigns often progress. But attorney Steve Cron says that's precisely the problem. He complains that all these new notification laws, which limit privacy, "come about as a result of one case that gets a lot of attention, and then they throw out the previous two hundred years or so of legal precedent and they say, Oh, we have to write a new law because of what happened in this particular case." Slowly but surely, he fears, that mentality will erode all of our freedoms as each new horror story sparks another set of antiprivacy laws. Still, you can understand why Carlie's grandmother thinks sending up a warning flare when a custodial parent is on a downward spiral makes all the sense in the world.

All of which brings us back to the issue of

secrets and trials. What's fair game and what's not? And what role do the media play? Should Susan's arrests have been kept secret by the media, out of a sense of fairness or sympathy for the grieving mother? My answer to that, as a reporter, is an emphatic no. Journalists do on rare occasions play the self-censorship game, but it's generally to shield the identity of a rape victim, to protect the identity of a minor, or to omit the address of someone who could be hurt or killed if his or her location was known. There are clear-cut guidelines at most major media outlets as to when and how information is to be suppressed. That the information is embarrassing to the subject is not one of those criteria.

To suppress merely embarrassing facts would open a Pandora's box and wipe out much of what passes for news these days. What actor Mel Gibson did and said when he was pulled over for his now-infamous Malibu DUI was certainly embarrassing. It was also, definitely, important news. That's why the website that broke the story got so many kudos. Who knows whether the public would have found out about Gibson's anti-Semitic tirade had TMZ.com not gotten hold of the deputy's original report?

In the case of Carlie Brucia, since her

mom wasn't famous, it wasn't until after her daughter's tragic murder that Susan Schorpen's problems became news. Had the Brucias in New York known about the troubled environment Carlie was living in before the crime, I have no doubt they would have pulled out all the stops to get that little girl out of Sarasota.

Still, there are at least two sides to every story, and in May 2006, it appears that Carlie's mother may have come out with hers. On the National Voice for Children website, a woman who insists that she is Carlie's mom responded to her critics, specifically addressing the organization's leader, Steve Eckmann, who has written blogs criticizing Susan's lifestyle. "Sue" asks:

Who the hell are you?? What gives you the right to even start this conversation using my name, my story and the legacy of my daughter?? God is my only judge . . . not you . . . I find it interesting that you have so much garbage to sling at me, my reputation, my family and the fate of my future. What does anyone stand to gain from this mindless thoughtless chatter. Haven't I suffered enough . . .

— Comment by sue (yeah, it's me), May 19, 2006 @ 6:08pm

In the wake of Carlie's gruesome murder, U.S. congresswoman Katherine Harris of Florida introduced legislation to the Congress that was known as Carlie's Law. It was designed to toughen jail terms and reduce parole opportunities for people convicted of sex crimes. While the proposal known as Carlie's Law never became an actual law, Carlie Brucia was one of the child victims mentioned in a far more comprehensive piece of legislation that became law in July 2006. This new law (H.R. 4472) has been hailed as the most important child protection bill in a quarter of a century.

The Adam Walsh Child Protection and Safety Act of 2006 was signed into law on the twenty-fifth anniversary of the abduction of six-year-old Adam Walsh. Adam was kidnapped from a shopping mall in Hollywood, Florida, in 1981 and found murdered about two weeks later. Tragically, no one was ever charged in his murder, though one notorious career criminal confessed and then recanted, exacerbating Adam's parents' already unimaginable torment. Adam's horrific killing jump-started a national missing-children's crusade.

Together, Adam's mom and dad, Reve

and John Walsh, helped put the National Center for Missing and Exploited Children on the map. Adam's dad also became the host of *America's Most Wanted,* a show that has helped recover more than forty missing children and capture nine hundred "wanted" individuals in its two decades on the air.

The Adam Walsh Act is massive, but among its highlights is the National Sex Offender Public Registry, a national public sex offender registry that any citizen can visit to get information on sex offenders. The website address of that registry is http://www.nsopr.gov, and I highly recommend you visit it and enter your zip code to see if you have any registered sex offenders living in your neighborhood. You can also search by name and address. It is run by the Department of Justice but taps into the various state sites.

Linda Spagnoli warns that the registry is "not a magic pill." Indeed, it is only as good as the information the states put in. The problem with sex offenders is that they tend to get "lost," especially when they move from state to state. According to the National Center for Missing and Exploited Children, there are more than 560,000 registered sex offenders in America and "at least 100,000 are 'missing.' " Now, that's scary!

The Adam Walsh Act tackles this issue by making failure to register a felony. Linda Spagnoli doubts that those who are demented enough to harm a child would worry too much about these threats: "Consider this. A person who would rape a child and bury them alive, do you think they're going to care enough to send a postcard to tell law enforcement where they live?" She's got a point. However, this new bill requires sex offenders to verify registration face-to-face with law enforcement instead of by mail. Short of locking up 560,000 people forever, this new law is a giant step toward ensuring that what happened to Carlie Brucia doesn't happen to another child.

THE CAMERA NEVER BLINKS

The Carlie Brucia case also illustrates how video technology is revolutionizing crime fighting. A camera is "the remote eyeballs of a police officer who's not there," says Joe Freeman, president and CEO of the J. P. Freeman Company, a leading research and consulting company in the security and automation industry.

Without that car-wash security camera identifying Joe Smith as the abductor of

Carlie Brucia, police might have never solved that case. Sure there was DNA evidence on Carlie's shirt, but had they not made that first link to Joe Smith when the abduction was caught on tape, they might never have learned the location of Carlie's body. It was Smith's brother who reportedly led police to the church grounds, after his brother told him the location.

After the World Trade Center collapsed in the 9/11 terrorist attack, security fears were rampant. We all wondered if it was safe to go through a tunnel, cross a bridge, or walk into a skyscraper. That universal anxiety jump-started the security camera trend and it took off from there. It's fitting, in a way. Carlie's grandmother, Andrea, calls killers like Smith homegrown terrorists.

As prices drop and the image quality of the cameras steadily improves, more and more businesses are installing them. Why would a car wash want one? To guard against theft or robbery, but also, suggests Freeman, to protect against false claims of damage to the cars being washed. If the fender dent was right there on tape when the car went in for a wash, it would be hard to falsely claim that the car wash inflicted the damage.

Most of these private security cameras

weren't put in to help the cops, but they are doing just that. The law of unintended consequences is in play. The impact of all these cameras on police work has been astounding. And the role of video is only going to get bigger as the technology improves.

FACIAL FINGERPRINTS?

Get ready! Intelligent video is on the horizon.

Just about every action movie has a scene in which the guard falls asleep in front of a bank of video monitors, allowing a key figure to sneak in. Soon, intelligent video will watch that monitor while the guard snoozes. Software is being developed that will recognize an unusual image and send an alarm signal telling the guard, "Now you better watch the monitor," says Joe Freeman, whose firm provides research, consulting, and design services to hundreds of corporations and several governments.

And each of us may soon have a digital ID. "In the next few years, you will see cameras that will identify you by name," says Freeman. "Let's say I have a pixelized pattern of your face and you show up at a store and it is known that you are a thief . . . that monitor is going to say, Hey . . . this is somebody we're looking for." And, he says, it will also provide clear instructions on what to do.

In the evolving field of biometrics, scientists are developing ways to read your eyeball, your wrist, your hand, or your face. "There's a lot of work being done now on facial technology," says Freeman. "There was an experiment done at one of the Super Bowls, as people were filing into the stadium, to determine just who they were, in terms of a facial fingerprint, if you will. They could then be matched to a computer file in . . . police departments, or the FBI," to determine if criminals or suspected terrorists were coming in.

I wonder if that was the same Super Bowl where Janet flashed her breast.

THE FUTURE IS NOW

"What we are going to see in our lifetime is cameras everywhere," says Freeman, noting that the one free zone may be inside the home. But even there, baby cams and other monitoring devices are already available. With cameras everywhere and other technological advances emerging, the circle is getting narrower for those who break the law.

Of course, everybody would like to wipe out crime once and for all. But at what cost?

Do we really want to live in a world where our every move is recorded? And let's not discount the audio components of such technology, which will undoubtedly be able to record much of what we say.

Wouldn't it be wonderful if we could find another way to tackle this plague of violence, to evolve beyond it?

BACK TO THE BREAST

Which brings me back to Janet's breast and the outrage it provoked. Breast as metaphor. What does that intense backlash say about us as a society? I really believe that one day historians will look back and laugh at how we, primitive society that we were, went berserk over a breast. As technology advances, we have to advance with it, psychologically and spiritually. We have to become as sophisticated as our technology.

I asked Carlie's grandmother what she thought the trouble with our society is, why so many men are committing horrific acts of violence against women and girls. She pointed to violence on television and in the movies. It's true, we're inundated with extraordinarily disturbing images of violence by men against women, in our movies and TV shows.

I'm a great believer in free expression in

the arts. I also believe in free expression of opinion. If violence in art is causing violence in reality, people have a right to question it. But I'm not sure that's the whole problem.

It seems to me that violent sex is more acceptable on television than loving sex. In violent sex scenes, a woman is often fighting back against a man who is trying to rape or brutalize her. This is all part of programming of men and women to be enemies. It's a warlike attitude toward sex. No wonder some men are waging war on women in the real world. These men *are* homegrown terrorists, and we need to ask ourselves, How and why is our society growing them?

What if we allowed nudity and more loving sexuality on television in place of violent programming? Could that have a subliminal impact on men like Joe Smith?

Let's imagine a little boy named Joe Smith watching that Super Bowl. Instead of being dragged away from the exposed breast and told it was a dirty thing, what if he was allowed to see topless women? What if they were commonplace? After all, there are plenty of topless men on TV. How would that change his attitudes toward women as he grew up? Would he look at them as exotic, shame-based objects that need to be either covered up or hunted, captured, and dominated? Or would he see them just as people who happen to have breasts?

We have a national neurosis about sex and we need to let go. We must stop demonizing our own bodies. The day sex stops being a crime in our own minds is the day we'll have fewer Joe Smiths walking around.

ANOTHER ANGEL

The fact is, Big Brother needs to find a way to track just the molesters, rapists, and killers and leave the rest of us alone.

Authorities are now using the latest global positioning satellite technology to do just that, thanks in large part to the involuntary sacrifice of another angel, Jessica Lunsford, who was also mentioned in the Adam Walsh Act. This nine-year-old Florida girl was abducted, raped, and murdered just about a year after Carlie's deadly ordeal.

I have no desire to compare the two cases to see which was worse. There is no "worse." They are both stomach-churning, nightmare-producing horror stories. There are certain details in Jessica's case that literally made me twitch in revulsion as I read through the research in preparation for a TV interview.

Jessica Lunsford was sleeping peacefully in her bed when she was kidnapped in

February 2005. According to the Citrus County Sheriff, forty-six-year-old John Evander Couey, a convicted sex offender, confessed to the crime. Couey took a lie-detector test, the sheriff told reporters, adding that immediately after, "He says 'you don't need to tell me the results, I already know what they are.' "

Authorities say Couey proceeded to tell investigators that he was smoking crack and drinking beer on the night he snuck into Jessica's house and abducted her to a trailer home just 150 yards away from where she lived. He admitted to keeping the girl in a closet for two or three days, feeding her hamburgers and water, while he sexually assaulted her repeatedly. Couey's half-sister, niece, and a friend were in the trailer home around the time of the abduction and have repeatedly insisted they were unaware of the girl's presence. Authorities do not believe those three were involved in little Jessica's death.

So Near and Yet . . .

Perhaps the most startling and gut-wrenching aspect of this case is that investigators went to the trailer home while canvassing the neighborhood for Jessica. During their first visit, Jessica may have still been alive, hidden in the closet. At least that's what Couey himself said, although authorities were skeptical.

Couey said he later buried the little girl while she was alive and conscious, putting her in garbage bags in the middle of the night. "She was alive. I buried her alive," Couey said in his confession. "Like, it's stupid, but she suffered. . . . Just covered a bunch of leaves over it where I dug the hole at and then went back in the house and went to bed."

But when he appeared in court, Couey pleaded not guilty to all the charges involving Jessica's kidnapping, sexual battery, and murder. Soon, his attorney was laboring vigorously to get Couey's confession tossed out on the grounds that he hadn't been allowed to consult a lawyer, as he reportedly requested. Still, prosecutors were convinced they had enough physical evidence, including DNA, to convict Couey even without the confession. Prosecutors pointed out that Couey also told a jail guard that he didn't mean to kill her, adding, "I never saw myself as someone who could do something like this." They rarely do.

There was so much pretrial publicity in this case that in July 2006, while in the final stages of jury selection, the judge presiding over Couey's murder trial suddenly dismissed the entire jury panel. The whole region seemed to be seething with outrage. One juror reportedly complained that someone yelled at him: You better convict him! or words to that effect. These kinds of cases generate such raw feelings that getting an impartial jury is tough. That's why defense lawyers often plead for a change of venue to a distant town or city that doesn't have such an emotional attachment to the case. But the rage so many felt was understandable. Couey's trial ended up taking place in Miami.

The autopsy results showed little Jessica was asphyxiated. Investigators say they found her body in a sitting position inside the garbage bags. Her hands had been tied with stereo wire and two of her fingers poked through the bags. She was found holding on to her favorite stuffed animal, a purple dolphin.

No Words

It's details like that which make you wonder about this life, about the existence of evil, and about what we can do to stop it.

In a show of incredible grace and courage, Jessica's grandmother told reporters, "All of us feel that the police did the best they could." In the aftermath of little Jessica's death, Florida lawmakers took action. They passed the Jessica Lunsford Act. It establishes a mandatory minimum sentence of twenty-five years behind bars for those convicted of the most serious sex crimes against children under twelve.

TRACKING EVIL

Child advocate Linda Spagnoli is enthusiastic about another provision of the Florida law. It requires lifetime tracking of the most serious sex offenders *after* they are released from prison, using GPS, the global positioning system. Police will now also have the capacity to match up crime data with the movements of these sex offenders: "If, for example, in West Palm Beach, a child's been raped, we can then take the data from the tracked sex offenders to see if any of them were in the vicinity of the crime at that particular time." Again, technology is giving police vast new powers.

Had John Couey, who was a registered sex offender, been wearing a GPS bracelet, detectives say they would have seen his proximity of 150 yards to the abduction scene and been on him in a flash. That technology could have saved that child's life. It will undoubtedly save other children in the future.

PARENT POWER

"Never underestimate the power of angry parents." Linda Spagnoli says this is her favorite phrase, which she first heard from a detective. Jessica's father, Mark Lunsford, has joined a long line of parents who have somehow, despite their unspeakable loss, found the strength not just to carry on but to crusade for change.

Mark has traveled the country seeking tougher laws to control child predators. One thing virtually all the experts in the field agree on is this: These sex offenders are almost never capable of rehabilitation. They will strike again.

"Lock 'em up and throw away the key," says Carlie's grandma, Andrea Brucia. She adds, "Our justice system seems to be broken." Carlie's family has already had to endure the trial, jury deliberations, the verdict, the sentencing phase, and then the judge's ruling giving Carlie's killer the death penalty. Now the appeals process has been automatically triggered. The frustration of Carlie's grandmother was palpable as she explained, "In Carlie's case they have Joseph Smith's DNA and Joseph was identified by his friends as Carlie's abductor. He confessed to his brother what he did to Carlie. It's irrefutable evidence. There's no room for doubt. So why does it immediately go into the appeals process when there is no doubt in anyone's mind this is the man who did this? I think all the money they've spent on these appeals cases, maybe the money should be spent on preventing crime." But how can we prevent these kinds of monsters from springing up in our midst?

UNIVERSAL THERAPY?

The one thing psychiatrists will tell you about criminals is that they are not solution-oriented. It's them against the world, kill or be killed. This kind of primitive thinking can sometimes be counteracted through education and therapy.

We need to tailor our educational system to teach people how to resolve their inner conflicts and negotiate the minefields of human interaction. Wealthy people can afford to go to psychiatrists to tame their inner demons. The "talking cure" should be available to everyone from grade school up, regardless of income bracket. Ironically, the very segments of society that need therapy the most — those struggling with financial, race, class, and self-esteem issues — are the very groups that have least access to the therapeutic process. How much would it cost to set up group therapy sessions in schools? Not much! And yet the benefits would be enormous. Imagine graduating a generation of students who have been taught to develop an awareness of their own unconscious motivations, desires, needs, and conflicts. Right now, we are churning out people who may know how to do long division but are flying blind when it comes to dealing with their insecurities and hang-ups. We need to revamp our schools and other institutions so that we're all invested in not just the problem but the solution.

The first thing we must do is admit we have a crisis. When we as a nation become determined to change, we can change our attitudes. Our society focused in on the dangers of smoking, and millions of people quit. Our attitude toward violence against females, whether children or women, must change *now*. The time for complacency has ended. Carlie and Jessie's killers saw to that.

12
SEX EDUCATION

Debra Lafave might as well be a movie star. The curvaceous blue-eyed blonde has websites devoted to her, national surveys taken about her, and T-shirts bearing her name. TV commentators, including me, have spent countless hours discussing her bizarre lifestyle choices. But though stunning to look at, Debra Lafave is not a movie star. She is a sex offender. The fact that she is a very good-looking criminal has made her the leading lady of America's latest crime trend: hot female teachers having sex with their young male students.

As Debra's case shows, when you get arrested, even the secrets your body holds are not sacred. Her saga is a dramatic illustration of how authorities, when armed with a search warrant, can pry into the most personal regions of your being, literally inspecting your private parts. Investigators got a search warrant to photograph her body in order to gather evidence of an underage boy's claims of having sex with the teacher. He described certain unique aspects of her private grooming that only a lover, or a bikini waxer, would know. The cops argued they needed corroboration to prove their case. A judge agreed and issued the body search warrant.

We'd like to think that we'd never find ourselves in such a vulnerable position, where even personal modesty gets thrown out the window. The fact is, it could happen to any one of us, sometimes for good reason, sometimes not. When the cuffs go on, your freedom is instantly relinquished. Your reaction is visceral. Getting arrested is usually a humiliating experience. For a woman it can feel especially degrading. But Debra Lafave was no ordinary woman. She was a knockout with dangerous desires.

PECULIAR PAGEANT

So many of these cute female predators have hit the spotlight recently, they could get together and hold a pageant. Debra would almost certainly represent Florida. She admitted to having sex with a fourteen-year-old boy, and according to the boy, they did it several times in different places, including at school.

Police say the relationship between the twenty-three-year-old teacher and the fourteen-year-old boy started with conversations during a school trip to Sea World Aquarium in Orlando. Debra then began taking him to his basketball practices and even to get his hair cut. According to the boy, they soon began having sex.

He told investigators that he and Debra had sex in a classroom at the school. The boy also said Debra performed oral sex on him in the home she shared with her new husband. Police say the two also had intercourse in the back of her SUV while the boy's fifteen-year-old cousin drove them around. According to what the young teen reportedly told cops, the newlywed Debra said she had marital problems and was turned on by the fact that the sex with the student was forbidden. Debra has since denied ever saying that. Prosecutors contended the relationship was so intense that the teacher made more than a hundred phone calls to her boy lover, averaging four a day.

After a long spate of legal wrangling in two counties, Debra ended up with a plea deal that gave her no jail time, three years of house arrest, and seven years of probation. Law enforcement sources told me she is only allowed to leave home for work or the necessities of life as determined by her community control officer. She can't work with children. She wears an ankle monitor and has a curfew. I'm told Debra was also required to complete a sex offender treatment program and, as an ongoing condition of her supervision, she must continue to see her psychiatrist and take all medicine as prescribed. She is classified as a sex offender. Listed under her maiden name, Debra Beasley, her photo and related information can be found on the National Sex Offender Public Registry, under Florida, at http://www.nsopr.gov/.

CARNAL KNOWLEDGE

Classically beautiful à la Candace Bergen, Sandra "Beth" Geisel would probably take the crown for Miss New York. The forty-two-year-old statuesque blonde was a Catholic school teacher and the estranged wife of a prominent banker when her scandalous sexual behavior made national news. Police say they caught the mother of four in a car having sex with a teenage boy. He was seventeen years old, which made their intercourse legal, since New York's age of consent is seventeen.

But then a *sixteen*-year-old boy came

forward and said he, too, had had sex with Geisel on three occasions, including at her home and in the press box at the school's football field. Because he was underage, Geisel was charged with rape.

The case became even more sensational as the media broke detailed reports chockfull of salacious secrets. The Smoking Gun website published a very graphic deposition reportedly taken by police. Its shocking content was widely disseminated. In it, the unidentified boy praised Geisel as a "good teacher." But that's not what made headlines. Returning from a field trip, he claimed he was told — by two other unnamed boys — that they "were sitting in the back of the bus with Mrs. Geisel and she gave them both a hand job." On another occasion, he said, they went to a party at her house, where Mrs. Geisel appeared drunk, and where — he claimed — he later had sex with her. He also described meeting Mrs. Geisel in the press box at the school's football field, where he said they had sex as she bent over a table. Rumors, he said, swept the school that Mrs. Geisel was "having sex with students."

In another shocker, after she was arrested and let out on bail, she was pulled over by police and charged with drunk driving. Geisel ultimately accepted a plea deal that allowed her to plead guilty to one of three rape counts, as well as driving while intoxicated. Geisel was sentenced to six months behind bars but was released sooner, in part because of time served and good behavior. She was immediately taken to an alcohol treatment center. She will remain on probation for ten years. She was required to register as a sex offender.

AMBER ALERT

Amber Jennings, a very pretty, hard-bodied, thirtysomething blonde, would undoubtedly wear the Miss Massachusetts sash. The high school English teacher, a married mother of two young girls, pleaded guilty to sending obscene photos and videos of herself to a sixteen-year-old boy with whom she was having sex. The prosecutor said the images revealed her breasts and vagina. Amber's attorney acknowledged that the relationship between his client and the student lasted several months, calling it consensual.

They first met when the boy was a freshman and she was his English teacher. The next school year, when he was not in her class, they began to talk on the phone, through e-mail, and in person. Eventually, say prosecutors, they began to have sex in various places, including her car, her house, and his parents' house. The assistant D.A. who handled the case said that at one point the boy asked Amber Jennings to use a video camera while they had sex, and she agreed. The police later found those images on the computers they seized. Even though her face was not on camera, prosecutors say the video caught Amber's tattoo, thereby proving it was her.

Although the sexual acts were not illegal because the age of consent in Massachusetts is sixteen, Amber broke the law when she allowed the videotaping of a person under eighteen engaged in sexual conduct. Her lawyer argued it was "incongruous" to say the sex wasn't illegal but the taping of it was. Amber finally reached a deal with prosecutors giving her probation for a single charge of disseminating harmful materials to a minor. She was also ordered to surrender her teaching license and stay away from the boy.

In a rash of similar cases, a host of other female teachers, from Tennessee to Michigan to California, have been accused of seducing students. Some media pundits began calling it an "epidemic" of teacher-student sex. Others say the May–September syndrome has always existed in schools and is just getting more attention because of a zero tolerance climate in our society today. But zero tolerance seems to wilt in the face of beauty.

Too Pretty for Prison?

Debra Lafave was a former model. In 1999, she was featured in *Makes and Models Magazine*. A photo of her that eventually appeared in the *New York Post* shows her posing in a bikini and high heels while clutching the handles of a Harley-Davidson. Her now ex-husband, Owen Lafave, told ABC News she had once dreamed of becoming a singer and had even dated Nick Carter of the Backstreet Boys. In court, the prosecutor was struck by how the cameras followed Debra as if she were "a runway model." He shouldn't have been surprised. In our culture today, the beautiful people reign supreme and often get away with a lot more than ugly people do.

Debra Lafave's lawyer crystallized the debate with a fascinating comment. Attorney John Fitzgibbons argued his client should stay out of the jail because "to place Debbie into a Florida state women's penitentiary, to place an attractive young woman in that kind of hellhole, is like putting a piece of raw meat in with the lions." Hello? What?

At first, the comment made me laugh. But milliseconds later — as the implications of it ran through my head — it infuriated me, and others. Was this attorney actually suggesting that only ugly people deserved to be incarcerated for their crimes? Carrying this argument to its extremes didn't take much imagination. If an ugly woman shot someone but then had plastic surgery to refine her features, should that be considered a mitigating factor, entitling her to more lenient treatment by the judge at sentencing? If two criminals robbed a store, should the handsome bandit get a shorter sentence than his less attractive partner in crime? The very fact that he would dare to use that kind of argument suggests that our system of justice doesn't even really pretend to be blind anymore. There was outrage among the media pundits!

But of course the media is guilty of the exact same prejudice. From watching news reports you'd think every teacher who touched a young boy was a bombshell. But it's just not true. Take Sharon Rutherford, a thirty-year-old high school teacher in Alabama. Prosecutors not only accused her of having sexual contact with students, but of drawing one of them into an unsuccessful plot to kill her husband. Her attorney called the charges completely false, categorically denying that she slept with a student and insisting there was absolutely no evidence of a murder plot. Still, in the summer of 2006, a grand jury indicted her on two counts of enticing a child to enter a room for immoral purposes and for solicitation of murder.

You'd think the entire national press corps would have devoted blanket coverage to this teacher accused of sexual shenanigans with a student, and — the capper — solicitation of murder. But the story didn't take off. Perhaps her mug shot had something to do with that. In it, she appears chubby and is wearing glasses.

Clinical psychologist Julia Hislop, author of *Female Sex Offenders: What Therapists, Law Enforcement and Child Protective Services Need to Know,* has studied many sex-offender registries. "I think the beautiful teachers are the ones coming to the attention of the media. I don't think they are representative at all of the women who are molesting children and adolescents," says Hislop. She assured me that most of the women she's seen who have committed sex crimes don't look like Debra Lafave: "They

515

are by no means beautiful. They certainly well represent the various sizes, shapes, and forms that women come in."

Hot Story

In the end, we have only to look at ourselves, the consumers, to know why the media focuses on the pretty teachers who cross the line. News executives try to program what is going to bring in the viewers, in sheer numbers and in the desirable eighteen-to-thirty-nine-year-old demographic, because their careers rise and fall on those ratings. They know very quickly when a story has captured the public's imagination from the numbers of people watching. This isn't guesswork. It's a science called the overnight numbers. If a story doesn't "rate," the coverage will be curtailed to its bare-bones "must cover" developments and will gradually disappear from the airwaves. If a story rates well producers will be doing backflips, eager to figure out all sorts of ways to stretch out the story, from new angles to national polls, from expert panels to viewer call-ins. Every so often a story comes along that has all the magic elements, like a delicious recipe or a captivating movie script. The Debra Lafave story was one of them.

While there are always exceptions, the

basic formula is that sex sells and fear sells. Criminal cases involving hot sex that feature attractive, affluent people can draw huge ratings. If a sexy star is involved in any sort of scandal, like a Mel Gibson, a Winona Ryder, a Robert Downey, Jr., or an R. Kelly, so much the better.

This is just the way it is right now. If we want to change what's programmed at us, we need to first change how *we're* programmed. People lie all the time about what they watch on television. If you believed what people told you, you'd think PBS was the number-one-rated network.

The teacher sex issue is a particularly acute example of ratings-based programming. The sexual details are so crucial to these stories that the news coverage can turn quite lurid, almost sounding pornographic at times. So a really sexy perpetrator can increase the story's sexual heat, which can boost readership, viewership, and ratings exponentially.

"Whenever we knew that Debra was going to be coming to court, or there was even the slightest movement of paperwork on her case, it would create an enormous flurry of activity in the courtroom pool," says journalist Candace Rondeaux, who now works for *The Washington Post* but who covered

517

the Lafave case as the Tampa court reporter for the *St. Petersburg Times.* "She's attractive and well dressed and gives off that kind of glamorous-meets-girl-next-door kind of air. . . . So, yes, I definitely think her attractiveness was a big factor in making this case such a huge media juggernaut."

The word "hot" even surfaced several times in Debra Lafave's arrest affidavit. One mother told cops "she overheard her son bragging about [the student] having sex with a 'hot' teacher from his school." A few paragraphs down, the police report said the boy "called him several more times and talked about the 'hot teacher' Ms. Lafave."

After talk of kisses, the police narrative turned X-rated. The fifteen-year-old boy who had been driving the SUV told cops that he saw Lafave having sex with his fourteen-year-old cousin inside the vehicle: She "laid down in the back with her head toward the rear of the vehicle. He observed [name withheld] take his pants off. He believed [ ] took her pants off, which he described as pink Capri pants, and placed them on the passenger's seat. He observed that her legs were spread and [ ] was between them. [ ] left his shirt on but he could see [ ] moving up and down as they were having sex and he could observe her legs as

518

well as his bare buttocks. He stated there was no talking. She moaned a couple of times, then laughed at something."

It struck me that the cops might have been working overtime on this report. *St. Petersburg Times* crime reporter Shannon Colavecchio–Van Sickler found it unusual as well. "I'd never seen an affidavit like that, frankly; it was very detailed. . . . more than other affidavits I've seen." Hmmm.

BRAGGING RIGHTS?

There seemed to be many double standards at work in this case. That it involved a hot female seemed to be a mitigating factor for some. In fact, some wondered aloud whether Debra Lafave even committed a crime, or was she doing this boy a huge favor, giving him something to brag about with his peers? That issue sparked a heated debate on MSNBC:

The Abrams Report, MSNBC,
March 22, 2006
David Schwartz, Criminal Defense Attorney: This really is a victimless crime, Dan, and I say victimless because you know what, this fouteen-year-old kid, she — that kid is walking around right now, he is the hero amongst his classmates, he

is a hero amongst that school, and you know, think back, his hormones are raging and she did him a favor. . . .

Susan Filan, former Prosecutor, MSNBC Legal Analyst: I am absolutely shocked. . . . I am shocked that you're going on national television and taking that position. I think that's shameful. . . .

Schwartz: It's not just me.

The radio chatter was even more blunt. Shock jocks were lamenting that they didn't have a chance to be "victimized" in high school. Letters to the editor were dripping with envy. "All of my female teachers in high school looked like Ernest Borgnine. . . . This kid hit the lotto!" The jokes were everywhere, says crime reporter Colavecchio–Van Sickler, which disturbed her because she was covering the story and saw the tragedy in it: "It's not funny, it's a real serious crime."

While not joking about it, defense attorney and TV pundit David Schwartz couldn't disagree more. He said he surveyed a hundred men and more than 90 percent of them agreed there was no victim in this case. Even respected mental health professionals disagree about the extent of trauma fourteen-year-old boys experience from sex with an adult female. I spoke with two such experts who had completely different takes.

Dr. Mohan Nair is a sexual deviancy expert who has testified in many cases. The psychiatrist told me that he's looked at numerous cases of adult sex with minors and believes that young female victims who have sex with adult males show a lot more long-term psychological trauma than young male victims who have sex with adult females. Younger females, he says, are often passive partners: "They don't have to participate. . . . They are passive recipients of the man's embrace or intercourse. There are various levels of coercion and actual physical force. . . . Threats apply to these situations. . . . That's not the case with boys. . . . It is almost always spoken about . . . as something along the lines of a conquest or something that they are really excited and proud about."

But Dr. Gilbert Kliman, a prominent forensic child psychiatrist, says trauma can surface over the course of the boy's life. He told me he has evaluated several boys who've had sexual experiences with their teachers and said, "I have found it had a fairly serious and sometimes extremely serious impact on their development." Dr. Kliman says when it comes to children between the ages of ten and sixteen, "Boys, just like girls . . . are not ready for the full emotional experience of a full adult sexual relationship. And they become, in many cases, overwhelmed, overstimulated, and handicapped by the great amount of passion and excitement that sexuality and romance involves them in, when they should be paying attention to school, sports, and peer relationships. So they lose a lot of their childhood."

Dr. Kliman, who is a senior fellow at the American Academy of Child and Adolescent Psychiatry, also described the fallout he has seen in many of these cases, saying it "led to a kindling of pathology in boys who had been less pathological in their behavior or had been reasonably well adjusted previously." He said moral corruption can occur, including pride in the deceit that had been practiced with the adult woman and a cold-hearted, utilitarian view of sex based on how the boy himself was used by the adult. A tendency toward substance abuse and alcoholism may also result.

In Dr. Kliman's experience, there is such a tremendous impact because "the development of ego ideals and what are called heroes and heroines are very active at that point [in a boy's development]. Kids are looking to follow the example of people outside their family and they come across a corrupt teacher, so they come up with corrupt ideals." Preadolescent and adolescent boys are very impressionable, and this sexual experience would seem to mark them with a tainted worldview.

"I had a Secret"

Who better to weigh in on this than a man who actually had a sexual affair with one of his female teachers when he was just fifteen years old? Now in his late forties, this man agreed to speak with me on the condition of complete anonymity. He told me his relationship also began on a field trip, when he noticed his teacher was crying and he tried to comfort her: "So I said, Let's take a walk. I kind of took control." He said what started that day with a kiss evolved into a full-fledged sexual affair that lasted more than a year. This teacher was also married with children. He told me he had sex with her in her house when her husband wasn't around.

He adds, "I don't feel like a victim. If anything, I felt extraordinarily special. That's what I took away from it, that I am different from all the other kids. Why would a person risk their livelihood, basically, to be with me sexually?" This man said the affair left him with a lot of confidence sexually and plenty of self-assurance in the company of women. But he also acknowledged that over the years, he's seen patterns in his life that he could trace back to this defining experience. Although he has been in a series of long-term relationships with women, he's never been married, never had any children, and doesn't want a traditional family: "I became very, very skeptical of marriage and all of the stuff we are fed. . . . I guess, at a very early age, maybe earlier than is healthy — I became very cynical. I became aware that many marriages are based on lies, and certainly this one was." His teacher was later divorced.

And there was the issue of secrecy: "I couldn't tell anyone and that was a bit of a problem. I had a secret. And I kept that secret." In analyzing his past, he feels that he may have unconsciously associated sexual excitement with secrecy and deceit, leading to a spotty track record with fidelity as an adult: "It does lay a foundation of deceit that's going to be a blueprint. In order to feel that same level of excitement, you have to do this stuff. You find that you want to maintain or reach that point again."

Dr. Kliman believes that a minor who has

sex with an adult is *doubly* traumatized when this person is a teacher because of the special status teachers hold in our society, what he calls "a position of special trust and authority, not very different from a parent or someone else on whom you are depending, like a doctor. . . . It's confusing to their moral development."

The anonymous man who experienced sex with his teacher as a teenager seemed to be describing the same thing in a different way. "I was introduced to sex and I learned about adults lying and the excitement of the possibility of getting caught. It's a very powerful combination," he says. The excitement of this first experience set the bar extremely high for future interactions of an intimate nature. He continues, "My subsequent relationships, both emotionally and sexually? It's going to be tough to match the excitement I had in junior high school. The boy who was with Mary Kay Letourneau, imagine him trying to — where the bar was raised for him — maintain that kind of excitement. He actually figured it out. Marry the one that raised the bar."

Except, according to the experts, you'd be marrying a woman with serious emotional problems. And the case of Mary Kay Letourneau would probably win the grand prize when it comes to strange and dysfunctional sexual behavior.

THE MOTHER OF THEM ALL

Today, Mary Kay Letourneau, in her mid-forties, and Vili Fualaau, in his twenties, are married and bringing up their two young daughters. You might say both of their children were conceived illegally. By law, she was the criminal, he was the victim.

Letourneau was a thirty-four-year-old suburban Seattle teacher and a married mother of four children when she crossed the line, embarking on an illicit relationship with Vili, a thirteen-year-old student, who soon impregnated her. She was charged with child rape. Not long after, she gave birth to the child the boy had fathered. After Mary Kay pleaded guilty, the judge gave her a seven-year sentence, but told her she would only have to serve about six months as long as she got treatment and stayed out of trouble. Staying out of trouble meant staying away from young Vili.

After a short prison stint, Mary Kay Letourneau was released. About a month later, police caught Mary Kay in a car with the very same boy, who had turned fourteen by this time. Not only had she violated the conditions of her probation, but to some it looked like she might have been trying to flee the country, what with the passport and several thousand dollars in cash she was carrying. This time Mary Kay was sent back to prison for seven years. Once there, it was discovered she was pregnant *again,* with her second child by Vili, her sixth child all told. Since Daddy was just a boy and Mommy was in the slammer, the two little girls lived with Vili's mother. Meantime, Mary Kay reportedly still tried to write to Vili and did time in solitary for it. Still she managed to send the boy coded messages. In 2001, while she was behind bars, Mary Kay Letourneau's father died. She wanted to attend his funeral. The powers that be said no.

Upon Mary Kay's final release from prison in August 2004, Vili was an adult. So their relationship became legal. They were married the next year. In June 2006, *Dateline NBC's* Josh Mankiewicz reported on the Fualaau family, which now included their two young daughters. One interesting observation: "The two growing girls and their loving parents seem downright . . . ordinary." Many have analyzed their odyssey as it progressed from the bizarre to the ordinary. Mary Kay and Vili are even listed as authors of their own book, called *Un Seul Crime,*

L'amour [*Only One Crime, Love*].

TAINTED LOVE?

An unlikely love story or a sign of serious mental illness . . . or both? Rational people can disagree. But a review of Letourneau's family history reveals a disturbing pattern of sexual secrets that she may have unconsciously been acting out. There is a psychological theory that children will reenact their family's most shameful secrets and traumas, handing them down generation to generation, disguised in new variations, unless and until the spell is broken with genuine transformative healing therapy. Could this be the case here?

Letourneau's father, John Schmitz, was an extremely conservative politician and college professor from Orange County, California. He served in Congress and ran for president of the United States in 1972 on the ultra-right American Independent Party ticket. As is so often the case, it turned out he was practicing the very kind of licentious behavior he publicly condemned. Mary Kay's mother, Mary Schmitz, was a conservative television pundit who crusaded against feminism and for so-called family values while she raised her seven children. Then scandal struck.

It was discovered that Letourneau's righteous dad was leading a double life and had fathered two children illegitimately during an affair with a former student and campaign worker. The careers of Mary Kay's parents fell apart. She was in college at the time and reportedly defended her dad through the waves of bad publicity. Gregg Olsen's book *If Loving You Is Wrong: The Shocking True Story of Mary Kay Letourneau* quotes Mary Kay as saying, "My father has a human side, an intimate side, to him too. That does not belong in the public. It should be kept private. He has needs — and I don't mean sexual — that are no one's business. I never asked about it and it wasn't my place to ask about it. It was none of my business." Or was it?

The commonalities between Mary Kay's story and her father's story are striking. Both had two children out of wedlock with a student when they already had large families. "I think it's identical," says defense attorney Anne Bremner, who represented the police in a civil suit Vili filed against them. Bremner's sense of it is that both father and daughter were narcissists who believed the rules did not apply to them: "I can tell you that Mary absolutely believes that what she did was absolutely right, that it was simply a moral lapse because she was married and a teacher. . . . She feels like she's the Joan of Arc of forbidden love and she likes the attention."

Mary Kay's behavior lends itself to the theory that children unconsciously feel compelled to act out their parents' secrets to bring the issues into the light of day. Even though her father's secret had been exposed to the world, it may not have been resolved in a way that allowed Mary Kay to learn and to grow from it. If it was okay for him to defy the rules, then it was okay for her to defy the rules. They were united by this. At least during her formative years "Mary was really close to her dad," Bremner told me.

Despite the father's scandal, it seems as if the family never experienced the catharsis of honestly coming to terms with their hypocrisy and double lives and changing their value system as a result. So Mary may have felt the unconscious compulsion to tell the story again. And the way in which Mary acted it out may have had a lot to do with an earlier trauma in her life.

Mary Kay was about eleven years old when her toddler brother was found dead in the swimming pool. According to the Gregg Olsen book and other published reports, at least one family friend believes

Mary Kay had been asked to watch him. If so, imagine the guilt that she carried with her through life. Even though Mary Kay has been quoted as saying it was a tragic family accident and no one was ever blamed, she was also said to be heartbroken, as she adored her kid brother. Imagine the ways her unconscious might have struggled to save a little boy's life. When she met Vili, she took the underprivileged boy under her wing. The deep wellspring of love that she's always claimed she felt for Vili may have been the thwarted love for her little brother redirected at this youngster. The scenario of being with Vili could have allowed her to unconsciously and symbolically undo the death of her little brother and simultaneously act out her family's drama of hypocrisy and double lives.

THE BIPOLAR DEFENSE

Is it coincidence that Mary Kay Letourneau and Debra Lafave both reportedly suffered from bipolar disorder? The illness is known to cause wild mood swings, from being manic or extremely "up" at one extreme to being depressed or very down at the other extreme. Severe behavioral changes can accompany these mood swings. The periods of extreme moods are called episodes. Some mental health professionals say manic episodes can cause hypersexual behavior, inappropriate acting out of a sexual nature.

But clinical psychologist Julia Hislop says many women have inappropriate sex for the very reasons people abuse other substances, "as a quick, but unhealthful fix to whatever is wrong — like people use compulsive gambling, compulsive spending, drugs, or alcohol." In other words, it's an escape.

What was Debra Lafave's history? "I tried to find out as much as I could about her life before and her family," says crime reporter Shannon Colavecchio–Van Sickler, who wrote about the death of Debra's only sister in 2001 in a car accident: "Her sister had died in a really terrible crash while she was pregnant. . . . The man who hit her, who was apparently drunk, they said, was in the military." The reporter learned that Debra was deeply traumatized by this sudden loss of her sister, a tragedy whose three-year anniversary roughly coincided with the illicit relationship with the boy. "It really crushed her and the whole family," said the journalist. Another reporter told me the unborn child, a girl, had already been named. Lafave's mother reportedly said the trauma of it all turned Debra into a "basket case."

Two Florida publications reported that Debra had told her then-husband, Owen, that she had been raped by an older boy in a classroom when she was thirteen years old. Debra confirmed that she had been raped as a young teen when she spoke out on *Dateline NBC* to Matt Lauer. While Debra's attorney, John Fitzgibbons, turned down my request for an interview, *The Tampa Tribune* quotes him as saying, "At trial, we were prepared to discuss the impact of the sexual assault when she was young."

Dr. Hislop says women who have sex with boys almost always have very traumatic backgrounds, and in some cases, "you'll find trauma at the same age as that of their target." So if a girl is raped at thirteen, when she becomes a woman she may take the role of victimizer *against* a young teenager. Therapists call this "identifying with the aggressor."

There is no science to explain this phenomenon, but mental health experts have often noted that human beings rework their most significant life traumas in many different ways, not always as literal reenactments, but sometimes in very disguised and oblique ways. The unconscious works in riddles. Sometimes only certain elements of a past trauma need to match up for the mind to make a connection.

FORBIDDEN LOVE?

Perhaps most interesting, a local television reporter for Tampa's *ABC Action News* got the exclusive interview with Casey Martinez, the woman who told investigators she dated Debra in high school. Martinez chose to speak only to Tampa's *ABC Action News* reporter Sarina Fazan. In an on-camera interview, Martinez claimed that a decade ago, she and Debra were romantically involved. Casey showed the reporter photos of her and Debra hanging out together as teenagers. She claimed they were sweethearts until Debra's disapproving mother broke them up. "We were young and in love and we had a happy time and good memories together. . . . Her mom withdrew her from school and sent her to [another high school]," said Casey. "It was very hurtful."

Parents enter a danger zone when they attempt to control the sexual leanings of their children. Sexuality is like a thumbprint. Everyone's is different. If you try to force somebody to be what they aren't, you may want to brace yourself for the backlash. Was Debra's sexual acting-out a consequence of what Casey has described as a premature termination of their same-sex relationship?

If, in fact, Debra was prevented from being with this *teenage girl,* who some might describe as a *tomboy,* did it set the stage for Debra to later seek out a *teenage boy?* Was she subconsciously trying to rewrite history and reclaim old passions by replacing one forbidden lover with another? "Casey said they were in a relationship like a teenaged boy would be in with a teenaged girl. . . . Casey feels that relationship would have continued on if Debra did not have to transfer schools," reporter Sarina Fazan told me.

Fazan says she is certain the relationship between Casey and Debra did happen: "I heard it was happening from so many of her friends in high school and so forth, but I wanted more concrete information as well." Fazan said she also interviewed Casey's parents, who confirmed it. "I met with Debra and her parents privately. They confirmed it as well."

I was never able to reach anyone from Lafave's family to confirm or deny the story. But Owen Lafave refers to this chapter in Deborah's life in his brilliantly titled book, *Gorgeous Disaster: The Tragic Story of Debra Lafave,* written with Bill Simon. In the book, Owen — who attended the same high school — claims Debbie and this girl "met at the house of a classmate, a girl who was, as we say, playing on the same team. Apparently Debbie found something pleasing in the sensual experience, because she came back for more. Several times." Owen adds that Deborah was badly teased. "Whispers spread around the school like wildfire: Deborah Beasley was making it with Maria." He uses the pseudonym Maria for Casey Martinez. He writes that not long after she was transferred out of that high school, "Debbie went into the bathroom at home, took a razor blade out of the medicine chest, and cut her wrists." He called it a cry for help.

Too Hot to Handle

But from what I saw of the national media coverage of this case, few cable TV outlets discussed this particular aspect of Debra's history. This is typical. Real-life tidbits that stray too far off script from what's considered normal sexuality don't get a lot of play. "I don't think we want to go there" is how I heard a TV producer once dismiss a suggestion that an alleged lesbian affair be included in a discussion of a movie star's life. Certainly, the producer may have had valid legal concerns regarding whether the claim was true, whether the story could expose them to charges of slander. But that doesn't stop the media from discussing other sensational and potentially libelous aspects of stars' lives. We never just say "Let's not go there" unless there's another dynamic at work.

Don't we need to go there if we want to have an honest discussion of why people do what they do? One reporter suggested to me that the national media didn't focus on Lafave's same-sex story because it seemed "too tabloidy." Oh, and graphic details about woman/boy sex in the back of a van aren't tabloidy? Homophobia is promoted in many subtle ways. Pretending same-sex relationships don't exist is one of the most common methods.

According to reporter Candace Rondeaux, the entire Lafave story offered the media "an interesting opportunity to discuss how sex offenders evolve into the person that they become." Sadly, the mainstream media barely scratched the surface because of their misplaced instincts that girl-on-girl relationships would make viewers uncomfortable. Guess what, girl-on-girl relationships are everywhere, and people are interested in learning about them. "People still stop and ask me about the story," says Sarina Fazan. "They want to know more details."

Fazan told me that Casey Martinez felt doubly traumatized, first by the sudden breakup with Debra years earlier, then again by the fear that she might be called as a reluctant witness in the trial and have her life turned into a spectacle as Debra's attorneys tried to establish an insanity defense. Here's my suggestion for an insanity defense: "I couldn't be who I really was, and it drove me nuts."

As it turned out, Casey would not have to testify. There would be no trial. Debra got a plea bargain in one county. In the other county, the one where she had sex with the boy while his cousin drove, the judge wanted a trial but didn't get one because prosecutors dropped the charges. It turns out the boy at the center of the case didn't want to testify, and his mother argued that it would traumatize him to do so.

SWEETHEART DEAL?

While many have expressed the sentiment that Debra got away with it as a result of her beauty, an inside peek at her distraught family paints a different picture. After losing one daughter to a drunk driver, this family then had to stand by helplessly as media from around the world dissected the most private facts of their other daughter's life.

Reporter Sarina Fazan says she met Debra's parents at the height of the case, when it seemed like the whole world was obsessed with the family. "To me it was heartbreaking. Her father had tears in his eyes . . . and her mother too." And what about Debra's now ex-husband? In his book, Owen Lafave describes being taunted by radio DJs about his sex life as he struggled to cope with a tsunami of media attention. He is now remarried and has successfuly moved on with his life.

Early in the investigation, Debra Lafave was forced to submit to an invasive and graphic photo shoot that left her feeling violated. Police were able to get a search warrant for her body after the boy described certain unique characteristics he noticed during their sex romps. Debra was forced to put her feet into stirrups as photos were taken of her genitals. Reporter Candace Rondeaux agrees with police who say genital photo identification is not unusual in sex crimes, but adds, "Just from a layman's point of view, that seemed a little bit out of hand. Because really what they were trying to do was see if she had a Brazilian wax." Tattoos and tan lines were other identifying marks. Lafave's attorney vehemently complained that police had gone too far.

So why didn't Debra Lafave try to prevent the snapping of pictures her lawyer called pornographic and a tremendous invasion of privacy? The attorney declined to be interviewed. But law enforcement sources told me the body search was done on Debra on the day of her arrest, raising the question of whether she'd even had a chance to strategize with her initial lawyer at that point.

What if she had refused on her own? Law enforcement officials say they are allowed to use reasonable force to gain compliance with a search warrant on someone's body, just as they can bust in the front door of a home when they're armed with a search warrant and the people inside refuse to answer the door.

Says Rick Ridgway, chief assistant state attorney for Florida's Fifth Circuit, "Your privacy, my privacy, anybody's privacy goes so far. But if there's evidence regarding the commission of a crime and a judicial officer determines there's probable cause to believe that evidence will be found, the court then authorizes a search for that evidence." While some legal experts say there are cases where defense attorneys have gone to court to try to quash a search warrant, it's rare. Noted

Massachusetts private investigator Tom Shamshak puts it this way: "The practicalities are . . . you want to fight it, you can do that afterward, but I got a warrant and I'm executing it right now. Now please comply." And reports are that in Debra's case a jail nurse was present and the photographs were taken by a female detention deputy, all proper procedure.

Debra Lafave described the experience to NBC's Matt Lauer in a *Dateline* special: "I can remember just shaking. And trying as hard as I could to clench my legs together to keep 'em shut. And, in fact, the nurse said — 'cause I was crying — she said, 'Honey, were you raped?' And I wanted to look at her and say, 'Yeah I've been raped. I was raped when I was thirteen. I'm being raped right now.' Forcing my legs apart and doing that. It was a complete violation."

Perhaps the most famous body search *ever* was the one conducted on pop star Michael Jackson back in 1993, when authorities got a warrant to photograph the superstar's body in a search for corroborating evidence in the child molestation accusation against him, which eventually settled out of court for millions with no charges filed.

In the wake of the photo session, Michael Jackson made a now-famous on-camera statement about the body search. Addressing the public, he said, "I have been forced to submit to a dehumanizing and humiliating examination by the Santa Barbara County Sheriff's Department. . . . They served a search warrant on me, which allowed them to view and photograph my body, including my penis, my buttocks, my lower torso, thighs, and any other area that they wanted. . . . It was the most humiliating ordeal of my life, one that no person should ever have to suffer. . . . It was a nightmare, a horrifying nightmare."

But back to Debra's body search. Even though there were no men in the room when the photos of Debra were taken, the speculation was that some male investigators surely looked at the photos, and have studied them a tad too carefully. Said one reporter, "I think we all surmised those pictures are out there somewhere, floating with the police in locker rooms and so forth."

When word of the photos surfaced, a very public legal battle was kicked off as news organizations unsuccessfully attempted to get hold of them, citing the sunshine laws. Debra's lawyer fought to keep them sealed and won that ruling. Still, it's a cautionary tale about what can happen when you get arrested. If they've got a search warrant, they can take a piece of you for testing, be it your hair, the dirt under your fingernails, or your saliva.

When they're searching for evidence, at least they need a warrant or a court order, absent the suspect's permission. In prison, the privacy violations, in the form of strip searches and the like, are a constant reminder of the loss of power that comes with incarceration. And in those cases, since they're searching for contraband, they generally don't need a warrant.

There was one more strange twist of a sexual nature in the Lafave story. As the case progressed, one of the three detectives who sought to have those graphic photos of Lafave taken was arrested on suspicion of soliciting a woman to commit prostitution. He was allegedly caught on tape paying a woman $140 to have sex with him.

According to the *St. Petersburg Times,* the manager of a Tampa lingerie shop complained that one of his models had been solicited twice by the detective. She reportedly agreed to help authorities catch the cop with a videotaped sting. Officials tell me he eventually got his criminal case dismissed after entering and successfully completing a pretrial misdemeanor intervention program for first-time offenders.

Still, this is a perfect illustration of how a highly publicized criminal case exposes the secrets of those on its periphery. After the officer's arrest, a police internal affairs investigation was launched. That probe allegedly uncovered further misconduct, all of which made the local paper. A Temple Terrace police spokeswoman told the *St. Petersburg Times* that the detective downloaded several images of adult porn and visited several pornographic websites from his work computer. In all, internal affairs investigators said they found a dozen violations. City officials announced the detective's resignation, and the Temple Terrace police chief announced he was "embarrassed and ashamed" of the detective's conduct, even though they found no irregularities with his work on the Lafave case. For law enforcement, the timing was awful.

The detective's arrest led some to wonder about the caliber of the cops assigned to investigate Debra and whether they had lost the moral high ground. Lafave's lawyer labeled the local Temple Terrace police headquarters a "wild and crazy place" and a "frat house."

The better it got in terms of a news story, the worse it got for the mother of the boy in question. As national news media lined up to cover the trial, she realized she did not want her son traumatized by having to be the star witness, forced to give an X-rated play-by-play of his sexual encounters with his teacher for the nation's entertainment.

Reporter Candace Rondeaux put it this way: "It just became more and more salacious, and I think, as these dribs and drabs came out in the press, it was becoming very apparent that this was a runaway train and nobody could control it. And that must have really frightened the mother of the victim in this case. And she said as much."

Since Debra's alleged sexcapades with the boy occurred in two Florida counties, this was a case that involved two jurisdictions. Ultimately, the case collapsed in the second county. Not wanting to subject the boy to the embarrassment and potential trauma of testifying in such a high-profile sex case, prosecutors folded. Debra was left with the lenient plea deal from the first jurisdiction, which gave her no jail time and house arrest. After it was all over, in late March 2006, Debra spoke to the media and scolded them.

Debra Lafave: My greatest regret would probably be the fact that I put this young man through this. I mean, the media has totally taken it out of proportion and he's suffering even more so by the media's actions. . . . He is a young man and his privacy has been violated. He has walked outside the door and has been approached by the media. His picture was published on the Internet. That's what I'm talking about.

No, Debra didn't sound very remorseful. She seemed to be passing the blame and only gave brief lip service to her part in the fiasco. It's always easy to slam the messenger who delivers the unwelcome news. The fact is, the mainstream media showed considerable restraint in protecting this young man's identity, much more restraint than Debra herself showed when it came to her own impulses.

Perhaps the final irony is that, after all of this, guess what Debra Lafave hopes to become?

Debra Lafave: Right now, I'm going through a class that's online for journalism. I think that I have, God has given me, a great outlet to write and I would hope that I could reach people through writing.

Unnamed Reporter: So after all this, you want to become one of us?!!

Debra Lafave: Yes . . .

Some predict she will make a great local news anchor. Except she might have to work on her voice, because she had a tendency to engage in baby talk with her student lover.

PINKY PROMISE

After police learned of the relationship between Lafave and the minor, they arranged for the boy to call her in the hopes of getting her on tape confirming the affair. Recordings of the calls reveal a woman who sounds like she's suffering from arrested development, a common syndrome in women who seek out underage boys. Psychiatrists say that emotionally, they may not feel much older than the children they're seducing.

Boy: So, what time are you planning on heading over?

Debra: Are you sure? Like, I just feel . . . I mean, I don't want you lying to your mom. I mean, it's like . . .

Boy: No, it's all right. She's gone in a sales meeting, like all day.

Debra: You sure?
Boy: Yeah. . . .
Debra: All right. Promise?
Boy: Yes.
Debra: Pinky promise?
Boy: Yes.
Debra: Say pinky promise.
Boy: Pinky promise.

13
THE POINT OF
NO RETURN

In the summer of 2005, there was a war.
There were corruption scandals in government and business, famines in Africa, a
devastating hurricane, and a dangerous
Avian flu. But if you had to pick the two
stories that intrigued Americans the most,
they would have to be the sudden disap-
pearances of teenager Natalee Holloway in
Aruba and honeymooner George Smith on
a Mediterranean cruise.

These two mysteries would keep millions
of viewers hooked to America's cable TV
shows for months on end, and still the
secrets of what really happened eluded the
captivated nation. Both cases featured good-
looking young Americans who had gone off
on exotic vacations and never come back.
Each had somehow reached the point of no
return. And in each case, the suspicion was
murder.

Natalee Holloway was a popular eighteen-year-old who loved being part of the dance team at her Birmingham, Alabama, high school. Beautiful and blond, she had just graduated and was among more than a hundred seniors who took part in an annual vacation tradition, a trip to the exotic island of Aruba, a country that is part of the Kingdom of the Netherlands and sits in the Caribbean Sea less than twenty miles off the coast of Venezuela. On the last night of the trip, after five glorious days of fun, Natalee disappeared.

"It's just agony. . . . I don't have any closure," Beth Holloway Twitty told me. Natalee's mother was on a cell phone at an airport when we spoke on Saturday, May 20, 2006. We were less than two weeks from the one-year anniversary of her daughter's disappearance. The airline had lost Beth's luggage and she'd just gotten word of a possible major break, a new arrest, in her missing daughter's case.

It was just another topsy-turvy day for a woman who had turned her life into a crusade for answers: "You know what, Jane, it's not just me. I think everyone is being dragged up and down. When I'm in the airport, in every state across the U.S., I just have so many people that . . . are also wanting answers and are so tired of the lack of a resolution in her investigation." Beth was not imagining things. Millions of people were religiously tuning in to the case coverage, tagging along on every turn of her tormented journey.

I could hear the anguish, frustration, desperation, and determination in Beth's voice, all rolled up into an otherwise gentle Southern drawl. From the moment she got word on May 30, 2005, that her daughter had failed to appear at Aruba's airport for the flight home, the once-average American mom has focused like a laser beam on finding out what happened to her daughter and bringing those responsible to justice.

Natalee had been part of a large group of young people partying it up at the "in" bar, Carlos 'n Charlie's, as the vacation came to a close. After last call at 1 a.m., Natalee's friends saw her leaving with three young men.

The family's prominent attorney, John Q. Kelly, told me that back at the hotel, the girls who shared Natalee's room kept expecting her to show up in time to grab her bags and make the flight: "They were just hoping, like eighteen-year-old kids, that she would come in with the messed-up hair and makeup and a little bit tired and none the worse for wear and be ready to go to the airport." But Natalee never appeared. As they all left for the airport, one of the seven adult chaperones stayed behind at the hotel, hoping Natalee was just running late.

Beth told me that after she raced to Aruba her heart fell upon seeing Natalee's bags just sitting there: "That's what I envision when I think about that first night when I entered her hotel room, was seeing her cell phone, sitting on her luggage, silent. She didn't have international calling. What if she had? What if she could have called me or what if she could have called a friend?" Beth has clearly tormented herself about what more she could have done to protect her daughter before the girl took off on what had initially seemed like an innocuous foreign adventure. But the truth is, even the best mother can't protect her daughter from all the dangers in the world.

THE SECRET LIVES OF TEENS

In her quest for answers, it didn't take long for Beth's laser to hone in on three locals: Joran van der Sloot and his two buddies, twenty-one-year-old Deepak Kalpoe and eighteen-year-old Satish Kalpoe. Joran was a tall, handsome seventeen-year-old boy of Dutch descent and the Kalpoe brothers were Surinamese, from the South American country formerly known as Dutch Guiana.

The three young men left Carlos 'n Charlie's with Natalee and hopped into Deepak's silver gray car, the two brothers in the front, Joran and Natalee in back. When some of Natalee's friends spotted her driving off with the trio, they shouted at her to get out of the car. She either ignored their warnings or couldn't get out, and the car sped off with her inside. Natalee was never seen again. She vanished without a trace.

A young man-about-town in Aruba, Joran was known for gambling at the local casinos and charming the pretty foreigners who came and went on the island. Joran first met Natalee and her friends earlier that last evening, at the casino inside the Holiday Inn, where the Alabama students were staying. The girls reportedly invited Joran to join them later at Carlos 'n Charlie's, which he did. Joran claims that at the bar Natalee came on to him, asking him to dance and do a "jelly shot" (or Jell-O shot) off her. Also known as a "body shot," it's a popular drinking game that involves licking booze, sometimes in Jell-O form, off a girl's belly button.

Anybody who has ever caught a TV news report on Florida's spring-break antics knows how wild teenagers can be when they get away from home and parental discipline. The kids who engage in this revelry are not bad kids. Psychologists say even the best-behaved teen is likely to succumb to the peer pressure to party it up if she finds herself in that sort of combustible environment. Thanks to videos like *Girls Gone Wild,* parents are intellectually aware of the dangers, but they go along with the fantasy that *their* child won't be swept up in the excitement, idealizing their teenager's ability to maintain control.

The fact is, parents don't always know their own teens as well as they think they do. That's because teenagers have secret lives that go well beyond the KEEP OUT signs on their bedroom doors and their secret diaries or weblogs.

Noted psychotherapist Dr. Judy Kuriansky says, "It's a natural part of child development to go through what's called *separation-individuation.*" This is the process whereby the child, first during the terrible twos and then again in the teens, separates from Mom and Dad and develops his or her own identity. Dr. Kuriansky says this intrinsic developmental process is "why they need their independence and why they have to assert it . . . sometimes by rebellion and strong acts . . . testing limits . . . not sharing or having secret lives." The therapist says this is a very healthy process that teens need to experience in order to grow up. However, sometimes other factors can make that process dangerous.

Consider the convergence of risk factors on that night. Natalee was away from her parents in a foreign country. Alcohol was flowing. It was the last night of her vacation, the last opportunity to experience this much freedom before returning to a more structured existence. And she was interacting with a practiced seducer of young women, a young man who was going through his own metamorphosis into adulthood and was also testing boundaries.

Though still underage for boozing and betting at seventeen, Joran didn't deny he frequented the island's casinos and bars, drinking, gambling, and hitting on females. The legal age of eighteen for both drinking alcohol and gambling is not widely enforced, according to a popular Aruban travel guide. Also, Joran looked older than his age and carried himself with more confidence than most minors. He told ABC News, "that was part of my lifestyle . . . being single and picking up girls . . . going out with them, having a good time, then saying good-bye."

The situation was primed to spin out of control. Dr. Kuriansky says Natalee "could have ended up being a victim out of her naïveté." Dr. Kuriansky notes that sometimes it's the most well behaved and obedient teens who get in trouble, because they haven't developed the street smarts to spot the red flags. Those good kids "develop a trusting nature and their guard is down. . . . The sweetest dog in the pack gets the worst hurt." In an interview conducted by the FBI, one of Natalee's friends on the trip says as much. The FBI summary of the friend's recollections reads "HOLLOWAY was a very good dancer and often attracted men because of her dancing. HOLLOWAY was probably the least experienced with boys out of all of [the interview subject's] friends."

So what did happen that night? Sadly, the mystery remains intact. Like the island's sand, Joran's story kept shifting. While Aruban authorities have not officially released transcripts of the many interrogations they conducted of Joran, a picture has emerged from numerous reports leaked to the media, investigations by Natalee's parents, and Joran's own public statements.

It's clear that Joran gave differing accounts of what he and Natalee did that night.

That's one of the main reasons her mother, Beth, is so convinced he is hiding something and knows what happened to Natalee. While Joran reportedly flip-flopped on details about twenty-five times, here are two of his most quoted explanations:

Story #1: At first, Joran said that after they left Carlos 'n Charlie's, the three boys drove Natalee back to her hotel, the Holiday Inn, and dropped her off there. Joran initially said she stumbled as she got out of the car, but that she wouldn't let Joran help her. He added that security guards approached her as the boys drove off. This claim would result in the arrest of two local security guards. The two men angrily protested their innocence, as did their families. It turned out they had alibis and were released.

After that, Joran admitted he had been lying and changed his story. This infuriated Natalee's mother, who told me she heard Joran's initial lies firsthand: "Within the first three hours I was on the island, Joran van der Sloot was very insistent, was just insistent on taking me to the Holiday Inn to show me where he had dropped her off. To show me how the security guards came up. . . . Nobody asked Joran to create this lie. And then he retracted it ten days later with the police. He totally derailed the investigation. What was he covering up? Why engage in that type of behavior if you have nothing to be responsible for?"

Story #2: Joran finally settled on this explanation, which he outlined in news interviews. Joran said that after stopping at his house but not going in, the Kalpoes drove him and Natalee to the beach near another hotel, the Marriott. Joran told Fox News's Greta Van Susteren that after they dropped him off, the Kalpoes said they would be willing to pick Joran up later. This seems odd, given it was past one in the morning at this point and it would be hard to imagine friends agreeing to come back in the predawn hours to pick a buddy up from the beach.

Once at the ocean, Joran said they walked on the sand, held hands, talked, and kissed. As they ambled, Joran said, they headed north, away from Natalee's hotel. He insisted in this interview that Natalee was not drunk; "she had something to drink but she seemed fine . . . she knew what she was doing."

He also said they did not have sexual intercourse because he didn't have a condom with him, although earlier he'd stated that his intention was to have sex with her.

To me, this doesn't make a lot of sense. Wouldn't he realize that he didn't have a condom before he got to the beach? Then Greta asked him, "You had some sort of sexual contact at some point, is that right?" "Yes." "Was that in the car or was that on the beach?" "That was on the beach too."

Joran insisted Natalee simply refused to leave the beach that night and, since he had school the next morning, he ultimately left her there on the sand in the dark of night.

Joran told a crew from the TV show *A Current Affair,* "The worst thing I did was leaving her there at the beach. That was the worst possible thing I could have done. And, then, lie about it to try and, yes, to try and make myself not look bad, I guess." Efforts to independently confirm what actually happened have been futile.

SEX, DRUGS, AND RECOLLECTIONS

The question of whether Natalee was drunk or had been incapacitated by some date-rape drug became a crucial issue. In a civil suit, Natalee's family argued that "Natalee was sexually assaulted, was fondled and was touched without her consent by Joran and his accomplices, over and over again, as she drifted in and out of consciousness." Natalee's father said he reached that conclusion after reading a statement from Joran.

> I read his deposition on one of the first statements and he indicated that she was falling asleep, waking back up, you know, right after she left the nightclub at Carlos 'n Charlie's. . . . So common sense will tell you that if you're falling asleep and waking back up, you're not in a condition to walk along the beach.
>
> — Dave Holloway, Fox News, *On the Record*, February 27, 2006

This claim contradicts Joran's public statements that Natalee had been drinking but was not extremely inebriated.

In court papers, Joran's attorney implied the Holloway family was "manufacturing untruths and distorting the law." Joran's attorney argued that the Twitty/Holloway lawsuit against the van der Sloots, filed in New York, should be thrown out. In the summer of 2006, a judge agreed, dismissing the case by saying New York was not the proper venue. Beth Twitty was said to be "crushed." Beth and Natalee's father later filed suit against the Kalpoe brothers in Los Angeles.

Joran has repeatedly condemned the Holloways for accusing him of being a sexual assailant, something he insists is absolutely not true. The Kalpoes have similarly accused the Holloways of harassing them. They have repeatedly maintained their innocence. As of this writing, the three young men have not been charged with any crime.

But because they still remained suspects, the debates and speculation continued: Did Natalee and Joran have sex? If so, was it intercourse or oral sex, were the Kalpoes in any way involved, and — if so — was Natalee too drunk to consent, therefore making it a crime? It would seem the devil was in the salacious details, which no one could confirm.

Vanity Fair interviewed local businessman Charles Croes, who says he talked to Joran the very night after Natalee disappeared. In the article, the businessman said Joran told him, "The girl was crazy. She was just crazy." As they were driving around, Natalee complained that "her mother was 'like Hitler,' that she was a virgin and that she was a lesbian. . . . She told him she wanted to have sex. 'Did you have sex with her?' Croes asked. 'Yeah,' Joran said. 'She gave me a blow job.' " The magazine said Joran told Croes the oral sex happened in the backseat of Deepak's car. Joran insisted to

Greta Van Susteren that the intimate contact had happened on the beach. Again, the stories of what Joran allegedly told people about what happened and where are all over the map.

BLAME THE VICTIM?

The drug issue turned heated in March 2006, when *48 Hours* got an exclusive interview with Deputy Chief Gerold Dompig, at the time the lead investigator on the Holloway case. Dompig made a stunning allegation, not against Joran but against Natalee Holloway herself, telling a CBS correspondent that Natalee was "using way too much alcohol in combinations which could basically be lethal." Dompig didn't stop there, saying, "We have statements claiming that she, that she had drugs." He wouldn't say what kind of drugs or that anyone saw her consume them, merely "that they saw her with drugs in her possession." Dompig went on to say that Natalee probably went into shock and collapsed and died and that whatever crime did occur was not a murder, but merely someone or a group illegally getting rid of her body.

Natalee's family was outraged, saying the authorities were trying to blame the victim. Said Beth Twitty's attorney, John Kelly,

"First of all, you don't even have Natalee, you don't know what happened to her, so how can you say it involves drugs or alcohol? There is absolutely no indication that played any role in it, and he didn't cite any basis for that statement, he just said it. It was totally irresponsible. . . . I'm not sure if he is incompetent, he may be covering things up." Dompig was soon replaced as the head of the investigation.

And Dompig's theory doesn't answer this question: Where is Natalee's body? As one TV commentator asked sarcastically, did she dig a hole and bury herself too? Considering the way the island's been turned upside down, had she been buried there, several experts suspect her remains would have probably turned up by now.

The notion of an intoxicated Natalee going for a late-night swim, drowning, and drifting out to sea was debunked by tests that showed tides would wash a body back to shore. And all boats that night were reportedly accounted for, as there is a radar perimeter around the island's waters designed to catch drug smugglers.

Natalee's family believes there was foul play, and that Joran and the Kalpoe brothers were involved. John Kelly, the Holloway lawyer, expressed his exasperation this way:

"It's just incredible that, whether it's Scott Peterson or guys who plan for years to murder wives or business associates . . . and still can't pull off the perfect crime. But here, there appears to be three kids who have pulled off the perfect crime. No evidence, no body, no witnesses to go on so far." Joran spent about three months in jail in Aruba and was repeatedly interrogated before being released. He has said he deserved to be behind bars . . . for lying.

Liar, Liar

Joran is probably the most extreme example of a compulsive liar since Scott Peterson. He had a track record of lying *before* Natalee went missing. He admits to lying to Natalee and telling her he was nineteen, when he was still seventeen. Others say he lied by leading the Alabama girls to believe that he was a student on vacation from Holland. He admits lying by omission to his own father that night, sneaking out of the house to go to Carlos 'n Charlie's without telling his dad. Then, he insisted, he lied about dropping Natalee off at her hotel because he didn't want to look like a cad for leaving her on the beach.

Joran has absolutely no credibility and cannot be believed. Period. When you lie continuously about little things, then no one can believe you on the big things. He's a guy who seems to lie for convenience and for the sheer fun of it. His parents were reportedly having a hard time controlling him around the time of this tragedy.

The exasperating thing about it is, his lying cuts both ways. You could argue that the only reason he had to lie was to cover up a crime. You could also argue that, as a compulsive liar, Joran would lie when a lie wasn't really necessary, just because he had developed the habit of not telling the truth and lying is how he dealt with most situations.

Because of this, some have criticized Natalee's family for focusing exclusively on Joran, claiming they never fully opened their minds to other possibilities, that a stranger could have abducted her from the beach afterward, or that she took a cab somewhere, or that someone in the Alabama group was responsible, or even that she ran away or was sold into white slavery, although this last possibility was dismissed as ridiculous. As the anonymous reporter told me, "The sex trade doesn't go to Colombia and Venezuela, it comes *from* Colombia and Venezuela to Aruba, where prostitution is legal, as it is in Venezuela." I was surprised to learn about the legality of prostitution on the island. "It's funny, it's not one of those things you read about in the tourist brochures," he said with a chuckle. The reporter added that the island is also in the middle of the superhighway of drug trafficking, and while there aren't a lot of murders in Aruba, drugs are plentiful, as are drug dealers and dens. And wherever you have drug dens, you have potential danger.

NEVER MIND

As the case dragged on, the media frenzy only increased, fed by a steady stream of intriguing developments that never quite panned out. In what *CNN Headline News* host Nancy Grace has described as a "catch and release" program, the authorities kept arresting people but ultimately letting them go. The security guards, Joran, the Kalpoe brothers, Joran's dad, a party-boat disc jockey — all were netted and then freed.

Then, almost a year after she disappeared, came word that a casino worker at the Holiday Inn who'd since moved to the Netherlands had been arrested. Could it be the big break we were all waiting for? It seemed possible, at first. Some published reports claimed this nineteen-year-old man knew Joran and had spent the day after

Natalee's disappearance with him.

But the new suspect's prominent European attorney reportedly convinced Aruban prosecutors that the evidence was extremely thin and they should let him go if he would remain available for questioning in the Netherlands. Another seemingly promising lead frittered away to nothing.

It struck me as odd that an island that was trying to step out of the negative spotlight would keep giving us new developments that seemed to lead nowhere. To arrest someone and then basically say "Never mind" seemed absurd and self-destructive. But then I learned there are stark differences between the Dutch and the American judicial systems. Aruban lawyer Benvinda de Sousa explained it this way: "The difference between the American system and our system, the Dutch Aruban system, is that you in America have an accusatory system. We have an inquisitory system. So when you [in the U.S.] bring a person in, you either charge them or you let them go. In our system, you bring them in and you see if there's enough evidence to continue the investigation. You hold them, but you don't charge them yet."

To illustrate just how radically different our two systems are, compare this. In

California, after you arrest someone you usually only have two days, or at most seventy-two hours, to charge them or they must be released. Contrast that with the Aruban Dutch system, where — if the evidence keeps mounting and a judge periodically approves — you can hold a suspect for over a hundred days without charging him. Says de Sousa, in Aruba "every time the extension is requested by the D.A., they need to come in with a little more evidence . . . to justify" holding the suspect longer. In America, police will often keep a suspect under surveillance, holding off on the actual arrest until they've gathered enough evidence to formally charge him. Scott Peterson's case is a perfect example of that.

SEARCH PARTY

Almost from the start of the Natalee Holloway case, the many and sundry search parties in Aruba generated their own media heat and controversy. After claims of possible Natalee sightings, a pond was drained, a landfill excavated, and sand dunes were studied for clues. Hundreds of tourists and locals joined together to conduct sweeps of the island. Critics accused one search group of trampling nesting grounds for endangered turtles.

The Netherlands sent F-16s to fly over the island with infrared sensors. Holland also brought in tracking dogs and more. "They brought in ground-penetrating radar. It was the same kind that they used in Bosnia to find mass graves," one journalist who wished to remain anonymous told me. He added that after all was said and done, the hot spots revealed the skeletal remains of buried dogs.

The American media went crazy when a bone that looked human washed up on the shore of Venezuela. The bone had been picked up by a Venezuelan dog and brought to its master, who then sent it to authorities, who had it tested. It was another red herring. "It just shows the insanity of this case and the way the investigation may have been mismanaged, looking at a bone washed up in Venezuela," said the reporter.

"A dog-and-pony show" is how some referred to it. The Aruban authorities, while putting on a formidable show of effort, may have allowed crucial evidence to slip away. While Aruban authorities insisted they quickly began surveillance, phone taps, and e-mail monitoring on the three suspects, American law enforcement experts complained about the lack of a swift and thorough investigation into the van der Sloot compound, where Joran lived in a separate apartment from his parents. "You've got forty-eight hours after a disappearance. After that, you are in the red zone and may never find the person," crime scene reconstruction expert Ron Watson told the Associated Press. He added, "They should have immediately done a forensic sweep of van der Sloot's house . . . his clothing, and done the same with the [Kalpoe] boys."

CULTURE CLASH

In general, people move at a much slower pace on islands. There are no commuters racing to beat traffic, few urgent deadlines. Aruba's main industry is relaxation, and thus, it is a way of life. It's precisely the reason people go there on vacation, to get away from it all and unwind. With daytime temperatures averaging 82 degrees, that sleepy attitude cannot be turned off in a flash. It's ingrained.

Americans are ingrained with the opposite values. We cherish efficiency, competence, and alacrity. That may be why we are the world's superpower. But as many Americans learn when they go to foreign islands and demand fast service, the more they insist on speed, the slower the service gets. Call it passive aggressive if you want, but that's just how most island people around the world react to our demanding nature. They view it as American arrogance.

This familiar culture clash was heightened by the emotional urgency of the situation, as Natalee's mother, her current husband, Jug Twitty, and her ex-husband, Dave Holloway, Natalee's father, all arrived on the island frantically seeking answers. Who can fault a mother or father who is desperate to find her or his daughter? But some locals did, calling the Americans overly aggressive and high-handed.

When I spoke with Charles Croes, the wealthy Aruban businessman who has been vocal on the issue, he told me Natalee's family would have gotten more out of the authorities with a softer attitude: "Give them your confidence, believe in them, and they will do miracles . . . because what you are doing is campaigning . . . and in campaigning everything changes and an aggressivity comes out because things are not happening at your pace."

Nonsense, responded Beth's attorney, John Kelly, "If Beth had showed up there, stayed for two days, accepted their way of doing things, and said, 'Oh, I'm going back to the States, call me when you learn something,' I'm sure nothing would have happened," he says.

Another compounding factor is that island authorities are used to tourists disappearing and then turning up a few days later with wicked hangovers and bad sunburns. Still, Natalee's dad claims the local authorities were not just lackadaisical, they were corrupt. Dave Holloway has written a book called *Aruba: The Tragic Untold Story of Natalee Holloway and Corruption in Paradise.* In it, Dave claims when he rushed down to Aruba and walked into the police station, the first thing the investigator asked him was "How much money do you have?" A perplexed Dave writes that the investigator then "insinuated that she [Natalee] had met someone and fallen in love. 'This happens all the time. She will probably show up in a few days,' he theorized. 'She was just partying hard,' he added. 'Don't worry. Just go down to Carlos 'n Charlie's and have a beer.' " Dave writes that he was stunned by the attitude of the police; the investigator "was so confident that she was just partying it up on drugs that he told us this particular bar would be the best place to find her. However, he did warn us to watch our drinks very carefully, adding that sometimes people put drugs into them." While waiting outside Carlos 'n Charlie's, Dave writes, he was approached at least ten times by pushers selling drugs.

RIPPLE EFFECT

The Holloway case became the Rubik's Cube of crime. With no firm answers, the door was wide open for speculation. It seemed like everyone in America had put on their Sherlock Holmes cap and was playing sleuth. But the people of Aruba increasingly felt a game was being played at their expense.

For many on Aruba, the other crime became the vilification of their island and the people on it. Charles Croes called the American media's saturation coverage of the Holloway case "totally out of control. It's totally out of balance and the priorities are not right."

It was interesting for me to hear that, because I was part of that saturation coverage, and therefore, in his eyes, part of the problem. I would be called to fill in for *CNN Headline News* host Nancy Grace, and I knew there was a good chance the Holloway story would be part of the program. Why? The viewers wanted to hear about the case. They were captivated by the ongoing

573

mystery and the secrets that nobody seemed capable of digging up.

As the coverage dragged on, tensions rose between Aruba and the United States, especially as calls for a boycott of Aruba continued to get lots of media play. Charles Croes told me that the islanders would turn on their TVs every night and become enraged: "Television is worldwide now. We don't just watch Aruba TV. We watch the same thing you watch."

In response, Aruban tourism and commerce associations banded together to form a "Strategic Communications Task Force" to fight back against what they considered a public relations war on the island. They set up a website called Aruba Truth and began talking back angrily on American television, pointing out the many unsolved cases in the United States that don't spark domestic boycotts. They have a point. Look at the JonBenet Ramsey case. After ten years, that case remains unsolved, and yet nobody is suggesting we boycott Colorado, where the six-year-old girl was brutally murdered.

Prominent Los Angeles defense attorney Dana Cole says he understands the frustrations of those who want answers in the Holloway case, but points out, "A missing body case, frankly, is always very, very difficult to investigate for the police, because they have none of the forensic evidence. . . . So right away, the police are at a disadvantage if they have no body."

WHY THE OBSESSION?

Ironically, it was partly because the Holloway case was mired in chaos and conflict that the TV ratings were so spectacular. It would seem the Natalee Holloway story had all the elements to lure even the most jaded viewer. "It has all the drama . . . the mystery unfolds live on TV," observed George McQuade. As a media expert with the Entertainment Publicists Professional Society, McQuade notes that cable news shows are now competing with network reality shows like *Survivor* and crime dramas like *CSI*. That, he says, is why cable news shows seek out the most dramatic real-life mysteries and stick with the ones that consistently rate well.

Robert Thompson, who heads the Center for the Study of Popular Television at Syracuse University, told me it's no accident that the Holloway case rated so well. He believes it had many of the key elements a story needs to "break out." His list includes: a mysterious crime or disappearance; a number of really attractive people; some kind of sexual dimension; a likeable and compelling spokesperson; a scandalous element like race, gender, drugs, or alcohol; larger implications for the authorities regarding incompetence or corruption; any kind of celebrity connection; and an alluring setting. Aside from celebrity, the Natalee Holloway case had it all. In fact, these cases have a way of creating celebrities of their own, with Beth Twitty and even Natalee herself having become famous as a result of the tragedy.

It may seem cold to break down a news story's ingredients in this manner, considering that it's not fiction, that it involves real people experiencing real suffering. But many people have demanded an explanation for the massive coverage of this case, which critics say squeezed out other important stories that also needed the air time, stories that also involved life and death, stories that sometimes involved thousands of people.

Thompson says it's easy for the news coverage of a sexy story to veer out of control and take on a life of its own: "The more equity you build up in these stories, the more people want to see how they turn out. If you anoint these stories with the value of being covered, then to some extent you make it necessary for them to be covered, not only by you but by everybody else." With the Holloway story, the final act never seemed to arrive; there were just more tantalizing new arrests that required still more coverage. News reporters are, after all, pack animals. The big fear in any news meeting is, The competition's got a hot angle and we don't.

Some cynics have labeled the coverage Missing White Woman Syndrome, noting that many individuals who are poor, minority, gay, older, or unattractive go missing all the time, with barely a peep from the media. Clearly, there's a double standard, but it's society's double standard. You are voting for this coverage with your TV remote. The cable shows cover what the rating numbers indicate people want to watch. Missing White Woman Syndrome rates. So that's what we're seeing. We have to look at ourselves and ask, Why are we so interested in the Natalee Holloway case, as opposed to a disappearance in South Central Los Angeles, or the search for a missing senior citizen who walked out of a nursing home and hasn't been seen since?

Psychologists would say the honest answer is not flattering to the viewer. We all enjoy looking at video of Aruba. It's a beautiful place, and every time we see the beaches, we feel like we just vicariously visited that exotic locale. But then we start feeling resentful about how hard we're working and how we can't go on vacation. Then we see that this glamorous vacation has turned tragic for someone else. So we don't feel so bad about not being there. Our dreary, mundane lives feel better by comparison with even the most glamorous life beset by tragedy. This isn't just an explanation of the Holloway case, it's an explanation of all news. We watch the suffering of others to feel better about ourselves. As long as someone out there is having a rougher time of it, we're winning the battle of survival.

Media expert Robert Thompson says programming news according to ratings is simply business: "When we made the decision back in the 1920s that broadcasting was going to be supported by an income stream coming from advertising, all of this became inevitable." Charles Croes says what bugs him is that in playing up the story as a public service and a search for truth, the media hides the secret reality behind the coverage: "What's this all about? It's about money."

But the counterargument is that the focus on Natalee Holloway has created a new awareness of and respect for the issue of missing people. It used to be, Put them on the milk carton and forget about them. Now missing-persons cases are getting special attention and coverage. A lot of that was prompted by the Holloway case. Beth Twitty says since Natalee's disappearance there has been a greater "missing-person awareness, just in general . . . That's something else I think is positive that's come out of this."

Beth has volunteered to work on other missing-persons cases. She traveled to Ocilla, Georgia, to help publicize the search for another missing woman, Tara Grinstead, a popular teacher who simply vanished without a trace in October 2005. Tara's family was overjoyed that Beth had taken time out of the search for her own daughter to help them.

Beth has also created a foundation to help raise awareness of travel dangers, called International Safe Travels Foundation. She travels to schools and talks to students about how to protect themselves when traveling anywhere, outside the United States or just to the local mall. "By presenting Natalee's story, we're showing how important it is to bring your evening agenda full circle," Beth told me.

When you're in the national spotlight, someone is going to criticize everything you do. Some have suggested the fear inspired by Natalee's story is an example of "deviancy amplification spiral." This theory suggests that rare events can be made to seem commonplace because of media overemphasis, creating an amplification of the issue beyond what it deserves in terms of the threat it poses.

THE REAL NATALEE?

My biggest criticism of the media coverage has been the lack of three-dimensionality in the portrayals of the main character, Natalee Holloway. She is not here to speak for herself. Meanwhile, the descriptions of her and her behavior that night have swung from one extreme to another. At first, she was deified. No one dared to delve into her partying or her interest in boys or her drinking or any of the other typical teenage behaviors she may have been displaying on that trip. Initially, she was portrayed as the perfect girl, pure and chaste. But even as I observed this coverage, I knew it was only a matter of time before the other shoe would drop, and it did.

In January 2006, the coverage swung to the opposite extreme. That's when the *Vanity Fair* article claimed that Natalee gave Joran oral sex and asked him if the Kalpoe brothers, who are dark-skinned, were his slaves. This was based on what Joran allegedly told businessman Charles Croes. But the door had swung open and Natalee had been knocked off her pedestal. Now many tabloids, journalists, and bloggers felt at liberty to dissect every juicy detail of every lurid claim anybody made about what Natalee did or didn't do that night. She went from good girl to naughty girl in the turn of a page.

To me, both extremes were disrespectful to Natalee. She was not a saint, nor should she have to be! She was a healthy eighteen-year-old girl intent on exploring the mysteries of being alive. Of course she is going to have sexual curiosity. Does anyone really think that is limited to teenage boys or girls of loose morals? *Everyone* has sexual curiosity at eighteen. She was partying — big deal! She was on the last night of her trip to paradise, and she may well have been trying to squeeze out every last ounce of fun she could before her carriage turned into a pumpkin. So what! Back in my day, we didn't do jelly shots, we did "snake bites."

Similar concept, except you had to suck a lemon wedge out of someone's mouth after doing a shot. Of course, my parents had no idea I was off doing snake bites. This is what young people do. Let's get real. It's not a crime. Killing someone is a crime.

We can say all we want about Missing White Woman Syndrome, but Natalee's also been the victim of sexist coverage in the media, which simply reflects societal attitudes. Had she been a missing teenage boy, we would never have treaded so carefully around her behavior initially, nor would we have come down so salaciously later. We need to realize girls are *just* as sexual as boys, and there is no shame in that.

Enduring all of this was Natalee's mom. To me, Beth Twitty is an inspiration who reminds me that one individual can have an enormous impact if she is willing to devote every molecule of her being to a cause. "She is always available," said one journalist who has covered the case from the beginning. Day after day, week after week, Beth went from dawn until midnight giving interviews on television, over the phone, in person, in any way, shape, or form. She never stopped. One TV viewer told me she felt like she had developed a relationship with Beth, that

Beth had become part of the family. Millions felt the same way. Beth has set a new standard for how to command media attention and, in doing so, has changed the face of media coverage. Whatever your cause is, study what Beth has done and see if there's a way to follow her example to get media attention to your issue, be it personal or political.

Beth's main lesson is that there's nothing like the pressure of press coverage to keep authorities focused on a crime they might otherwise toss into the cold-case file.

The family of George Smith, who disappeared from a cruise ship, learned that lesson well. I spoke with George's sister, Bree, who told me that, like Beth, she and her parents have forged ahead, demanding answers. "Together, united, we've had the strength and the courage to fight. . . . We need to keep the story out there in order to get it solved, and we really learned that from Natalee Holloway's family."

Both the Holloway and the Smith cases seem to offer the tantalizing promise of the perfect crime, in which critical secrets remain intact despite the Herculean efforts of loved ones to uncover them. In both cases there are missing pieces of the puzzle that just cannot be found. Is someone who is still alive simply not talking, or has the truth gone to a watery grave, never to be dredged up?

Double-Action Intoxication

While we were celebrating America's independence on July 4, 2005, newlyweds George and Jennifer Smith were partying it up on the *Brilliance of the Seas,* a Royal Caribbean cruise ship making its way around the Mediterranean. The future seemed fabulous for the Connecticut couple. Both twenty-six and strikingly attractive, George and Jennifer had just experienced the glamour of Monte Carlo and the magic of Mykonos and were headed for Turkey as July 4 wound down.

Late that night, the Smiths found themselves in the ship's disco and were drinking heavily with a group of men. According to numerous published reports, they were drinking absinthe, a very strong alcohol that is illegal in the United States. On the Absinthe Buyers Guide website, one of the frequently asked questions is, What does absinthe do to you? The answer: "Drinkers of absinthe experience a double action intoxication. This intoxication combines the separate effects of strong alcohol and thujone. The alcohol produces a sedative effect in absinthe drinkers while the thujone is reported to cause hallucinations (both visual and auditory) as well as excitation." Thujone is "a chemical compound . . . a colourless liquid . . ." found in various plants. Wow. That's what they were drinking that fateful night, and it undoubtedly played a role in how events unfolded. Suffice it to say, secrets have a safe place to hide when absinthe is in the mix.

No one seems to dispute that Jennifer and George were quite drunk. Several witnesses told the Associated Press they saw George and Jennifer get into an argument, purportedly over her alleged flirtation with another man. According to witnesses, Jennifer was leaning on a guy. "We were afraid a fight was going to start. . . . She was flirting with him," said a Phoenix teacher on the cruise. The witnesses said Smith began calling his wife names and that's when Jennifer kicked her husband in the groin and stumbled out of the bar. "I was very surprised by their behavior, that a honeymoon couple would act that way," said the teacher. Another passenger said Smith was in pain from the hard kick, as he "bent over for quite a while."

According to the Associated Press, Jennifer has called the suggestion that she kicked her husband "ridiculous" and "outlandish. . . . That's not something I would do to my husband." She has not commented on claims that, as she left the bar, the man she'd been leaning on followed her out. That man, reportedly a ship employee who worked as a manager, later hired a lawyer, who insisted to *48 Hours* that ship records prove his client was already back in his room while Jennifer was still in the disco. Jennifer and her lawyer have also said publicly that she soon became unconscious and has *no recall* of what happened later that night.

As in the Holloway case, the risk factors on the night of George Smith's disappearance were enormous and the situation was primed for trouble. Honeymoons are sexually charged events, in which jealousies can easily boil over into rage. Take some flirtation, mix it with high-test alcohol, add rowdy strangers who become drinking buddies, put it all on the high seas, and you've got the perfect storm.

EARWITNESS

According to CBS's *48 Hours,* which took an in-depth look at the case, there were four young men with George that last night, a California student and three Russian Americans. George was reportedly so drunk that the young men had to help him back to his room. The teacher put it this way: "His pupils were dilated. . . . I'll never forget that look in his eyes."

Once in his room, George saw that his wife wasn't in the cabin and reportedly wanted to go search for her. That is when the first loud debate erupted, according to a lawyer for one of the Russian men. According to the *48 Hours* report, the men said they took George to look for Jennifer, couldn't find her, and returned Smith to his cabin at 4:02 a.m. (Helping to establish a time line, the ship's sophisticated logs mark the exact time a lock is turned with a key.) The Russians contended they laid George on the bed and then the four young men left together.

Royal Caribbean, which had come under attack by Jennifer and the Smith family in the wake of George's disappearance, issued a detailed time line of what they say happened. The ship time line states that at 4:05 a.m., a complaint came in about "loud voices and drinking game noises coming from the Smith cabin." The complaining passenger, Clete Hyman, was a deputy police chief from Redlands, California, and, as such, his recollections tended to be quite detailed.

Hyman said that after he phoned in the complaint, he also banged on the wall. He said the voices continued, but not as loudly, until it seemed like some people were leaving the Smith cabin, because the voices moved outside the cabin door. Clete Hyman told MSNBC that, after that, things calmed down. While he could still hear male voices, they seemed engaged in normal conversation. However, after a few minutes, another commotion erupted.

Clete Hyman: And then we heard what sounded like arguing out on the balcony . . . couple of male voices arguing . . . Then, I heard a voice just repeatedly say "good night" and my first assumption was that someone was trying to usher these people that were arguing out of the cabin. . . . So, I waited for a couple of seconds and then opened the door and looked out. . . . I saw *three* younger males walking down the hallway.

If Clete saw three young men leave, did that mean a fourth man stayed behind with George? No, says the attorney for one of the Russian American men, insisting all four left together. Some suggest that with the ship's corridors being so narrow, Clete's view of the fourth man could have been blocked by the other three.

After that, said Hyman, he heard what sounded like furniture moving and thought perhaps someone was cleaning up the room. Then he heard furniture moving on the balcony. Finally, it got very quiet for about three minutes, followed by what Hyman called a "horrific thud" shortly before 4:30 a.m.

By the time Clete Hyman heard that ominous thud, all four of the guys were already back in one of their cabins, says an attorney for one of the Russians. However, if someone was inside George's cabin at the time of the thud and slipped out, the ship's system would not note that. It only notes when a key is used and you would not need a key to leave.

Clete Hyman said that just a couple of minutes later, the ship's security arrived to check out the complaint. But, says Royal Caribbean, "the noise had already stopped and there was no answer to our knocking."

At almost exactly the same time, Jennifer "was found sleeping on the floor of a corridor on the other side of the ship and a significant distance from her cabin," according to Royal Caribbean.

Now, here's where it really gets strange. At 4:48 a.m., according to the ship's time line, two crew members went to the Smith cabin to see if anyone was around to help Jennifer. "They knocked and, not getting a response, looked inside the cabin, found it empty, and saw nothing amiss." How could there possibly be so much partying, arguing, furniture moving, and various other noises and thuds with nothing appearing amiss afterward? According to the earwitnesses, the room was being trashed.

At 4:57 a.m. Jennifer was taken back to her cabin in a wheelchair by two security guards and a female supervisor. Said the company's time line, "She was placed on top of her bed and asked if she was all right. She answered that she was okay, and the security personnel left the room. George Smith was not present, and nothing appeared amiss."

George's sister, Bree Smith, told me her family later became estranged from Jennifer: "I think that what was frustrating for my family is that we had been told that she provided a wealth of information to the FBI, and she had not provided a wealth of information to us. And as the parents and the sister of the missing and presumably . . .

dead passenger, we should know as much as possible. . . . We know rumors from the media and that's about it."

Federal authorities have told the Associated Press that Jennifer is cooperating with the investigation. While Jennifer did appear at a congressional hearing on cruise ship safety, she has apparently not commented much beyond her complaints against the cruise line and her explanation that she doesn't remember what happened that night. She told MSNBC's Joe Scarborough that she's following the FBI's instructions not to talk publicly about that crucial time period until the case is solved. After an in-depth look at the Smith case, NBC News reported, "The FBI, which is conducting the investigation into George Smith's disappearance, has made a point of letting it be known that Jennifer is not a suspect in any theory of foul play."

One plausible explanation is that after Jennifer left the disco, she became disoriented, couldn't find her cabin, and passed out, while, unbeknownst to her, George was meeting his demise at the other end of the ship.

It was only the next morning, when a big splotch of blood was discovered on the ship's metal canopy beneath the Smiths' cabin and George still could not be located, that there was the first suspicion he'd gone overboard. Jennifer was found in the ship's spa. She had woken up and gone there, she said, thinking her new husband would meet her there for their scheduled massages.

Bree Smith told me, "I have a theory that my brother met up with the wrong people, that he was too trusting, that he had a few drinks and let his guard down, and that there was a fight in his cabin. That seems fairly clear from the earwitness accounts from either side of his stateroom. I'm not saying who did it. I can't point a finger. . . . All I know is that this fight ended up with my brother being thrown overboard." That was Bree's take. But the FBI, despite a lengthy investigation, remained mum, offering no theories or potential suspects, leaving open the possibility that George could have jumped or fallen off *on his own.*

Ship of Fools?

As if all of this weren't enough, there was another drama on the very same ship just a few days later, allegedly involving the same Russian American guys. "There was an alleged gang rape several days after my brother's murder and it was videotaped . . . and the Russian Americans were thrown off the boat in Naples, Italy," Bree told me.

In *Vanity Fair*'s April 2006 article on the case, an attorney for one of the Russian American men acknowledged that his client took part in the alleged rape, but insisted the sex was consensual. The magazine says, "The rape allegation was reviewed by a magistrate in Naples. According to an Italian newspaper article, the magistrate, after viewing the videotape, found no evidence of a crime." But *Vanity Fair* cited others as saying the Italian judge found his court had no jurisdiction and turned the case over to the American consulate. The attorney for one of the Russians told *48 Hours,* "That whole escapade was noncriminal in nature. The tape itself revealed that." No charges were filed in this incident.

As the investigation into Smith's disappearance dragged on, month after month, with no arrests, the tensions rose. In a pattern similar to the Holloway case, charges and countercharges erupted, except this time they were between the Smith family and the Royal Caribbean cruise line. With the cable news shows pitting the two sides against each other, televised shouting matches were only one part of the public relations war.

One basic complaint of the family also

echoed a theme from the Holloway case, that crucial evidence was allowed to slip away in the early hours and days of the investigation. A key issue was the bloodstain on the ship canopy and whether it was removed too soon. Bree complained that it was "removed before the FBI entered that cruise ship. They claim they washed it away at six at night because people were looking at it. Well, that is a very poor excuse for why they did not preserve a crime scene."

Royal Caribbean responded to these and other criticisms with an unprecedented press release entitled "Top 10 Myths Regarding Royal Caribbean's Handling of the Disappearance of George Smith," designed to debunk what the company called unfair criticisms.

"Myth 1. Royal Caribbean engaged in a deliberate cover-up, which impeded the investigation. The company washed down the canopy in the morning, before the authorities even arrived and then painted over the blood. This is false. . . . The Captain took immediate steps to preserve the scene, including the sealing of the area and stationing a guard outside the cabin." The cruise line claims Turkish police told them on the afternoon of July 5 that their forensic investigation, including photographs, fingerprints, blood samples, and the collection of other evidence, was complete and there was no need to further preserve anything in the cabin or the canopy. It was only after that, says the cruise line, that they washed off the blood "with high-pressure hoses at 6:15 p.m." Still, Bree Smith said her experts have told her a tarp should have been placed over the bloodstain to keep the evidence while not disturbing other passengers.

AMERICA FIRST

But the biggest question was why the investigation of the apparent death of an American citizen was left in the hands of Turkish authorities, who, in all probability, did not have the technological sophistication that American investigators have. Again, this echoes a refrain from the Natalee Holloway case, namely that Americans see the rest of the world as incompetent when measured against our own standards. As much as we may come off as arrogant, a lot of time, it's the truth.

Royal Caribbean responded, "The ship and its passengers were under the jurisdiction of Turkish authorities since they were in a Turkish port. This is no different than the jurisdiction U.S. authorities exercise over foreign ships when they are in U.S.

ports." The FBI is said to work in conjunction with the local authorities, who do the initial probe and turn the results over to the Bureau.

To add to the mess, the FBI was shown up when TV reporters from syndicated news shows interviewed several passengers who offered crucial information, only to learn those passengers were wondering why the FBI hadn't contacted them yet. Again, in a parallel to the Holloway case, journalists often seemed ahead of the official investigators.

The fact is, journalists are highly competitive and scrambling for scoops. For many on a big story, a dearth of exclusive interviews can be a career ender while a huge "get" can be a career maker. How can that level of zeal be matched by anyone working for a measly salary at a government agency? This is why the news is often ahead of everyone else on a story like this.

CRUISE CRUSADE

The cruise industry says the crime rate is much lower on cruise ships than on land, and that taking a cruise is safer than staying at a motel. But for those who have lost loved ones on cruise ships, the larger issue is how the industry can improve so that other passengers don't vanish mysteriously in the future.

The Smith family, and the relatives of other victims, want Congress to impose tougher government regulations on the cruise ship industry. Due to pressure from the Smith family, congressional hearings were held on cruise ship safety. Some of the stories were heartbreaking.

Michael Pham says that on May 12, 2005, both of his elderly parents simply vanished while on board a cruise ship run by a different company. Pham told me all they found were two pairs of sandals and a purse near where his parents had been sitting on deck: "It was such a nightmare for our family. We couldn't get any answers from the cruise line. . . . There is absolutely no accountability. If you lose a piece of luggage there is a phone number to call. . . . Well, we lost our parents. We call and nobody calls us back. Nobody gives us an answer."

Pham is crusading to get independent law enforcement officers on board all cruise ships, similar to the air marshals that fly on commercial jets. He also wants to see laws changed to ensure better reporting, investigation, and prosecution of crimes that occur on cruise ships. And he wants to make it easier to sue cruise companies for negligence.

Pham has joined the nonprofit organization called International Cruise Victims that was spearheaded by Bree Smith. One of her key issues is booze on the cruise. "I think they make a lot of their money through alcohol sales on the boats and they push alcohol. If you are going to have an aggressive alcohol sales policy, then you need to take care of your passengers, much like if you are on land, you have to know when to stop serving."

While Royal Caribbean refused our repeated requests for an interview, it must be noted that the absinthe the Smiths were reportedly drinking that night was not sold on the ship. It was apparently brought on by one of the passengers. One attorney even claimed George brought it on.

CRUISING FOR A BRUISING

That raises the ultimate issue: personal responsibility. So many Americans forget to pack common sense and self-restraint when they travel abroad. Americans are so overworked and overstressed in our daily routines that when we go on vacation, we often try to make up in a couple of weeks for all the wild times we miss the other fifty weeks of the year. We are a workaholic nation. And like all addicts, we veer from one extreme to the other. When we finally get time off, we feel compelled to party as hard as we work. This is the new American ethic.

For these and other reasons, Americans often do things in foreign countries and on cruise ships that they would never for a moment consider doing in their own hometowns. We naïvely regard foreign travel as a no-consequence zone. *Au contraire.* We often face more consequences when we're off on our own, without our normal support systems there to catch us when we go overboard, physically or metaphorically.

And for those left to pick up the pieces, there are no vacations from the grief and rage and loss; as Bree says, "Not only is my brother missing and never been found, but we don't know what happened to him." In the year since her brother disappeared, Bree left her job as a lawyer in Hong Kong and moved in with her parents in Connecticut to help them cope. Her toddler son remained with her. Her husband, back in Hong Kong, filed for divorce. "Our lives are unrecognizable," she sighed. And still the secret of what happened that night has not been cracked.

599

AUTHOR'S NOTE

As a reporter, I have heard countless crime victims say, "I never thought it could happen to me." Even the criminals mired in these brutal and terrifying cases will tell you they are baffled that their lives ended up the way they did.

It's often impossible to say exactly when we first set foot in the quicksand of a toxic situation. It's only after we're neck-deep in trouble that our missteps become obvious to us.

We can avoid being blindsided by violence. We can strive to become more self-aware and take honest inventories of ourselves and our relationships. As we go through life, we all suffer traumas. It's up to each of us to work through our unfinished business, even if it means going to a therapist or a twelve-step program. Never feel shame about getting help!

Likewise, we must face the truth about

those we love and accept that we can't change them unless they want to change. We must avoid magical thinking, especially in personal relationships, where being in denial can be deadly.

Each of us has the power to develop a sixth sense that can warn us when somebody, even a stranger, is being false and possibly setting us up for catastrophe.

Wouldn't it be a relief if we could be less secretive as a society? Our current social structure rewards superficiality and hypocrisy. We demand that people deny their sexual proclivities and identities so they can appear "normal." We turn a blind eye as our children torment one another in the schoolyard. Our slow-moving bureaucracies expose children to retaliation if they speak up about abuse in the home. We scold women for being out late when they become victims of violent predators.

Our society instills a love for prestige, power, and money so great that people will lie, cheat, and kill for it. Our culture of deceit can spark rage in those who feel betrayed by double-talk and double standards. Phoniness comes packaged as politeness. Intolerance often takes the form of moral rectitude that leaves many feeling judged and rejected.

We have seen how resentment and alienation can lead to violence. And so a cycle ensues, for generation after generation: injustice, revenge, punishment. Over and over.

Is there a way for us to evolve, as a society, beyond crime and punishment? Is there a way for us to circumvent the pain before it turns homicidal? The answer is up to each and every one of us. In every decision, throughout the course of every day, we choose in which direction this world will move, toward peace or violence, toward acceptance or intolerance, toward love or hate, toward honesty or secrets. Please choose peace, acceptance, love, and honesty. I will try to do the same.

VICTIM'S RIGHTS WEBSITES

If these stories upset you, there is something you can do. Get involved!

www.carliescrusade.org ▶ Named in Carlie Brucia's memory, this organization teaches children self-defense.

www.carolesundfoundation.com ▶ The Carole Sund/Carrington Memorial Reward Foundation raises public awareness about people who have gone missing under suspicious circumstances, and victims of violent crimes.

www.CodeAmber.org ▶ Code AMBER Alert Ticker provides every website owner with the ability to display AMBER Alerts on their site by adding the Alert Ticker.

www.internationalcruisevictims.org ▶ The International Cruise Victims Organization (ICV) provides support to victims of cruise ship crime, and pushes for legislative reform to protect passengers from crimes.

www.internationalsafetravelsfoundation.org

▶ The Safe Travels Foundation informs and educates the public to help them travel more safely. Founder Beth Holloway Twitty personally presents the Safe Travels Student Safety Awareness message in high schools and colleges around the country.

www.jmlfoundation.com ▶ The Jessica Marie Lunsford Foundation has been established to help children in crisis and to promote legislation that protects children from predators.

www.JusticeforImette.com ▶ Justicefor Imette.com was created by friends of Imette St. Guillen in New York City as a clearinghouse for information relevant to the case.

BIBLIOGRAPHY
AND SOURCE LIST

CHAPTER 1: WOMEN AS PREY

The Abrams Report, March 2, 3, 6, 7, 8, 10, 13, 15, 22, and 23, 2006, MSNBC Transcript.

"Match in New York City Murder Case," *Anderson Cooper 360°,* CNN, March 13, 2006.

"Darryl Littlejohn, in His Own Words," CBS News, New York, March 22, 2006.

Janice Shaw Crouse, "Commentary: Sex and Society. She Had Every Right . . . But Now She's Dead," UPI, Religion and Spirituality, March 7, 2006.

"A Break in the Murdered NYC Student Case," *Dateline NBC,* March 12, 2006.

"Meeting Imette's Family," *Dateline NBC,* March 11, 2006.

Chris Faherty, "Last Call: What the Bartender Saw the Night Imette St. Guillen Was Drinking at the Falls," *New York,*

March 27, 2006.

Adam Goldman, "NYPD: Bouncer's Blood Linked to St. Guillen Slaying," Associated Press, March 13, 2006.

Nancy Grace, *CNN Headline News,* March 3, 6, 7, 9, 17, and 22, 2006.

Nancie L. Katz, Jonathan Lemire, and Corky Siemaszko, "He Can't Look Family in the Eye," New York *Daily News,* March 24, 2006.

Larry King Live, CNN, March 6 and 13, 2006.

Robert McFadden, "Police Say DNA Links Bouncer to Body of Slain Student," *The New York Times,* March 13, 2006.

Rita Cosby Live & Direct, March 2, 6, 7, 8, 9, 13, and 14, 2006, MSNBC Transcript.

Christina Silva and John R. Ellement, "Friend Joins Appeal for Help in NYC Slaying Case," *The Boston Globe,* March 2, 2006.

Laurel J. Sweet and O'Ryan Johnson, "Woman's Friend, Kin Unite in Grief, Fond Remembrance," *The Boston Herald,* March 2, 2006.

CHAPTER 2: DESPERATE HOLLYWOOD

"New Details Emerge in Spector Murder Investigation," Agence France Presse,

December 10, 2003.

Anthony Bruno, "Phil Spector: The Mad Genius of Rock 'n' Roll," Court TV Crime Library.

Anthony Bruno, "Spector: Did He Murder Fading Movie Actress Lana Clarkson," Court TV Crime Library.

Celebrity Justice, February 3, 4, 2003.

"Coroner's report: Victim in Spector Case May Have Fired Shot," CNN, May 7, 2004.

Linda Deutsch, "Music Producer Will Contend Shooting Was Accidental, Friend Says," Associated Press, February 11, 2003.

Jean Guccione, "Spector Said He Shot Actress by Accident, Officer Told Grand Jury," *Los Angeles Times,* January 7, 2005.

Edna Gundersen, "Music's Spector Charged with Murder," *USA Today,* February 4, 2003.

Caitlin Liu, "Women to Testify in Spector Case," *Los Angeles Times,* May 24, 2005.

"Lana Clarkson," LivingDollProductions .com.

Edward Lozzi and Associates, "News Release: A Message from the Lana Clarkson Camp," May 7, 2004.

Carlton Smith, *Reckless,* New York: St. Martin's Press, 2004.

"Search Warrant and Affidavit," The Smoking Gun, document: Search Warrant Affidavit Details Record Producer's Activities on Evening of Murder.

Lisa Sweetingham, "Guns, Depression, and Rock 'n' Roll: Documents Show Twilight of Spector's Life," Court TV, updated January 31, 2006.

"Legend with a Bullet," *Vanity Fair,* June 2003.

Richard Williams, *Phil Spector: Out of His Head,* Omnibus Press, 2003.

CHAPTER 3: THE TEXAS CHILDREN MASSACRE

Heather Bell, "Michael Woroniecki Preaches Jesus, Not Murder," *Central Michigan Life,* March 22, 2002.

Andrew Cohen, "Tale of Two Killer Moms," CBS, April 4, 2004.

"Pastor Blames Demons, Not Mental Illness," ExChristian.net, February 16, 2006.

Nancy Grace, "Andrea Yates Granted Bail," *CNN Headline News,* February 1, 2006.

"Encore Presentation: Interview with Rusty Yates," *Larry King Live,* CNN, January 16, 2005.

"Jury Will Now Decide if Yates Should

Receive Death," *Newsnight,* CNN, Aaron Brown, March 12, 2002.

"Mother Accused in Drowning Deaths Attempted Suicide Because She Feared Hurting Others," *News Tribune,* September 1, 2001.

Suzanne O'Malley, *Are You There Alone? The Unspeakable Crime of Andrea Yates,* New York: Simon & Schuster, 2004.

Katherine Ramsland, "Andrea Yates: Ill or Evil?" Court TV Crime Library.

Amanda Ripley, reported by Deborah Fowler/Houston and Alice Park/New York, "A Mother No More: A Woman Tells Police She Drowned Her Five Children. What Could Have Led Her to This Act of Madness?" *Time,* July 2, 2001.

Rita Cosby Live & Direct, March 15, 2006, MSNBC transcript, March 16, 2006.

Timothy Roche, with reporting by Anne Berryman and Deborah Fowler/Houston, Hilary Hylton/Austin, and Greg Fulton/Atlanta, "The Yates Odyssey," *Time,* January 28, 2002.

Suzy Spencer, *Breaking Point,* New York: St. Martin's, 2002.

Suzy Spencer, "The Crime in Writing True Crime: An Author's Notebook," Center for Individual Freedom.

Lisa Teachey and Ruth Rendon, "Yates'

Medical Records Indicated Little Progress," *Houston Chronicle,* September 1, 2001.

CHAPTER 4: EXPENSIVE SECRETS

"Billionaire Robert Durst Back in Jail," *The Abrams Report,* MSNBC, January 25, 2006.

"Durst Murder Trial: Not Guilty," *Anderson Cooper 360°,* CNN, November 11, 2003.

Charles V. Bagli, "Durst Severs Ties to Family in Return for $65 Million," *The New York Times,* February 7, 2006.

Charles V. Bagli, "Durst Tells Murder Case Jury of His Life on the Run," *The New York Times,* October 23, 2003.

Charles V. Bagli, "For Heir Accused of Killing, a Loyal and Tough Ally," *The New York Times,* September 20, 2003.

Matt Birkbeck, *A Deadly Secret: The Strange Disappearance of Kathie Durst,* New York: Penguin/Berkeley Books, 2002.

Anthony Bruno, "All About Millionaire Murderer Robert Durst," Court TV Crime Library.

Anthony Bruno, "Millionaire Murderer," Court TV Crime Library.

"Mystery of Robert Durst," CBS, September 8, 2004.

"Across the Nation," *Detroit Free Press,* September 30, 2004.

Nancy Grace, "Nancy Grace Transcript," *CNN Headline News,* July 15, 2005.

Bill Hewitt, Alice Jackson Baughn, and Matt Birkbeck, "Heir of Mystery: His Wife Disappeared Years Ago. Now Robert Durst Faces Charges in a Texas Murder," *People,* November 5, 2001.

Bill Hewitt and Matt Birkbeck, "Resuming the Search; Police Reopen the Case of Kathie Durst, Who Vanished 18 Years Ago," *People,* December 4, 2000.

Craig Horowitz, "The Perils of Jeanine," *New York,* February 27, 2006.

"End of the Road: Thanks to a Stolen Sandwich, Pennsylvania Cops Catch Murder Suspect Robert Durst," *People,* December 17, 2001.

Richard T. Pienciak, "Views of How Durst Did It," New York *Daily News,* October 1, 2003.

Ruth Rendon, "Juror Visits Durst in Jail: After Assurance of Innocence, Chat Takes an Odd Twist," *Houston Chronicle,* January 31, 2004.

Ruth Rendon, "Logs Show Juror Met with Durst Five Times in Jail," *Houston Chronicle,* February 4, 2004.

Leslie T. Snadowsky, "Butcher Bob," *New*

York Post, October 2, 2003.

Leslie T. Snadowsky, "Durst Jury Wants Answer to Loaded Question," *New York Post,* November 8, 2003.

Leslie T. Snadowsky, "Naked Durst's Dirty Dancing," *New York Post,* October 13, 2004.

Scott Williams, "Durst Released from Federal Prison," *Galveston Daily News,* July 16, 2005.

Ned Zeman, "The Fugitive Heir," *Vanity Fair,* February 2002.

CHAPTER 5: SAVAGE SUBURB

"Vitale Murder Suspect's Dark Life," CBS News, October 25, 2005.

"Horowitz Says He Knew Wife Was Dead as Soon as He Found Her," CNN, October 19, 2005.

"Letter by Susan Polk on March 16, 2001," Court TV.

"Susan Polk Case Coverage," Court TV, March 2, 8, 9, 16, 21, and 30, 2006; April 3, 2006; October 17, 2005.

"Scott Dyleski," *On the Record with Greta Van Susteren,* Fox News, October 27, 2005.

Bruce Gerstman and Kelli Phillips, "Friend Casts Suspicion on Dyleski," *Contra Costa*

Times, February 12, 2006.

Nathaniel Hoffman, "Neighbor Offers New Theory in Slaying," *San Jose Mercury News,* October 29, 2005.

"Horowitz Federal Crime Defense Team," Horowitz website, www.federalcrime.us/index.html, www.federalcrime.us/pages/1/index.htm.

Virginia McCullough, NewsMakingNews.com, August 30, 2005; March 27, 2006; October 11, 2006.

Keith Morrison, "Murder in the Midst of a Murder Trial," NBC News, *Dateline NBC,* October 23, 2005.

"Daniel Horowitz Story," NBC News Transcripts, October 17, 2005.

Kelli Phillips and Matt Krupnick, "Clues Sought at Lafayette Death Scene," *Contra Costa Times,* October 18, 2005.

Ashley Surdin and Bruce Gerstman, "Brutal Details Released in Vitale Murder Case," *Contra Costa Times,* November 17, 2005.

Lisa Sweetingham, "Judge: Sufficient Evidence to Try Scott Dyleski for Woman's Vicious Murder," Court TV, February 21, 2006.

Lisa Sweetingham, "Susan Polk Fires Her Closest Ally and Defense Aide," Court TV, April 3, 2006.

Chapter 6: The Blood-Spatter Boys

The Abrams Report, February 2, 2006, MSNBC transcript, February 3, 2006.

"Massachusetts Murder Mystery," *Anderson Cooper 360°,* CNN, February 7, 2006.

"Hopkinton Woman and Infant Are Shot," *The Boston Globe,* January, 24, 2006.

"The Alibi: Disturbing the Peace," CBS News, *48 Hours Mystery,* January 22, 2005.

John R. Ellement and Suzanne Smalley, "Apparent Slayings Shock a Town,"

"Perfect Union?: Examining the Marriage of David and Kim Camm," CBS News transcripts, October 11, 2002.

Robert Falcione, "I Saw Neil Entwistle," *Hopkinton News,* 2006.

"The Case Against Neil Entwistle," *On the Record with Greta Van Susteren,* Fox News, February 19, 2006.

John Glatt, *One Deadly Night,* New York: St. Martin's Press, 2005.

Nancy Grace, "Neil Entwistle," *CNN Headline News,* January 31, 2006; February 7, 10, 15, and 16, 2006; March 2, 2006.

Steve Huff, "Neil Entwistle No Stranger to Sex and the Web," Court TV Crime Library.

Lisa Hurt Kozarovich, "What's Next for Convicted Camm?" *New Albany Tribune* and *Jeffersonville Evening News,* March 4, 2006.

"David Camm Timeline," *Louisville, KY, Courier-Journal,* 2006.

Hoyer Meghan, "Testimony Shows Camm Still Cheated: 8 More Women Tell Court About Relationships," *Louisville, KY, Courier-Journal,* January 31, 2002.

"Murdered in Their Bed," *People,* February 13, 2006.

Grace Schneider, "The Camm and Boney Murder Trials," *Louisville, KY, Courier-Journal,* January 24, 2006.

"David Camm Timeline of Major Events," WAVE 3 News, www.wave3.com, 2005.

"Sentencing Hearing: Text of Debbie Karem Written Statement," WHAS11.com, March 28, 2006.

CHAPTER 7: MOTHERS WITHOUT BORDERS

"Scott Peterson Talks to ABC News' Diane Sawyer," ABC News, January 28, 2003.

Keith Ablow, M.D., *Inside the Mind of Scott Peterson,* New York: St. Martin's Press, 2005.

"Death Penalty Is Sought in Modesto Killings," Associated Press, April 27, 2003.

"Scott Peterson's Parents Take Witness Stand, Defend Son," Associated Press,

October 26, 2004.

Anne Bird, *Blood Brother,* New York: HarperCollins Publishers, 2005.

John Bradshaw, *Family Secrets,* New York: Bantam Books, 1995.

Catherine Crier and Cole Thompson, *A Deadly Game,* New York: HarperCollins, 2005.

Michael Fleeman, *Laci: Inside the Laci Peterson Murder,* New York: St. Martin's Press, 2004.

"Timeline: The Scott Peterson Trial," Fox News and Associated Press, July 12, 2004.

Amber Frey, *Witness,* New York: HarperCollins, 2005.

Nancy Grace, "Laci Peterson's Mother Speaks Out," *CNN Headline News,* January 10, 2006.

"Interview with Sharon Rocha," *Larry King Live,* CNN, January 9, 2006.

Nick Madigan, "Modesto Police Seek to Identify Bodies on Shore," *The New York Times,* April 16, 2003.

"National Briefing/West: California: Peterson Autopsy Sealed," *The New York Times,* June 7, 2003.

Sharon Rocha, *For Laci,* New York: Random House, 2006.

Chapter 8: Rawhide

"Newsman Ranch Suspect: Abused?" Associated Press, July 9, 2004.

"Posey Guilty of Murders," Associated Press, February 8, 2006.

"Statistics Teen Murder," Center on Juvenile and Criminal Justice.

"Homicide at Sam Donaldson's Ranch," Court TV transcript, February 8, 2006.

"Transcript of Cody Posey Sentencing," Court TV, updated February, 23, 2006.

Felicia Fonseca, "Case of Teen Accused of Killing His Family on Donaldson Ranch Goes to Jury," Associated Press, modified February 6, 2006.

Emanuella Grinberg, Court TV, updated January 27 and February 9, 2006.

"The Joe Factor," *People,* December 12, 2005.

Susan C. Smith, "Abused Children Who Kill Abusive Parents," *The Catholic University Law Review,* 1992.

John Springer, "Psychiatrist: Teen Who Killed Family Had Post Traumatic Stress Disorder," Court TV, February 21, 2006.

Chapter 9: Dirty Tricks

American Morning with Paula Zahn, CNN, "Interview with Bakley Family Lawyer,"

February 27, 2003.

"Newly Acquitted Robert Blake Seeks Work," Associated Press, March 17, 2006.

"Robert Blake Thanks Barbara Walters for Saving His Life," Associated Press, March 22, 2005.

"Timeline: Robert Blake Trial," BBC News, March 17, 2005.

"A Question of Guilt: The Bakley Murder," CBS, August 5, 2002.

"Press Release: Statement from the Jerry Lee Lewis Family," Chuck Berry website, May 8, 2001.

Linda Deutsch, "Actor Robert Blake Discloses High Cost of High-Profile Trials," Associated Press, May 25, 2006.

Linda Deutsch, "Bakley's Daughter Testifies Against Blake," Associated Press, January 27, 2006.

Alex Johnson, "Kissing Cousins," MSNBC, March 1, 2005.

"Handyman Denies Involvement in Murder," KABC-TV, Los Angeles, September 2005.

Gary C. King, "Robert Blake," Court TV Crime Library.

"Robert Blake Working as Malibu Ranch Hand," KUTV.com/Associated Press, March 20, 2006.

"Interview with Robert Blake," *Larry King*

Live, CNN, May 16, 2005.

Dennis McDougal and Mary Murphy, *Blood Cold,* Hammondsworth: Penguin Books LTD, 2002, p. 210.

Wayne Petherick, "Victimology," Court TV Crime Library.

"Eyeing Robert Blake's Accusers," The Smoking Gun archive, www.thesmoking gun.com/archive/blakestuntmen.html.

"Hi, I Hate to Tell You This but the Pill Did Not Work for Me," The Smoking Gun, document: Original Letter from Bonny Bakley to Robert Blake.

"July 2000 Letter Sent by Bonny Lee Bakley to Robert Blake: She Demands That the Couple Get Married," The Smoking Gun, document: Original Letter from Bonny Bakley to Robert Blake.

Lisa Sweetingham, "Housekeeper: Strange Man Watched Blake's House Before Wife Was Slain," CNN.com/Court TV, February 16, 2005.

CHAPTER 10: TEENACIDE

"Excerpts from Court Filing in Murder Case Against David Ludwig," Associated Press, November 21, 2005.

"The Dark Side of Homeschooling," CBS, October 13, 2003.

"Pa. Teen Taped Another Murder Plan,"
CBS/Associated Press, November 18,
2005.

"Updates, Thoughts, and a Timeline: David
Ludwig and Kara Beth Borden," Free
Republic, freerepublic.com, November
29, 2005.

Nancy Grace, *CNN Headline News,* November 17, 2005.

Carma Haley, "Home School Controversy,"
iParenting.com.

Bill Hewitt, Nicole Weisensee Egan, Tom
Duffy, Michelle York, Sean Scully, Shia
Kapos, "Desire Turns Deadly," *People,*
April 21, 2006.

Adam Hunter, "When Murder Hits the Blogosphere," special to MSNBC.com, December 1, 2005.

Jessie Klein, "Teen Killers Feel Trapped by
Masculine Stereotypes," *USA Today,* November 11, 2003.

"Ludwig Attorneys' Press Release," KTVU
and *Bay Insider,* November 16, 2005.

"Ludwig Family Statement," KTVU and
Bay Insider.

"Night Patrols," Look Who's Tattling Now
website, Optymyst.com, November–
February, 2006.

Brett Lovelace, "Ludwig Drove Away with
Another Girl," *Lancaster Intelligencer,*

November 19, 2005.

"Violence — Quick Statistics," National Youth Violence Prevention Resource Center.

Martha Raffaele, "PA Teen Remains in Care of Relatives," Associated Press, November 20, 2005.

Katherine Ramsland, "Young Killers," Court TV Crime Library.

Cindy Stauffer and Janet Kelley, "Secret Liaisons?" *Lancaster New Era,* November 16, 2005.

Zan Tyler, "Dr. Phil Speaks Out on Homeschooling," Lifeway. www.ugarmy.com

Hans Zeiger, "A Defense of Home Schooling," *Renew America,* October 18, 2003.

CHAPTER ELEVEN: ANGELS OF JUSTICE

The Abrams Report, March 15, 2006, MSNBC transcript, March 16, 2006.

"Death for Carlie's Killer," *Anderson Cooper 360°,* CNN, March 15, 2006.

Jess Andrews, "Troubled Life Had Divorces, Drug Use," *Sarasota Herald-Tribune,* February 7, 2004.

Samuel Bruchey and Theresa Vargas, "Family Promises to Keep Carlie's Case in Spotlight," *Newsday,* 2004.

"A Letter from Carlie's Grand Parents,"

carlieslaw.org/grandad.html.

Robert Eckhart, "Carlie's Stepfather Arrested on Domestic Battery Charge," *Sarasota Herald-Tribune,* last modified May 5, 2004.

Robert Eckhart and Mike Saewitz, "Man Indicted in Death of Carlie," *Sarasota Herald-Tribune,* February 23, 2004.

Dan Kadison, "Carlie's Last Ride — Borrowed Car Shows Signs of Death Struggle," *New York Post,* February 9, 2004.

Dan Kadison, "Ex-Wife of Carlie's 'Killer': Let Him Fry," *New York Post,* February 10, 2004.

Rita Cosby Live & Direct, March 15, 2006, MSNBC transcript, March 16, 2006.

Todd Ruger, "Susan Schorpen's Brother Dies," *Sarasota Herald-Tribune,* March 23, 2006.

Mike Saewitz, "Making the Case," *Sarasota Herald-Tribune,* updated November 6, 2005.

Mike Schneider, "Prosecutors Play Tapes of Suspect Talking About Florida Girl's Death," Associated Press, November 15, 2005.

Mike Schneider, "Smith's Defense Raises Questions About Reliability of FBI Lab," Associated Press, November 15, 2005.

Thomas Alex Tizon, "80 Eyes on 2,400 People," *Los Angeles Times,* March 28, 2006.

Abby Weingarten, "Beloved Carlie a Shining Light," *New York Post,* February 8, 2004.

Chapter 12: Sex Education

"Debra Lafave's High School Lover Breaks Her Silence," *ABC Action News* Report, February 10, 2005.

The Abrams Report, March 21–24, 2006, MSNBC transcript.

"MySpace Page Puts Teacher Back in Jail," Associated Press, April 12, 2006.

"Worldwide Ages of Consent," Avert, avert .org.

Shannon Colavecchio–Van Sickler and Abbie Vansickle, "Lafave Case 'Over for Good,' " *St. Petersburg Times,* March 22, 2006.

Shannon Colavecchio–Van Sickler, "New Loves Bloom from Lafaves' Failed Union," *St. Petersburg Times,* March 16, 2006.

Jessica Fargen, "Sex, Truth & Videotape: Teen-tryst Teacher Admits to Naked Pix," *Boston Herald,* September 29, 2005.

Nancy Grace, *CNN Headline News,* August 4, 2005.

Nancy Grace, "Tennessee Teacher Back in Jail," *CNN Headline News,* May 5, 2006.

Thomas W. Krause, "Spouse Says Lafave Radically Changed Before Her Arrest," *Tampa Tribune,* November 23, 2005.

Owen Lafave and Bill Simon, *Gorgeous Disaster: The Tragic Story of Debra Lafave,* Phoenix Books, 2006.

Josh Mankiewicz, exclusive interview with Mary Kay Letourneau and Vili Fualaau, *Dateline NBC,* June 2, 2006.

Bill McGinty, "Detective Investigating Debra Lafave Has Also Been Arrested," WTSP, Tampa Bay's 10.

Melba Newsome, "Dangerous Liaisons," *Time,* April 10, 2006.

Denise Noe, "Mary Kay Letourneau: The Romance That Was a Crime," Court TV Crime Library.

Gregg Olsen, *If Loving You Is Wrong: The Shocking True Story of Mary Kay Letourneau,* New York: St. Martin's, 1999.

On the Record with Greta Van Susteren, Fox News, March 22, 23, 2006.

Rita Cosby Live & Direct, December 9, 2005, MSNBC transcript, December 10 and 30, 2005, and May 2, 2006.

Candace Rondeaux, "Judge Keeps Lafave Photos from Public View," *St. Petersburg Times,* September 21, 2005.

Candace Rondeaux and Catherine E. Shoichet, "Lafave Deal Rejected in Marion," *St. Petersburg Times,* December 9, 2005.

"Student Statement to Police Regarding Sandra Geisel," The Smoking Gun.

Chapter 13: The Point of No Return

The Abrams Report, March 24, 2006, and April 6, 12, and 24, 2006, MSNBC transcript, March 27, 2006.

Bryan Burrough, "Honeymoon Over," *Vanity Fair,* April 2006.

Bryan Burrough, "Missing White Female," *Vanity Fair,* January 2006.

"Cruise Tragedy Opens Family Feud," CBS News, March 7, 2006.

"Love Lost: What Happened to Missing Honeymooner George Smith?" *48 Hours Mystery,* CBS, April 8, 2006.

"Transcript: Dave Holloway Reacts to Joran van der Sloot Interview," Fox News, February 28, 2006.

Nancy Grace, *CNN Headline News,* April 17 and May 22, 2006.

Dave Holloway with R. Stephanie Good and Larry Garrison, *Aruba: The Tragic Untold Story of Natalee Holloway and Corruption in*

Paradise, Nashville: Nelson Current, 2006.

"International Cruise Victims Organization Submitted Recommendations to Congress for Changes to the Cruise Industry," ICV Press Release, March 12, 2006.

"Cruise Booze," *Inside Edition,* April 27 and 28, 2006.

"Arrest in Aruba Connected to Holloway Disappearance," *Larry King Live,* CNN, April 17, 2006.

"Interview with Family of George Smith," *Larry King Live,* CNN, December 13, 2005.

Charles Lipcon interview on the George Smith Case, *Scarborough Country,* MSNBC, August 9, 2005.

Dennis Murphy, "The Smith Family Speaks Out," NBC News, January 23, 2006.

On the Record with Greta Van Susteren, Fox News, March 1–6, 14, and 24, 2006; February 13 and 14, 2006; and April 13, 2006.

"Top 10 Myths Regarding Royal Caribbean's Handling of the Disappearance of George Smith," Royal Caribbean press release, official site: www.royalcaribbean .com, January 27, 2006.

ACKNOWLEDGMENTS

This book would not have been possible without the insight and wisdom of my amazing editor Nancy Hancock. She took a leap of faith when she decided to entrust me with this project and followed up with expert guidance every step of the way. I am honored to have had the opportunity to collaborate with such a delightful yet diligent wordsmith. It's also been wonderful working with my Touchstone editor, Trish Grader, who has taken this project under her very able wing. Editorial assistants Sarah Peach and Meghan Stevenson have also been terrific.

Thanks also to Nancy Grace. Her many invitations to appear on her widely watched *CNN Headline News* show have given me an extraordinary opportunity to weigh in on the biggest criminal cases of our times. It's been an exciting ride. Her entire staff is exceptionally talented. I would especially like to thank executive producer Dean Sicoli, supervising producer Elizabeth Yuskaitis, producer Naomi Goldstein, CNN producer Eric Marrapodi, and editorial producer Ellie Jostad. Much thanks to CBS *Early Show* producer Jennifer Simpson.

A tremendous debt of gratitude goes out to Sandra Mohr. As my partner as well as my researcher on this project, she worked hard and fast, securing vital information and interviews, always with the utmost professionalism, courtesy, and kindness, particularly for those going through the agony of missing a loved one.

Everyone I interviewed for this book took time from their extraordinarily busy schedules to impart their considerable knowledge. I was struck by how generous these individuals were with me: victims' family members, lawyers, reporters, psychologists, forensic scientists, and all the professionals who offered their opinions. Los Angeles psychotherapist Dr. Bethany Marshall provided me with thought-provoking insights, as did L.A. trial consultant Molly Murphy, psychotherapist and cultural mythologist Dr. Martha Velez, and noted clinical psychologist Dr. Judy Kuriansky. Private investigator Scott Ross offered a wealth of behind-the-scenes information. Jennifer

Lewi of AP Images was indispensable. Publicist Gillian Sheldon and media consultant Ceri Williams are masters at getting the word out. Author Cynthia Kersey was always there with great advice, as was my good friend and fellow journalist Shoshanah Wolfson.

I must thank a few people who are very important in my life and have helped me evolve personally and professionally: TMZ .com executive producer Harvey Levin, who thinks faster than the speed of light; my agent at N. S. Bienstock, Carole Cooper, who has filled my life with exciting career adventures for decades; *Extra* senior executive producer Lisa Gregorisch-Dempsey, who has given me so many opportunities; Dr. Roman Anshin, whose fatherly advice has been priceless; true friend and TV producer Stephen Doran, who inspires me to think for myself; dear friend Jane Langley, a source of wisdom and laughter; and my sister, Gloria Vando. A gifted poet, Gloria is always there for me with love and acceptance, as are her children, Lorca Peress, Paul Peress, and Anika Peress, and her husband, Bill Hickok. And, of course, thanks to my mom, Anita Velez-Mitchell, a dancer and playwright who has shown me, through example, how to dance through life.

ABOUT THE AUTHOR

Jane Velez-Mitchell frequently guest hosts for Nancy Grace on CNN Headline News and has reported for the nationally syndicated Warner Brothers/Telepictures show *Celebrity Justice.* A former reporter/anchor for WCBS-TV in New York City and KCAL-TV in Los Angeles, Velez-Mitchell has won numerous awards, including two Emmys for her work in New York City and Los Angeles. She lives in Los Angeles. Visit her Web site at www.secretscanbemurder.com.

The employees of Thorndike Press hope you have enjoyed this Large Print book. All our Thorndike and Wheeler Large Print titles are designed for easy reading, and all our books are made to last. Other Thorndike Press Large Print books are available at your library, through selected bookstores, or directly from us.

For information about titles, please call:
(800) 223-1244

or visit our Web site at:
www.gale.com/thorndike
www.gale.com/wheeler

To share your comments, please write:
Publisher
Thorndike Press
295 Kennedy Memorial Drive
Waterville, ME 04901